Omnipotent Fantasies and the Vulnerable Self

THE LIBRARY OF CLINICAL PSYCHOANALYSIS

A SERIES OF BOOKS EDITED BY
STEVEN J. ELLMAN

This series is intended to show the depth, flexibility, and vigor of contemporary Freudian thought. It is by no means a series that can be equated with classical psychoanalysis or ego psychology, but rather we intend to show how contemporary Freudians are able to meaningfully integrate a variety of positions into the scaffolding of Freudian tenets. Goldman's and especially Bach's work show the richness and depth that can be achieved within such a framework.

Freud's Technique Papers:
A Contemporary Perspective
Steven J. Ellman

In Search of the Real:
The Origins and Originality of D. W. Winnicott
Dodi Goldman

In One's Bones:
The Clinical Genius of Winnicott
Dodi Goldman, Editor

The Language of Perversion and the Language of Love
Sheldon Bach

Omnipotent Fantasies and the Vulnerable Self
Carolyn S. Ellman and Joseph Reppen, Editors

Omnipotent Fantasies and the Vulnerable Self

Edited by
Carolyn S. Ellman, Ph.D.
and
Joseph Reppen, Ph.D.

JASON ARONSON INC.
Northvale, New Jersey
London

Production Editor: Elaine Lindenblatt

This book was set in 11 pt. Granjon by Alabama Book Composition of Deatsville, Alabama, and printed and bound by Integrated Book Technology of Troy, New York.

10 9 8 7 6 5 4 3 2 1

Library of Congress Cataloging-in-Publication Data

Omnipotent fantasies and the vulnerable self / Carolyn S. Ellman and
Joseph Reppen, editors.
p. cm.
Includes bibliographical references and index.
ISBN 0-7657-0046-8 (alk. paper)
1. Fantasy. 2. Psychoanalysis. 3. Freud, Sigmund, 1856–1939.
I. Ellman, Carolyn S. II. Reppen, Joseph.
BF175.5.F36046 1997
154.3—dc20 96-38978

Printed in the United States of America on acid-free paper. For information and catalog write to Jason Aronson Inc., 230 Livingston Street, Northvale, New Jersey 07647-1731. Or visit our website: http://www.aronson.com

Contents

Acknowledgments

We wish to express our deep appreciation for the support of the New York Freudian Society in this important endeavor. The New York Freudian Society and Psychoanalytic Training Institute was founded in 1959 to provide training and a professional community for psychoanalysts from many disciplines. It is to the Society's credit that it continues to seek new and interesting ways to challenge intellectually its candidates and members. We thank the Society for acknowledging the importance of this topic.

We would like to give individual thanks to Anni Bergman, Ph.D., who co-chaired with distinction the Scientific Program Committee from 1990–1994. Her dedication and intellectual rigor helped bring to fruition the idea of a series on omnipotence. We would like to acknowledge the dedication and effort of the Scientific Program Committee: Carolyn S. Ellman, Ph.D. (co-chair), Rita V. Frankiel, Ph.D., Marvin Hurvich, Ph.D., Katherine Oram, Ph.D., Lilo Plaschkes, M.S.W., and Iris Sugarman, M.S.W. Special thanks are due Dr. Frankiel, who not only chaired the actual meetings during 1994–1995 but originated the idea of using *omnipotence* as the year's topic of exploration. Her contributions to the committee were truly original and her work as chairperson from 1994–1996 was exemplary.

We are grateful to the staff at Jason Aronson, especially our copyeditor, Judy Levin; our production editor, Elaine Lindenblatt; and Michael Moskowitz, Ph.D., whose editorial judgment and enthusiasm make editing as painless as possible.

Finally, appreciation is due Francesca Reppen for her editorial skills and to Steve, Peter, and Lauren Ellman who always find a way to be wonderfully supportive.

Contributors

Richard Almond, M.D., a psychiatrist and psychoanalyst in private practice in Palo Alto, California, is a faculty member of the San Francisco Psychoanalytic Institute, and Clinical Professor of Psychiatry, Stanford University School of Medicine. He is the author of *The Healing Community: Dynamics of the Therapeutic Milieu* (1974) and *The Therapeutic Narrative: Fictional Relationships and the Process of Psychological Change* with Barbara Almond (1996).

Steven J. Ellman, Ph.D., is Professor of Clinical Psychology, City University of New York, and Fellow of the Institute for Psychoanalytic Training and Research where he was president from 1994 to 1996. Dr. Ellman is Visiting Professor at the New York University Post-Doctoral Program in Psychoanalysis and Psychotherapy, author of *Freud's Technique Papers: A Contemporary Perspective* (1991), and editor with J. S. Antrobus of *The Mind in Sleep* (1991).

Rita V. Frankiel, Ph.D., Training and Supervising analyst with the New York Freudian Society and Chair of the Scientific Program

Committee (1994–1996), is Associate Clinical Professor at the New York University Post-Doctoral Program in Psychoanalysis and Psychotherapy where she offers a course on object loss. Dr. Frankiel is the editor of *Essential Papers on Object Loss* (1994) and has published papers on Anna O, Freud's treatment of Little Hans, countertransference, universal fantasy, and the game of hide and seek. She originated the idea for the New York Freudian Society series on omnipotence.

William M. Greenstadt, Ph.D., is Assistant Clinical Professor in the Department of Psychiatry of the Mount Sinai School of Medicine, Chairman of the Interdisciplinary Colloquium in Mythology and Psychoanalysis of the New York Psychoanalytic Institute, a Training and Supervising analyst at the New York Freudian Society and the National Psychological Association for Psychoanalysis, Past-President of Section 1 (Psychologist-Psychoanalyst Practitioners) of the Division of Psychoanalysis of the American Psychological Association, and Past-President of the New York Freudian Society.

Otto F. Kernberg, M.D., is Associate Chairman and Medical Director, The New York Hospital–Cornell Medical Center, Westchester Division; Professor of Psychiatry, Cornell Medical College; and Training and Supervising analyst, Columbia University Center for Psychoanalytic Training and Research. Among his many honors are the Mary S. Sigourney Award for Psychoanalysis in 1990 and the Distinguished Service Award from the American Psychiatric Association in 1995. He is the author of six books and co-author of five others including *Borderline Conditions and Pathological Narcissism* (1975), *Severe Personality Disorders: Psychotherapeutic Strategies* (1984), *Agression in Personality Disorders and Perversion* (1992), and the most recent *Love Relations: Normality and Pathology* (1995). Dr. Kernberg is President-elect of the International Psychoanalytical Association.

Henry Krystal, M.D., is a psychoanalyst in private practice in Michigan. Professor Emeritus of Psychiatry, Michigan State University, and a faculty member of the Michigan Psychoanalytic Institute, he has been honored as one of four pioneers in the field of trauma by the International Society for Traumatic Stress Studies. Dr. Krystal is the author of *Drug Dependence* with Herbert Raskin (1970) and *Integration and Self Healing: Affect Trauma Alexithymia* (1988), and the editor of *Massive Psychic Trauma* (1968).

Zvi Lothane, M.D., is Clinical Associate Professor of Psychiatry at Mount Sinai School of Medicine, Senior Member of the National Psychological Association for Psychoanalysis, and Fellow of the Institute for Psychoanalytic Training and Research. He is the author of *In Defense of Schreber: Soul Murder and Psychiatry* (1992) as well as numerous articles.

Jack Novick, Ph.D., and **Kerry Kelly Novick** are child and adult psychoanalysts on the faculty of the Michigan Psychoanalytic Institute. Both trained at the Anna Freud Centre in London. Jack Novick is a child and adolescent supervisor at the Michigan Psychoanalytic Institute, a Training and Supervising analyst with the New York Freudian Society, and Clinical Associate Professor of Psychiatry at the University of Michigan and Wayne State University Medical Schools. Kerry Kelly Novick is Clinical Director of Allen Creek Therapeutic Preschool and formerly Lecturer in Psychoanalysis with the Department of Psychiatry, University of Michigan Medical School. The authors of several papers, their most recent book is *Fearful Symmetry: The Development and Treatment of Sadomasochism* (1995).

Paul H. Ornstein, M.D., is Professor of Psychiatry Emeritus and Professor of Psychoanalysis Emeritus, and Training and Supervising Analyst with the Cincinnati Psychoanalytic Institute. Co-director of the International Center for the Study of Psychoanalytic Self Psychology, Dr. Ornstein is the editor of the four-volume work *Heinz Kohut: The Search for the Self* and author of numerous papers.

Jerrold M. Post, M.D., is Professor of Psychiatry, Political Psychology, and International Affairs, and Director of the Political Psychology Program at George Washington University. Dr. Post's career has been devoted to the field of political psychology; he was formerly with the United States government, where he founded and directed the Center for the Analysis of Personality and Political Behavior. Vice-President of the International Society of Political Psychology, he is co-author of *When Illness Strikes the Leader: The Dilemma of the Captive King* with Robert S. Robins (1993) and author of the forthcoming *Political Paranoia: The Psychopolitics of Hatred*. He developed the Camp David Profiles of Begin and Sadat for President Carter and was awarded a civilian Medal of Merit in 1979.

Introduction

Omnipotence is the result of human helplessness. We are all born in a helpless position, dependent on the outside world for nurturance and survival, and we all face the ultimate annihilation of the self at the end of life, through death. The human being is thus constantly in a struggle to maintain a sense of power in the face of total vulnerability.

If some analytic theorists are correct, infants construct a fantasy of "oneness" and "omnipotence" by feeling that they are at one with a "powerful other" during a most vulnerable time, following birth. For these theorists children slowly internalize the omnipotent parent and then, only over time, are able to give up this "fantastic" image in order to face the reality of their own weakness and vulnerability as well as that of the parent. Developmentally, at the end of life, one is again faced with helplessness and attempts to negotiate reality and fantasy. Whether or not one resolves this problem through religion and a belief in God, or develops a fantasy of living on in some other way, such as through children and creative or philanthropic works, considered a healthy resolution by many people, the question remains:

Does one ever really give up some omnipotent protective fantasy related to the self and other?

When the topic of omnipotence appears in psychoanalytic writing, it is usually connected to more disturbed patients and psychopathology. It is rare to read an article either on borderline or narcissistic pathology in which the term "omnipotent fantasy" is not used to describe some aspect of the patient's inner world. In many studies patients are viewed as struggling with disappointment and pain around pathological relationships and they attempt to deal with rage and powerlessness by developing fantasies of self-sufficiency, power, and control. Frequently these traits are attributed to another and they partake in the other's fantasied power while at different times they act as though or fantasize that power resides in their self. Whether these fantasies are always the result of painful experiences, whether they exist from the beginning of life, and whether they are fantasies constructed much later as a result of trauma and disappointment are crucial issues. How these fantasies develop and why they are sometimes put into action at the hands of pathological leaders and whether there are healthy fantasies of omnipotence are some of the many important issues with which this volume deals. There are many possible avenues of exploration, such as the relationship between religion and omnipotence, the increased interest in reincarnation, and what we have learned about the infant's inner world.

This volume presents a series of papers read at scientific meetings of the New York Freudian Society in 1994 and 1995. In the announcement for these meetings the following questions were asked:

Do infants fantasize being omnipotent?

Is the working through of fantasies of omnipotence central to the termination process?

Does trauma increase or decrease fantasies of omnipotence?

To what extent can omnipotent fantasies be analyzed in certain extreme character pathology?

Are omnipotent fantasies ever adaptive?

The papers attempt to answer, in different ways, many of these questions. Unfortunately, one of the presentations and its discussion could not be published because of issues of confidentiality. We have, however, included an additional paper on omnipotence and power that surveys the question of omnipotence and presents a number of significant clinical vignettes. The program committee, influenced by one of its members, Dr. Rita Frankiel, was profoundly attracted to the topic of omnipotence.

We hope that this volume will provide a stimulus for future studies of a topic that, although a little less neglected as a result of this contribution, remains elusive, challenging, and, in the end, rewarding.

Carolyn S. Ellman, Ph.D.
Joseph Reppen, Ph.D.

1

Omnipotence and Power*

Richard Almond, M.D.

Editors' Comments

Richard Almond's chapter looks at omnipotence and power in three realms: 1) clinical analytic process, 2) research studies suggesting that infants and children have considerable control over their interpersonal environment, and 3) the work of major psychoanalytic theorists who have conceptualized omnipotence. Almond's excellent review of the literature (from Freud's "On Narcissism" through Kohut's contributions) seems an appropriate place to begin the discussion of omnipotence.

Almond differentiates omnipotent fantasy from power. He says: "The internal state of omnipotent control is represented in a range of displaced and translated forms in adult life as we . . . see in clinical examples. In these situations, it is the use of power that we can

*The author is grateful to the following for their helpful suggestions and comments: Adrienne Applegarth, Stanley Coen, Lee Grossman, Alan Skolnikoff, and the members of the Palo Alto Writers Group.

observe, not the omnipotence fantasy." Almond shows that 1) omnipotence has a distinguishable development; 2) omnipotence manifests in normal development; 3) the need for a sense of power, or subjective omnipotence, continues throughout life, side by side with reality testing; 4) each individual approaches the search for power in his or her life in a characteristic manner; and 5) concepts of power and omnipotence are valuable in dealing with the here-and-now transference.

Clinical examples constitute the center of Almond's chapter. They show how power-related, interactive aspects of process play an important part in every analysis. In each instance, examination of the way power emerges clinically makes it possible to infer an underlying omnipotent fantasy. It is with the interplay of the intrapsychic conflict over this fantasy in the transference that Almond bridges a theoretical gap between the intrapsychic and the interpersonal. In each example omnipotence is an element in the power relationship with the analyst and in each case omnipotence is expressed in a different way. Almond's remarks about how to allow the patient to maintain a certain amount of control in the analytic situation are particularly timely.

This chapter was not part of the original series read at the New York Freudian Society but is included because of its salient contribution to the topic.

Despite clear instructions to *associate* and report experience, patients want to *bring about effects* on the analyst (Freud 1914a). Our patients are continually trying to *do* things to us and get us to *do* things to them—to get us to *answer* or *ask* them questions or *make* us feel things toward them. Analytic exploration of the meaning of such motives often reveals that the patient's thinking and behavior derive their compelling quality from a wish to actualize a fantasy in which a sense of power is central. We usually designate this sense of power, or wish for it, *omnipotence*, or *omnipotent fantasy*. It is at the heart of much neurotic conflict and compromise. To maintain certain gratifications and to protect against certain imagined dangers, the individual must control internal object relations. This control is expressed externally in the form of actions that give the patient a sense of power in relation to the analyst.

Freud did not use the word *power* in his psychoanalytic vocabulary. Adler did (see below), but in a way that had more to do with omnipotence than power itself. While the term has major significance in other social sciences, *power* may not have become a psychoanalytic term because it has strong social, interactive connotations. Analytic language generally describes *intra*psychic phenomena. When analysts discuss power they tend to use the term *omnipotence*, usually referring to the infantile quality of power wishes and fantasies. Power is also implicit in discussions of ego capacities and strengths. Yet, as Freud noted (see below), such capacities have their roots in early omnipotent experience.

Omnipotence is also more suggestive of an internal state than *power*. Thus, for our purposes omnipotence is a subjective state—a sense of complete control or influence—that the individual tries to bring about through action and/or fantasy. Although the terms are often used interchangeably, grandiosity can be distinguished from omnipotence as more affected, a pose, an attempt to create or substitute for the internal feeling of omnipotence. Some authors use the term *pathological omnipotence* to describe processes that are similar or related to grandiosity (Beiser 1979). *Efficacy, competence, confidence*, and *self-esteem* are all terms related to a healthy sense of omnipotence. The internal state of omnipotent control is represented in a range of displaced and translated forms in adult life as we will see in clinical examples. In these situations it is the use of power that we can observe, not the omnipotent fantasy.

Power is a central concept in the social sciences: political science, sociology, anthropology, history, law. The disjunction between analytic discussions of omnipotence and the idea of power in other fields limits potentially valuable contributions to those fields from depth psychology. The elaboration of such linkages (see, for example, Mack 1986, 1994) would be a major study. Here I wish to consider the clinical interplay of omnipotence and power. I will discuss how these concepts have been developed in the psychoanalytic literature, and then present a number of clinical examples to explore how power and omnipotence play out in analytic process and in human development.

Freud

Freud's discussions of omnipotence contain references to both its pathological and ego-adaptive aspects. "On Narcissism" (1946) laid the groundwork for the idea that a desired aspect of psychic life—self-esteem—arises from omnipotence: "Every remnant of the primitive feeling of omnipotence which his experience has confirmed, helps to increase his self-regard" (p. 75). This observation has been elaborated extensively in recent years both in psychoanalytic developmental theory and in theories that foreground the concept of self and states of self (see below). Freud also related omnipotence to aggression and the death instinct. In "Civilization and its Discontents" (1930), Freud says, "[The death instinct] can be seen in the blindest fury of destructiveness . . . the satisfaction of the instinct is accompanied by an *extraordinarily* high degree of narcissistic enjoyment, owing to its presenting the ego of a fulfillment of the latter's old wishes for omnipotence" (p. 121). He then goes on to discuss the sublimation of such impulses: "The instinct of destruction, moderated and tamed, and, as it were, inhibited in its aim, must, when it is directed towards objects, provide the ego with the satisfaction of its vital needs and with control over nature" (p. 121). In other words, Freud assumes that there is an "original omnipotence" (my term) derived from aggressive energy that is the source of gratification to the ego (here Freud is using the word in the sense of "self"). This view leads naturally to his ideas about omnipotence in development.

Freud (1913) assumed that the stages of autism and primary narcissism are accompanied by high levels of omnipotent experience, levels that can only decline with time. In this model, the infant begins life in a blissful, protected, and self-absorbed state, provided for by mother in what the infant experiences as an automatic and subjectively omnipotent manner. Freud deduced this model from clinical inference, speculation, and possibly some unreported infant observation. As such, his model is subject to the distortions of his own infantile amnesia and repression, and the methodological limitations of his "infant research."

Following from this beginning of omnipotent experience in the maternal matrix, Freud suggests, there is a developmental sequence for the "vicissitudes of the omnipotence of thoughts." In "Totem and Taboo" (1913) he compares this sequence to the evolution of religious thinking. In the earliest stage omnipotence is ascribed to the self. Freud likened this to the animistic thinking of primitive cultures. That is, any element of the outside world can be brought under one's (subjective) control through magical knowledge. In the second stage, that of secondary narcissism, the ego (self) is invested with power, and specific objects are idealized and then brought under ego control. This is analogous to the development of monotheism, and the corresponding division between sacred and secular. There is now a recognition of the existence of other centers of control that can be influenced by the right behaviors. In the final stage omnipotence is relinquished, or at least severely delimited. What remains takes the form of faith in mind, which can then "grapple with the laws of reality." Psychologically, this stage corresponds to full ego development, with reality testing and the predominance of secondary process thinking. In short, ego development and reality testing lead to an ever-diminishing sense of omnipotence.

In portraying the developmental line of omnipotence in this way, Freud enriched developmental theory. But he also laid the groundwork for the pathologizing of omnipotence in adult personality and treatment by saying that the "earlier, narcissistically tinged forms of omnipotence are more primitive, less mature" (Freud 1913). In this respect *omnipotence* denotes psychopathology, regression, or arrested development.

Although Freud did not use *power* as a concept, it is implicit in his discussions of resistance. The term itself implies a struggle by the patient in relation to the analyst and the analytic process. While his early writing about resistance concerned the patient's efforts to prevent unconscious material from surfacing, by the time of "Inhibitions, Symptoms and Anxiety" (1926) resistance described all aspects of the patient's part in the analytic process. Any of the mental structures could be used in the service of resistance. That Freud retained the term *resistance*, when *analytic process* would have been more appropriate, indicates, I believe, his continuing recognition of the interplay of power in the relationship. For all his emphasis on neutrality and surgical objectivity, Freud knew that patients struggled to resist change, and that treatment required the analyst's engagement in that struggle.

Adler

Of Freud's immediate followers, Adler elaborated ideas about power and omnipotence. In Adler's view, the infant's primary experience is one of inferiority and consequent humiliation (Ansbacher and Ansbacher 1956). This engenders a set of motives that include striving for superiority (the masculine protest: "I *am* a man!"), striving for power, and striving for perfection. Although superiority, power, and perfection have external referents, for Adler they are primarily internal states of mind. He does not refer to omnipotence per se, but these constituent elements suggest that he has something like omnipotence in mind as that for which man (the self) strives.

For Adler, drive is non-specific; libido and aggression are colorations of a basic impulse that characterizes *all* motivation. Thus, it is as basic to speak of striving for power or perfection as it is to speak of libido. Freud had taken the first step by adding aggression as a second drive; now Adler was suggesting that the "urge upwards" toward an omnipotent ideal is the core of drivenness.

Winnicott

Melanie Klein and her followers, with their emphasis on reconstructions of early development, have developed Freud's assumption of infantile omnipotence (Klein et al. 1983). In Klein's system omnipotence is discussed entirely as intrapsychic, particularly in its role of protecting the good object, or part-object, from the (projected) aggression of the bad object. Winnicott (1947), influenced by Klein, extends the more ego-developing aspect of Freud's thinking about omnipotence. Building from Freud's comment that, in speaking of the infant, one should include the assumed presence of the maternal caregiver, Winnicott portrays omnipotence as a product of the child's creativity and the mother's good-enough mothering. For example, the "breast" in its internally meaningful sense as a part-object is "created" through myriad experiences of active, successful clamor, search for the nipple, and discovery that sucking produces milk. The *activity* of the child is a critical element, as is the appropriate complementarity of the supplying mother. Thus the breast is *created* in a transitional space, where, with mother's cooperation, the infant experiences omnipotence.

By emphasizing activity and creativity, Winnicott alters and extends the Freudian paradigm. Omnipotence is not inbuilt, but achieved. It requires a partnership of infant and mother to bring this about, so possibilities for disturbances can easily be imagined. Winnicott's "false self" personality organization, for example, results from a failure of the mother-infant interaction to be sufficiently confirming to the child's omnipotence. The child learns to evoke the mother's "gesture" (i.e., the response that the child *can* elicit), to retain some sense of control, some remnant of omnipotence.

For Winnicott (1960), omnipotence remains a *lifelong* aspect of internal experience. "In psychoanalysis . . . there is no trauma that is outside the individual's omnipotence. . . . In infancy, however, good and bad things happen to the infant. . . . [T]he capacity for gathering external factors into the arena of the infant's omnipotence is in the process of formation" (p. 590). Winnicott argues that in analysis we create a situation that allows the patient to rekindle wishes for, and experiences of, omnipotence. Take, for example, patients' anger about analysts' vacations. Whatever a particular patient's specific fantasy, the analyst's vacation generically exposes and frustrates the sense of omnipotent control invited by the analytic situation. The analysis of, and gradual mastery over the affective impacts of the analyst's vacations eventually brings the separation experience within the patient's subjective control, or, as Winnicott would put it, his omnipotence.

Winnicott (1965) does acknowledge the evolution of modifications to infantile omnipotence. "[T]he good-enough mother is able to meet the needs of her infant at the beginning . . . so that the infant, as emergence from the infant-mother relationship takes place, is able to have a brief experience of omnipotence" (p. 57). While Winnicott is using a paradigmatic image from early development, his frequent references to the clinical situation suggest that he is talking about a general psychological issue: that humans require a "subjective" matrix of experience where they feel omnipotent in order to tolerate momentary contacts with reality, or objective experience. From this experience they form a more realistic sense of themselves in the world. This view casts an interesting perspective on the psychoanalytic situation, suggesting that it is designed to encourage omnipotent experience. This implication of Winnicott's work foreshadows the ideas of Heinz Kohut.

White

White (1963), following Hartmann's interest in adaptation and independent ego energies, developed the concepts of *efficacy* and *competence*. Using the developmental data of Piaget and others, White, like Winnicott, argued that it is the child's experience of effectiveness in its activity that leads to the build up of self-esteem. One aspect of this experience is the parents' praise. For this praise to create solid self-esteem, it must be matched to the real accomplishments of the child, not be bestowed without reason. Efficacy begins in the maternal relationship, but remains an issue throughout development. Initially, the emphasis is on influencing the object world; later, the management of internal impulses in the form of more or less healthy defenses becomes a significant factor in self-feeling. The sense of competence would then contain a combination of satisfactions: the ability to seek ends effectively along with the ability to contain raw impulse in the process.

Kohut

The theme of omnipotence is central to the thinking of Heinz Kohut (1971, 1977, 1984). Both aspects of Kohut's "bipolar self"—ambitions and ideals—have omnipotent attributes. The "ideals" pole develops healthily when the parent, sensing the child's need, performs functions the child desires. These functions range from physical caretaking to psychological functions like soothing and empathizing. When the parent does these things well, the child experiences momentary merger with the parent's capacity—a sense of owning the parent's power to help—a psychic structure Kohut first called the *Idealized parent imago*. As a consequence of the parent's attuned functioning, the child feels soothed, cared for, protected, powerful, and, in later manifestations of parental function during the oedipal phase and beyond, inspired. These experiences are ultimately internalized as a part of the self.

The ambitions pole (earlier, the *grandiose self* [1971]) requires mirroring from the selfobject. Mirroring is a complementary reaction by the selfobject that confirms the assertive, expressive, exhibitionistic behavior of the child. Mirroring gives the child a needed sense of omnipotence and grandiosity to support its appropriate ambitions. Without the omnipotence that the selfobjects provide, there is depression, fragmentation, or devaluation of the self. In Kohut's view of psychopathology, when there are developmental deficiencies in one or both of these self-experiences, there will be a regression to "archaic" self-structures. In effect, Kohut is arguing for the motivational, that is, driven, quality of a desired self-experience, especially its omnipotent component. It is for this reason that he originally designated such motivations as "narcissistic libido" (1971).

Kohut's contributions, for our purposes, can be summarized:

1. The wish for, and attribution of, omnipotence is ubiquitous, particularly in the first relationships of life and in the emerging self.
2. A sense of omnipotence is a normal part of psychic life. It is not outgrown but rather finds acceptable outlets and forms as development proceeds. Selfobjects, and the omnipotence that they provide are needed throughout life, not given up as a part of childhood.
3. Omnipotence can be experienced in oneself and also vicariously through attribution to a parent imago.
4. Frustration of the omnipotent wish (drive) leads to "regression" to developmentally earlier forms.

It is my view that the superstructure of self psychology is not necessary to acknowledge that omnipotent strivings have motivational power and developmental consequences. In fact, by expanding "self" to embrace all of personality, and by linking omnipotence to so much else, Kohut makes it more difficult to sort out the *particular* role omnipotence plays in psychic life.

While omnipotence plays a limited role in Freud's metapsychology, it is carried to the other extreme in Adler's and Kohut's theories, where, through the omnipotence implicit in the striving for power or the need for the functions of the selfobject, it is everywhere. Winnicott is somewhere between these two, indicating that omnipotence is of particular importance to experiences he places in the realm between self and other, between fantasy and reality. Similarly, White places omnipotence alongside ego capacities and defenses in the development of a sense of competence. But even Freud—who links omnipotence to aggression, self-esteem, narcissism, and ego development—indicates a wide range for the concept. I believe the explanation for these different views is the ubiquity of issues of power and omnipotence in human psychology and everyday life. Despite this, omnipotence itself has not often been the central focus, as it is in this volume (Beiser 1979, Kernberg 1975, Levin 1991).

Definitions

In the following discussion we shall use the term *omnipotence* to designate an intrapsychic sense or fantasy of unlimited influence over aspects of the self, the object, and the external world. *Power* will refer to actual influence in the external world, potential or enacted, as opposed to fantasy. *Control* can refer to both realms, as a more localized form of real or potential influence over the self or the other.

Power and Omnipotence in Analytic Process: Illustrations

To introduce the ways in which omnipotent experience manifests externally in the form of power, we can turn to clinical experience. It is here that we should see the translation of internal omnipotent psychic structure into power-related interactions. In the following vignettes I have deliberately chosen examples in which the power issues were relatively subtle. These cases are within the usual range of psychoanalytic practice, and the phenomena I shall describe can easily be phrased in terms of transference and resistance. That is specifically my point: that in the most typical psychoanalytic situation the interactive aspects of process will show us power at play, and in turn illuminate omnipotent intrapsychic fantasy. Each example presents a particular aspect of omnipotent thinking. These will include (1) *control over the other*, and (2) *control over the self*, (3) *timelessness* (the sense of power over time); (4) *omnipotent thinking*; (5) *masochism* (omnipotence through the entitlement consequent to suffering); and (6) *drivenness* (control through the power of driven behavior itself). While this is not necessarily the only way to subdivide omnipotence in action, these divisions illustrate the varieties of mental activity and action consequences that may be imbued with omnipotent meanings.

Omnipotence Through Power over the Object

Almost no analytic hour passes without the expression of a wish, usually verging on conviction, that the analyst should do or feel or think something that the patient wants. Often the wanting is clearer than what it is that is wanted. By virtue of the generally nongratifying behavior of the analyst, the desire for control and power over the analyst—and the assumption that such desire will be satisfied—emerges more vividly than in daily social intercourse, where unwritten social rules protect people from exposing too blatantly the desire to control the behavior of others.

> Mr. Adams spent the initial forty minutes of each hour describing in painful detail his anxiety and self-criticism, along with his futile attempts to get relief through compulsive rituals and intellectualization. Near the end of each hour he would turn to me and ask, "What are you thinking about this? You must have some ideas that would help me understand this better." The emotional pressure of the accumulated unhappiness was sufficient that, on some occasions, I offered some thoughts about what was going on, particularly my impression that Mr. Adams was, in fact, generally doing well in his life, and that this might be arousing some guilt or anxiety. This sort of response seemed to lead to momentary clearing of his anguish, but in the next session the pattern would begin all over, as though nothing had happened.
>
> Over a protracted period we came to understand the layered meanings underlying this state and the interaction it led to between us. For example, Mr. Adams was making me a transference critic like his rigid, never-satisfiable mother. His earnest request for help covered a hidden disdain for abusive authority, and his "unhelpability" was his means of retaliating. At the same time, Mr. Adams was turning passive into active by showing me how useless my interventions were, playing the part of his mother to my attempts to "please" him by being helpful.
>
> What was central to this process was Mr. Adams's acting in the analytic relationship in a way that was designed to elicit a response from me. The form of his action—his repeated questions to me, with the accompanying affective pressure—gave him an unconscious sense of control with me. A situation that had been

unbearable to him in childhood was being played in the analytic relationship, but reversed, and under his control. Subjectively, this control created a sense of omnipotence vis à vis his mother.

In the next case this mode of omnipotent control was more obvious:

> Mr. Booth reported that his mother was a cold, controlling person, recognizing her children only when they were dutifully filial. He described his father as relatively uninvolved. Many years of therapy had enabled Mr. Booth to develop a professional career. He came to me around anxiety that limited his corporate advancement. Once an analytic relation was established, it became clear that Mr. Booth expected me only to listen and agree. He firmly rejected any questioning of his ideas, or proposals of my own. Mr. Booth felt the analyst's role was to agree with and reflect the patient's thinking. The treatment could only proceed when I acceded, at least temporarily, to his demands, and limited myself to interventions of a reflective nature.

As with Mr. Adams, this transference enactment bespoke Mr. Booth's use of identification with the aggressor, turning passive into active by making me do what he wished, rather than think of himself as the object of his mother's demands. This gave him a sense of control over me and probably defended him against rage stemming from transference projections of mother. Another function of his demand for control in the analytic situation was to undo his inner feeling of powerlessness over the other and his conviction that, when I acted spontaneously, I controlled him as his mother had. As long as he could maintain omnipotent control over me, this anticipated traumatic re-experience was forestalled indefinitely.

Both Mr. Adams and Mr. Booth illustrate another aspect of omnipotence—its close connection with action. For both patients it was significant that, once in the treatment situation, they were compelled to structure the relationship in a certain desired way. Omnipotence in action may create a sense of potentially broadened efficacy. That is, through taking action with me on a wish involving power in one *particular* respect, they created a sense of power that could be, in fantasy, generalized. For the moment, old unsatisfactory object-related experiences came under control and were made right. Both mental activity and interaction were necessary parts of omnipotent experience. Similarly, Mr. Booth could tolerate the analytic situation only by taking action on his need for direct control. By controlling the power relationship with the analyst these patients reverse their internalized sense of passivity and weakness in the face of a parent's superior power. We see this process in identification with the aggressor, and in turning passive into active.

Omnipotence Through Control over the Self

Mr. Charles came to analysis with a complaint of "living in a Nirvana World," as well as a block in sustaining close relationships and advancing in work. He found any financial transaction painful, and arranged his life so that he could feel that he never asked others for money, or did so only under duress, that is, when someone else (his credit card company, or his analyst, for example) required him to. Such arrangements pervaded his life. In the analysis, while he produced material freely, he did not "take" improvement from the process.

Exploration revealed that not changing served multiple functions clustered about a quality of "holding still": by avoiding full exchange with his world, Mr. Charles postponed long warded-off affects. Childhood traumata could be averted; memories of his fear around parental fights was suppressed; anxieties about his own greed could be fended off; his need for love from me or others could be denied. Core to all these, and clinically the source of greatest difficulty, was a stubborn holding onto an illusion of self-sufficiency. This illusion allowed Mr. Charles to live in the world, aloof from the painful reminders of its limitations, and gratified by fantasies that were kept open from testing against reality through his avoidance of feelings.

Mr. Charles: [During the third month of analysis; in the previous hour he had threatened to terminate for financial reasons.] I was going to . . . I guess . . . yesterday was a strange session. The idea of having to purge myself of some need or desire. I'm not sure what that is, but it seems . . . an idea of dependency seems pretty involved in it. [He reports a dream in which he walks by derelicts, whom he identifies with, but his mother says they are "bad" people. His first associations are that he must not want to leave his parents, and that he was defined all his childhood as a "dependent" by the military.]

During his second year in analysis Mr. Charles began acknowledging that that he had a strong involvement with me, but he maintained a wall of control between that idea and associated feelings, as in the following exchange:

Mr. Charles [after a silence]: I still owe you for last month. I'd like to put off payment for a week. What about that? The reason why . . . funds are tight . . . I'm expecting a check any time. I'm feeling indebted.

R. A.: You mentioned several thousand you haven't billed.

Mr. C.: Yeah. I'm going to have to . . .

R. A.: Can you explain more about that—the pull to be in debt—you're pointing out that now it's happening with me.

Mr. C.: It guarantees you'll need me . . .

R. A.: How will I need you?

Mr. C.: I guess, if I owe you, you need to keep contact with me. If I decide to leave, it will pay you to keep in touch.

Mr. Charles is an example of what Modell (1975) describes as the narcissistic defense against painful affects through the feeling of self-sufficiency. Mr. Charles created a sense of omnipotent control by avoiding real contemporary experiences, such as the feelings he had about wanting money or wanting to be close to me. Mr. Charles's "Nirvana World" was of long standing; as best we could reconstruct its origins, it may have begun with overzealous toilet training begun at age 12 months by a compulsive mother. We reconstructed that in childhood Mr. Charles had responded by being compliant and good, hiding from himself and others his impulses to be messy, angry, or controlling. His compromise, developed and refined over many years, was retention of a sense of power by keeping his internal experience separate from external reality. Otherwise his affects were too dangerous, his sense of disappointment too great. One function of Mr. Charles's omnipotence was to deny the passage of time, to retain a world in which he was "not yet" furious about having to give up control. This form of omnipotence is central in the next illustrative vignette.

Omnipotence Through Controlling the Experience of Time

> Mrs. Dalton was the daughter of an intrusive mother who also seemed to have conveyed ambiguous messages about the value of her fifth and youngest child. These messages influenced Mrs. Dalton's early gender identity, so that she felt demeaned and damaged as a girl. During latency a traumatic event occurred in the family: her vigorous and successful father suicided. My patient's grief reactions seem to have been lost sight of in the general family crisis. She became anxious and possessive; her mother responded protectively, forming an excessively interdependent bond between them. Mrs. Dalton felt she had a special status as long as she remained close. There was strong evidence in the analytic material that Mrs. Dalton felt singled out as a replacement for her father in specialness to her mother, creating difficulties both in gender concept and separation. Most importantly, she never affectively acknowledged the loss of her father.
>
> A long period of psychotherapy in her twenties enabled Mrs.

Dalton to separate from her mother, to marry, and to establish a career. She returned for psychoanalysis when she recognized the anxious, immature, and "co-dependent" nature of her relationship with her husband, and her difficulty taking action in many areas of adult life: fears of penetration during sexual intercourse, of deciding about child-bearing, of making major purchases, such as a house or new car.

In analysis a central theme emerged: Mrs. Dalton's fear of change. She was highly motivated to please me, or at least to conform with what she took to be the "rules" of psychoanalysis. Her hours were not only rich with material, but affectively convincing of her intense involvement in the treatment relationship.

After a year, however, I recognized that like a hound pursuing a clever fox, I was being deftly led in circles amidst all this meaningful work. Somehow Mrs. Dalton was avoiding using analytic experience. Mrs. Dalton admitted she did not want to act on any understanding she had gained in analysis because then something would "happen": she would become aware that time was passing. To acknowledge this meant accepting her father's death. This in turn, signified to her arrested, 8-year-old mind her failure as a girl to be attractive enough to retain her father's interest.

Mrs. Dalton feared being overcome by the affects of the "past," that is, by the childhood rage and confusion that had, in collusion with her mother, been avoided. Ultimately, she feared being the passive, damaged female that her mother had found unattractive and her father had abandoned. All these concerns, which Mrs. Dalton anticipated would be too intense to tolerate, were defended against by her construction of *timelessness*. She admitted that she believed she would have another life, in which she would take action in many of the areas she now avoided. In *this* life there was thus no need to act.

Mrs. Dalton, like Mr. Charles, made a bargain with life. If she denied herself enough, if she struggled against every pressure and impulse toward developmental progression, then she could retain her inner world, one in which she had not been rejected forever by her father, in which she was not damaged, in which penetration, with its fearful meanings, could be avoided. The "power" to bring this about resided primarily in her form of omnipotence, the halting of time. By fending off the passage of time in the analytic relationship, Mrs. Dalton once again possessed her lost father. To maintain this fantasy around the transference she needed to avoid analytic progress.

I believe this mechanism is quite widespread in individuals who have been seriously traumatized (Levine 1991). A variety of symptoms and behavior patterns can be recruited in the service of denying the passage of time, or, more specifically, of asserting omnipotent control over time so that one can believe one has stopped time prior to the trauma. This requires "regression," that is, the creation of a psychological condition at an earlier age than the trauma or traumatic period. That the person is not in fact truly regressed is revealed in the frequent alternation of levels of functioning or, as with Mrs. Dalton, the coexistence of adult and childlike functioning at different moments.

The appeal of the Faust story derives from this same theme of struggle against the passage of time. In Goethe's (1808) version, Faust's first speech begins:

> Philosophy, medicine, law, theology:
> I have studied them all thoroughly,
> with great pain.
> Here I stand, poor fool,
> Just as clever as before! [p. 28]

Faust's pursuit of knowledge is an attempt to retain *omnipotentiality* (Pumpian-Mindlin 1969); he hopes that by knowing all, he can control all, especially his feelings. The drama develops the lesson that one must experience and suffer, that affects cannot be avoided, nor can disappointment. Faust has tried an omniscient solution. By amassing knowledge and defeating time, Faust gains omnipotence in the form of a sense of *immortality*. This plays into his confidence about the bet with Mephistopheles. In their contract he promises:

> If I were to say of any moment:
> Wait! You are so beautiful!
> Then you may ring the funeral knell. [p. 59]

Mephistopheles exposes Faust to affects: lust, love, grief, and, eventually, more attenuated, sublimated feelings associated with civic involvement and true productivity. With a sense of the fulfillment of these extensive, real accomplishments Faust can now relinquish omnipotentiality for mortal experience.

Omniscience: Omnipotence Through Thought

In certain situations thought itself becomes invested with omnipotent meaning:

> Mr. Edwards quickly sensed what psychoanalysis was about and became involved with me in an intense and positively tinged relationship that I felt spoke of his long-standing wish for closeness with his withdrawn father. He made steady progress, both in the analytic situation and outside. Gradually I became aware that a feature of this progress was that he needed to "do it himself," that Mr. Edwards usually experienced my ideas as disturbing intrusions, rejected out of hand, though digested later. What we came to understand about this was that ideas were powerful and dangerous. When I intervened, I was not only father competing, but also mother demanding center stage. Mr. Edwards had to hold back his mind at work because it could damage others competitively and narcissistically. At the same time he became aware of an inner world in which he gloried in the total power of his thought process. He could tolerate his work itself, because it involved solitary technical activity that confirmed omniscience. When this work led to real world opportunity and success, he experienced

the combined dangers of having some real power and not having enough power. The former led to castration anxiety, the latter to narcissistic rage.

In the analysis Mr. Edwards used his mental agility to keep me at bay, while acknowledging that he knew he had strong feelings about me. Like Mrs. Dalton, he held back part of his involvement. He employed the compromise to retain omnipotence while gaining confidence about using power in the external world.

Mr. Edwards avoided physical exercise and competitive sports. These would make him aware of his body—his tangible, physical strength or weakness relative to others. Remaining within an arena of mind made the task of preserving omnipotence far easier. His verbal skill enabled him to parry or neutralize statements by me that threatened to create a sense of real power at play between us, with consequent experiences of vulnerability and weakness or of real—and, in fantasy, dangerous—power and control. Of course, to the extent such specialization is successful it is the source of limitation and anxiety. Major life areas must be avoided or specially defended because they threaten to make one aware of body strength, sexual desire, or aggressive impulse, or even the defenses that indicate the presence of impulse.

The magical, omnipotent power of thought characteristic in obsessional defenses not only guards against impulse, it also supports the validity of belief in one's omnipotence: "If I am so anxious there must be real danger here!"—a secondary gain from the fantasy of having great power and potential destructiveness.

Masochism: Omnipotence Through Suffering

Omnipotence can also be obtained through a self-image that is damaged, that is, through masochism.

Mr. Ford came to treatment because he wanted a normal life, not the painful relationship he was in with a partner of several years.

Although he was the more successful of the two, contributing disproportionately to shared expenses, it was Mr. Ford who took the blame in the couple's frequent arguments. In analysis it became clear that what was played out externally as a submission to an irrational wife represented a control over her in fantasy. This sense of power was abetted by the fact that Mr. Ford did indeed have the power to "pull the plug" financially in the relationship. Even after he gave up this destructive bond and married a woman who was far more mature and appropriate for him, Mr. Ford found himself feeling exploited by his wife, while not getting the emotional support he wished for.

In the analytic relationship Mr. Ford was an ideal patient. It was only after several years that we elucidated effectively that this was another form of his masochistic control: he would sacrifice doing what *he* wanted in the analytic situation to provide me with the steady stream of associations he knew I "wanted." By doing this, Mr. Ford defended against the vulnerability he might feel were he to experience feelings about me directly. He also remained psychologically engaged in his relationship with his mother, a bond characterized by struggles for control.

Mr. Ford's "plastic shield" (his term) between himself and me was seriously shaken by an external event. A workman on a ladder outside my office window fell several feet to the ground and lay crying out in pain. I ran out for a few minutes to help deal with the emergency. When I returned, Mr. Ford was sitting on the edge of the couch. He lay back down, resuming talking where he had left off. When I brought up the incident he admitted that it had upset him, and he wanted to avoid discussing it. When I pursued it further, he admitted being flustered. Should he have come with me? Had the workman needed help from him, too? Would that be intimate, break the analytic frame? What would he learn about me in the process?

The next hour after this event, Mr. Ford folded down the small piece of carpet I keep at the foot of the couch. He explained that he was allergic to wool, and that the carpet had been causing rashes on his calves since the beginning of the analysis several years back. It was only after processing the incident with the workman that Mr. Ford was willing to act on his allergic problem. To do so earlier signified a realness in the relationship with me that was threatening on a number of transference counts. His position of suffering silently had elements of controlling the self, but the suffering in particular was associated with fantasies of ultimate gratification and dominance in his relationship with me.

Analysis of these incidents, along with a myriad of others in his outside life, made it clear that suffering, caretaking, accepting the short end in relationships had the hidden purpose of according Mr. Ford a secret sense of superiority, power, and entitlement (Cooper 1973, Novick and Novick 1987). The way he enacted this with me was "invisible" for the most part until the outside event revealed that being a good analytic patient was disguising Mr. Ford's difficulty being openly involved with me.

Omnipotence Through Drive

Directly expressed libidinal or aggressive derivatives have an omnipotent quality because of their infantile associations. At some level there is no compromise; wishes are never given up. The implicit omnipotence of the self in relation to the object emerges most clearly in the analytic situation, as Winnicott pointed out. This quality is obscured by defensive maneuvers that protect the self from renewed exposure of humiliating limitations. When the maternal relationship is more difficult than usual, however, this yearning for direct power over the desired object may not only persist, but driven activity itself may become the way in which a sense of power is implemented.

Ms. George formed a highly explicit erotic transference to me. She also interrupted the treatment repeatedly for months at a time, which she justified by her particular job requirements. Years of psychotherapeutic work led to fewer departures. As she remained in treatment for longer periods of time, Ms. George began to understand that her behavior defended against frustration, disappointment, and rage in both maternal and paternal relationships, particularly rage at her mother's demanding closeness. In treatment, the erotic transference served to maintain a sense of power over me, through a fantasy of seduction, much as Ms. George felt her mother had had over her. It also fended off fears about the dependent meaning of her loving attachment to me.

When we were able to analyze Ms. George's seemingly positive attachment to me, especially its more demanding, seductive side, she was able to access angry, destructive fantasies about me. This, in turn, led to a more balanced relationship, in which both positive and negative feelings were accessible, but in less exaggerated forms.

Many of the cases I have discussed involve *aggression* as an important aspect of the dynamic that creates and maintains a sense of power. This is particularly true in those more severe character disorders where aggression may be an ego-organizing activity engaged in to create a feeling of control. For such individuals, the need for omnipotence takes on far greater importance. Dramatic acting out, suicidal threats, and disruption of the therapeutic frame all may represent the patient's use of aggression to restore omnipotence.

To summarize: omnipotence, or the need for a subjective sense of power and control, has many clinical manifestations. My examples include direct control over the object; control over the self; arresting the passage of time; moral masochism; and drive-dominated, aggressive erotic transferences. In each case, omnipotence was also an element in the power relationship with the analyst. We can note that each individual dynamic involved a different *emphasis* in the way in which omnipotence was expressed, but that often several aspects of omnipotence could be seen in the same person. In fact, the clinical material suggests that the different aspects of omnipotence may act as proxies for one another. A clear example is Mr. Ford, whose masochism enabled him to deny the passage of time, to forestall oedipal and pre-oedipal loss, and to avoid acknowledging vulnerability that would make him prone to humiliation in the analytic relationship.

In all these examples of major transference resistance patterns, the patient actively created in the analytic situation conditions that would allow a sense of control in the relationship in some way, and by inference a subjective experience of omnipotence. That is, the internal state required an external situation in the analytic relationship that the patient could interpret as creating or adding to his or her power. In many respects the analytic situation is set up to facilitate this. We do not quickly challenge the way the patient is structuring the relationship, and our general unintrusiveness promotes the patient's continuing use of power to maintain unconscious fantasies of omnipotence. We may interpret the patient's behavior, once we recognize it, but this does not end the behavior. Freud recognized this early on in his description of working through. Recent observers of psychoanalytic process using clinical or research bases are emphasizing the importance of the patient's active part, not simply as a relayer of associations, but as a participant who forms the analysis and then learns from analytic interactive experience (Renik 1993, Weiss and Sampson 1986). A central force driving this process is the patient's need to exert power toward the goal of maintaining the internal sense of omnipotent control in achieving gratifications and defending against danger. In other words, people work hard to maintain an internal equilibrium around their feelings of omnipotence. This leads to questions of how the sense of omnipotence comes to exist and how children deal with power.

Development

A psychoanalytic understanding of omnipotence and power in development can be enriched by examining recent research. Developmentally oriented psychoanalytic researcher-theorists now present a picture of infancy in which vivid subjective and interpersonal experiences occur from the first day forward (Stern 1985). This new work provides observations that can serve as rudimentary "data points" for a line of development concerning omnipotence. More properly, this developmental line has to do with the sense of power, competence, and efficacy (Beiser 1979, Erikson 1959, A. Freud 1936, Hendrick 1943, White 1963).

Early Months of Life

Infant research has vastly enriched our understanding of the nature of the abilities, interests, and responses of babies in the first months of life (Lichtenberg 1989, Stern 1985). From the beginning of life, infants seek sensory stimulation, have preferences about stimuli, form hypotheses about their world, and experience affects along with cognitions. For example, 3-week-old babies who suck blindfolded on two differently shaped pacifiers are able afterwards to distinguish *visually* the one more recently sucked on. We can infer that such activities are the forerunners of a sense of efficacy and control.

In its social world the newborn infant displays an ability to control others with cues so subtle that parents react without consciously registering the stimulus (Stern 1985). Thus, an infant exerts power in the social world from the earliest moments of life. Further, parents quickly begin to facilitate the infant's sense of power by reacting to the child enthusiastically. As we noted earlier, Winnicott suggested something similar in his description of the infant's creation of the breast part-object. In each of these situations the child is an active initiator of events which, in turn, lead (by our inference) to a sense of power.

What is of particular significance in this new view of the infant is how different it is from the Freudian infant with respect to activity-passivity and the source of initiative. Freud's newborn was undeveloped, sensitive, and passive, requiring the input of milk, love, and protection. Stern's newborn is an active and skilled participant in its world. While we cannot know for sure whether there are accompanying subjective experiences of this competence, we cannot escape the image of an individual with both abilities and the motivation to use them in the world.

"Symbiosis"

Mahler (1975) retained a Freudian framework, while elaborating the complexity of self–other interplay between 6 and 36 months. She followed Freud in her conceptualization that the child's consciousness emerges out of a relatively undifferentiated physiological-psychological condition of the first 3 months. Central to Mahler's developmental model is the establishment of a symbiotic relationship between mother and child beginning at about 6 months. For the child this phase involves a growing recognition of the mother as a separate individual, but one who is attuned to meeting most of the needs of the child. On this base of parental support established during the symbiotic phase, the child begins to venture boldly into the world away from the mother. The symbiotic bond is relinquished reluctantly and complexly over the next two to three years. Symbiosis, for Mahler, provides a past psychological time of omnipotent experience with a relationship. However, Mahler also showed how the symbiotic relationship serves as a launching platform for the child's forays into autonomy and individuation.

If one asks parents about different stages of development, many or most will describe this phase—3 to 9 months—as an idyllic time. Infants are delightful during this period, occupied with sedentary play, crawling, and a vital interest in people. If parents and others are delighted with the infant, it seems probable that the infant is experiencing a complementary sense of pleasure, not because of being passively attended to, but because it has brought about others' attention and interest, and can *elicit* the parents' special affection and approval. This mutuality—the fact that *both* adult and child are intensely engaged—makes this phase crucial. "Symbiosis" has, unfortunately, become equated in many people's minds with ideas of merger or massive dependency, or undifferentiated interdependency. What seems to make this phase developmentally significant is that both parent and child experience a sense of great accomplishment in their learning of signals and cues that bring about significant responses from the other toward the self. Put less technically, the child and the parents(s) fall in love. As in the oedipal, adolescent, and young adult phases to follow, the child experiences the romance of "symbiosis" as an exhilarating achievement, learning how to create a sense of delight in oneself through expressing feelings toward another.

The actual experience of each partner is somewhat different. For the parent, the delight is in the child's interest, pleasure, responsiveness; inferentially, for the child there is likely a large component of satisfaction at the growing capacity to *influence* the adult, and at the adult's increasingly accurate and immediate responsiveness. Again, observational and experimental data indicate that during the "symbiotic" phase babies are actually getting increasingly clear about their internal constructs of what is self and what is other. From the power perspective, there is little question that the child must experience with pleasure its capacity to elicit emotional reactions and various specific behavioral sequences from the parents. Or, to put it in terms of pathogenesis, we frequently reconstruct how the absence of such power experiences in the interplay of parent and child during the first years have led to significant, lasting distortions and affective distresses in areas of self-appraisal and object-relatedness.

Toddlerhood

Stern's (1985) studies of the phenomena that he named "affect attunement" identify a fascinating next step in the development of a sense of power. Stern noticed a particular sort of interaction sequence when mothers and children from 9 to 14 months were observed in an unstructured dyadic play situation. Immediately following certain brief behaviors of the child, mothers acted in ways that resemble some aspect of the child's behavior, but usually in a different mode. If the child *bangs* a toy rhythmically, the mother may follow with a *vocal* sequence in the same rhythm. These "attuned" responses convey to the child that mother is reacting *internally* to its behavior. Pure mimicry would tell the child little about mother; the transformation to a different modality tells the child the mother has an inside that reacts and responds in a confirming way. A further striking observation by Stern is that the child appears to react noticeably only to *unattuned* maternal responses (e.g., variations in tempo or intensity from the mother's usual response); otherwise the child goes on with what it was doing. It seems that attuning is something like a pat on the back for the child's curiosity, activity, expressivity. We can infer that when the mother is acting in an "attuned" way, the infant experiences subjective pleasure in efficaciousness, in its power.

Margaret Mahler may have been describing a similar phenomenon with her observation of what she called "refueling" in this early toddler phase. In refueling, the child returns to mother for contact and reassurance following a foray into the environment. Mahler's observations suggest that the infant, when away too long, experiences some sort of depletion, possibly the absence of the short-term impact of an attuned mother. Refueling may consist of obtaining attuned responses after increasingly longer periods of autonomous activity.

I have kept "symbiosis" in quotes because contemporary developmentalists question the accuracy of the term in describing the young child's bonding and individuation. "Symbiosis" implies a complete dependence, or interdependence. It tends to minimize the role of the child in actively recruiting and demanding what it needs from the parent (although a close reading of Mahler's work gives the child due credit).

The Anal Stage; Rapprochement

Here I will briefly underscore certain aspects of our understanding of sphincter control and toilet training, developed first by Freud and extensively by others (recently, for example, see Shengold 1988). What makes anality unique is its combination of bodily pleasure/unpleasure with the child's behavioral impact on parental satisfaction. There is, with anality, a large multi-dimensional matrix of possible outcomes involving sphinteric holding back versus letting go, giving versus withholding, body and non-body, and pleasure versus unpleasure. In grappling with these and the accompanying ideational processes of early sexual theorizing, the child must find a solution that works for its particular situation and history. Because of the link with body and control, the working out of the anal situation is likely accompanied by a more complex set of experiences of power, in which relation to the body may conflict with or complement the power relation to the other.

Mahler's (1975) "rapprochement crisis" at about 18 months epitomizes this aspect of the anal stage situation, and may well be the developmental sequel to affect attunement. The child cannot go through life with mother literally confirming the child's behavior once a minute (as Stern's mothers do for their 1-year-olds). In some way the child must move away, while increasingly experiencing (and perhaps creating) a portable, internalized, attuned mother. The clinging and tantrums of this phase may attest to the difficulty of this, and the child's attempts to "have it both ways": to control the source of attuning responses, and to move away from direct physical dependence on her.

What these newer psychoanalytic perspectives on early development reveal is 1) an infant born with capacities to evoke responses from the world, and the desire to do so; 2) a child–parent collaboration to develop and enhance the child's feeling of specialness and influence; and 3) the complexity of disentangling the sense of power from the earliest relationships so that the child can feel autonomous and effective at the same time.

The following discussion of subsequent developmental phases does not involve recent research data, but is included in order to suggest how issues of power continue to emerge throughout the life cycle.

Later Developmental Stages

The oedipal phase. Both Freud (1909b) in "Little Hans" and, more recently, Kohut (1977) emphasize positive feelings as part of the child's oedipal experience. The child's wish to possess one parent and be rid of the other reflects not only impulse, but also expansiveness, optimism, and creativity. Certainly, one aspect of the oedipal phase is conflict/defense, but our clinical experience also tells us that the more thoroughly a patient has entered and engaged in oedipal activity, the better for the subsequent phases of latency and puberty (Loewald 1960). The general shape of successful oedipal resolution (identification, as opposed to continued murderous feelings toward the competitor) also reflects a capacity for *fantasy* about power. For, after all, from a 5-year-old's perspective, a "realistic" delay of gratification is unimaginable. Instead, substitutive fantasy goes on, along with ambitious peer group activity (which is a preparation for adult roles). Making a shift to fantasy and peer relations worthwhile requires a capacity for self and object concepts that is "larger than life."

The extensive subliminatory activity of *latency* years is fueled by unconscious, unfulfilled desires, as well as by a desire to attain greater real control in the world. At the same time, regression to earlier types of defensive activity bolsters a feeling of power by recalling a time when one could successfully win the approval of parents without danger. The child's interest in heroic figures and in stories of children who are gratified after mastering the demands of the adult world testifies to the continuation of omnipotent mental activity (Almond 1990), as does the extensive "superhero" play of this period.

The *adolescent* must master adult sexuality relatedness, and the challenge of beginning adult autonomy from the family. The defenses of idealism and asceticism (A. Freud 1936), which often characterize this period, serve to create or maintain a sense of control and competence in the face of the immense developmental tasks of this phase. The risk-taking activity of adolescents has many functions, among them the assertion in action of *invulnerability* and *immortality*. At the same time, the dire behavior of anorexics shows us that the need to maintain control can be greater than the survival instinct. The intensity of such behavior speaks to the importance to the adolescent of creating an inner sense of power in the face of the challenges of this period.

Pumpian-Mindlin (1969) introduced the term "omnipotentiality" to describe an aspect of psychological life of adults in their *early to mid-twenties*. He felt young adults may show a regressive return to the illusion of being able to be anything, of not having to commit to one selective future that excludes other possibilities. Omnipotentiality denies the facts of development, that growth excludes some paths, just as it enhances abilities in specific areas. The psychopathology of early adulthood frequently involves blockage in the capacity to complete academic or career-starting hurdles, along with difficulty "settling down" with one partner. These choices mean a significant loss of omnipotence, often a loss too great to accept.

Marriage and parenthood, the major challenges of *early adult development*, involve significant fantasies of omnipotence. Choice of a mate frequently involves acquisition, by proxy, of certain characteristics, with an unconscious belief that these qualities are now part of oneself (Benedek 1959). This is the reciprocal of omnipotentiality: missing, undeveloped aspects of the self can be magically obtained—vicariously. The adult sustains a sense of omnipotence by imagining that the partner, or the dyad together, will embody all one's missing capacities and qualities. In *parenthood*, there is both the opportunity for reliving vicariously the omnipotence of childhood and for reworking early developmental phases with an enhanced sense of omnipotence by virtue of being in the influential parental position. The child also enables the (omnipotent) solution to old developmental conflicts through its narcissistic, as opposed to object-related, function for the parent. ("My child will fulfill my own unmet ambitions.")

In *middle and old age* omnipotence comes into play around career ambitions and the search for immortality, as well as through the continuing vicarious satisfaction of children and grandchildren. Through one's descendants, one's creations, and one's influence in the social matrix, the older person seeks to maintain the sense of power that earlier has been associated with the building up of abilities and roles.

To summarize: if we combine this necessarily summary review of significant moments of development with the earlier discussion of clinical material, we have strong support for a changed understanding of omnipotence in psychological life. This view sees the sense of power as developing early and remaining crucial throughout life, requiring ever-more elaborate psychological processes for its maintenance, as the child, and later the adult, encounters new issues. I believe the capacity to feel powerful has a normal and enhancing role in personality development (Levin 1986). It may be one of the significant activities of solitude (when it is enjoyable, rather than dominated by loneliness): the replenishing of a sense of personal efficacy in the face of the deflations of daily experience. The search for personal power may in fact be an ego function, one which we usually dress up in the more acceptable garb of "self-esteem maintenance." If this is the case, then the development line of omnipotence, instead of following Freud's route of gradually yielding to reality testing, is a process of equilibration between the hard facts of limitations and an internal sense of sufficient power over self and world. The work of development then would be learning to *create and maintain* a sense of specialness, greatness, entitlement, and uniqueness, while at the same time accepting compromises required by reality. Put another way, the capacity to compromise in the face of reality requires an *unrealistic* view of oneself. This "unrealistic" view contains an enhanced sense of worth and an intense valuation of one's powers.

Summary

I believe there are significant, though tentative, conclusions we can draw from this review of theoretical, clinical, and developmental material. The first refers back to the question of what omnipotence is, and draws upon all three of these areas: omnipotence, as evidenced by its ubiquity, may be a major way in which we *experience* drive, subjectively. When a drive is operating, the ego generates fantasy, attached to a specific goal. We experience, "I want it!" which, in the unambivalent style of primary-process thinking, becomes "I can and must have it!" Pine (1985), in the same vein, has suggested that drives are not primary, but rather are the aggregation of groups of motivated impulses and behaviors. It is this drive-related quality of omnipotence that makes its definition so difficult. Perhaps the lesson is that we need to be specific about the usage of the term "omnipotence," indicating the source and purpose of the fantasies and activities that have reference to creating subjective feelings of power.

Second, omnipotence is a lifelong issue. It seems to be the center of a significant equilibration process related to self-esteem, object relatedness, and efficaciousness. This centrality corresponds to the importance of power in human affairs. If we think of the infant crawling or toddling towards a goal, fueled by mother's affect-attuned reactions, we may have an idea of "proto-omnipotence," an inner state that seems critical to developmental progress on a moment-to-moment level. I have tried to give some hints of the earlier and later vicissitudes of this line of development. Such a model fits with Freud's idea that earlier successful omnipotent, aggressive experiences—by which he no doubt meant all past experiences of subjective efficacy—form the basis for self esteem. This model of the place of omnipotence also fits with Kohut's assertion of a lifelong need for selfobjects.

The importance of omnipotence and its derivatives is clear when we think of how much time and effort goes into political activity, both at the level of government, and within organizations and small groups. It would seem a moot point to debate whether this adult striving for status represents sublimated oedipal desire, or whether the oedipal struggle manifests omnipotent internal strivings at an early point.

Third, considerations of omnipotence can be seen as an important focus in recent clinical theory. For example, an appreciation of the importance of omnipotence can provide an integrating perspective in the schism between self psychology and mainstream psychoanalysis, the polarization between the respective roles of defense/conflict interpretation and empathic reflection. Although my dynamic formulations of the cases cited here were not in self psychological terms, the pervasiveness of the theme of omnipotence demonstrates how easily that point of view could be applied to the same material.

Recent technical contributions from ego psychology indicate a growing attention to the specifics of "tact, timing, and dosage." Implicit in these new clinical contributions is an acknowledgment of the patient's need to maintain equilibrium around the internal sense of power and/or control. Davison and colleagues (1990), for example, recommend that the analyst's interventions be made "on the down-slope of the assertive-reactive curve." In terms of omnipotence this could be restated as waiting until the patient has sufficiently established his sense of power in relation to the analyst, before interpreting. Otherwise, a precipitous intervention, while accurate, may be experienced as a deflating challenge or attack.

Paul Grey's (1990) recommendation that interpretation focus on the patient's conscious defensive activity also shows a sensitivity to power. If the analyst interprets what is unconscious, he puts himself in an omniscient position, from the patient's point of view. The patient can submit or fight back. This authority imbalance reduces the likelihood of the patient's integrating the analyst's idea. But if, as Grey recommends, the analyst refers to conscious, reported experience, the patient may feel his omnipotence less disturbed, his defensive activity uncritically acknowledged, and may be more able to assimilate new ideas.

The clinical vignettes bring out other important and apparently paradoxical features of omnipotence. The tenacity of neurotic structure suggests that the particular route taken by an individual to omnipotent experience is delimited at some point in development. Among my clinical examples, each patient had a *particular* way of being omnipotent, and clung to it tenaciously in outside life and in the analytic situation. This individual style of enacting power provides a *general* sense of omnipotence, accounting perhaps for the "omni-" part of the term. For example, Mrs. Dalton's "ability" to stop time gave her a feeling that *all* of life's problems and *all* her conflicts were in her control. How a particular fantasy and mode of relating to the world is "chosen" for creating the feeling of omnipotence is an interesting question, no doubt involving the infantile neurosis and the development of character structure. In psychoanalysis these characteristic modes of dealing with omnipotence emerge vividly in the enactments of the transference. With greater understanding of the need for internal operations involving omnipotence, modern clinical theory may help us understand and interpret these phenomena better.

Finally, the analysis of the power–omnipotence junction provides one way to look at the relation between intrapsychic and interpersonal levels of understanding. Clinical discussions among psychoanalysts are increasingly concerned with interaction, but we lack concepts that create a bridge between the two conceptual realms. I have tried to trace the path of external power alongside discussions of the intrapsychic vicissitudes of omnipotence. A far more extensive study and vocabulary will be needed to take us further into this new area.

References

Almond, B. (1990). The Secret Garden: a therapeutic metaphor. *Psychoanalytic Study of the Child* 45:477–494. New Haven, CT: Yale University Press.

Ansbacher, H., and Ansbacher, R. (1956). *The Individual Psychology of Alfred Adler*. New York: Harper & Row.

Beiser, H. R. (1979). The problem of infantile omnipotence. *Annual of Psychoanalysis* 7:113–132.

Benedek, T. (1959). Parenthood as a developmental phase. *Journal of the American Psychoanalytic Association* 78:389–417.

Cooper, A. (1973). The narcissistic-masochistic character. In *Masochism: Current Psychoanalytic Perspectives*, ed. R. A. Glick and D. I. Meyers, pp. 117–138. Hillsdale, NJ: Analytic Press.

Davison, W. T., Pray, M., and Bristol, C. (1990). Mutative interpretation and close process monitoring in a study of psychoanalytic process. *Psychoanalytic Quarterly* 59:599–628.

Erikson, E. (1959). Identity and the life cycle. *Psychological Issues* 1. New York: International Universities Press.

Freud, A. (1936). *The Ego and the Mechanisms of Defense*. New York: International Universities Press.

Freud, S. (1909a). Notes upon a case of obsessional neurosis. *Standard Edition* 10:155–318.

——— (1909b). Analysis of phobia in a five-year-old boy. *Standard Edition* 10:5–152.

——— (1913). Totem and taboo. *Standard Edition* 13:1–161.

——— (1914a). Remembering, repeating and working through. *Standard Edition* 12:145–156.

——— (1914b). On narcissism. *Standard Edition* 14:73–104.

——— (1926). Inhibitions, symptoms and anxiety. *Standard Edition* 20:87–172.

——— (1930). Civilization and its discontents. *Standard Edition* 21:64–145.

Goethe, J. W. (1808). *Faust*. Munich: Wilhelm Goldman Verlag, 1958.

Grey, P. (1990). The nature of therapeutic action in psychoanalysis. *Journal of the American Psychoanalytic Association* 38:1083–1098.

Hendrick, I. (1943). Work and the pleasure principle. *Psychoanalytic Quarterly* 12:311–329.

Kernberg, O. (1975). *Borderline Conditions and Pathological Narcissism*. New York: Jason Aronson.

Klein, M., Heiman, P., Isaacs, S., and Riviere, J. (1983). *Developments in Psycho-Analysis*. New York: Da Capo.

Kohut, H. (1971). *The Analysis of the Self*. New York: International Universities Press.

——— (1977). *The Reconstruction of the Self*. New York: International Universities Press.

——— (1984). *How Does Analysis Cure?* Chicago: University of Chicago Press.

Levin, R. (1986). Infantile omnipotence and grandiosity. *Psychoanalytic Review* 73:57–76.

Levine, H., ed. (1991). *Adult Analyses and Childhood Sexual Abuse*. Hillsdale, NJ: Analytic Press.

Lichtenberg, J. (1989). *Psychoanalysis and Motivation*. Hillsdale, NJ: Analytic Press.

Loewald, H. (1960). On the therapeutic action of psychoanalysis. *International Journal of Psycho-Analysis* 41:16–33.

Mack, J. (1986). Prologue: Aggression and alternatives in international relations. *Psychoanalytic Inquiry* 6:135–142.

——— (1994). Power, powerlessness, and empowerment in psychotherapy. *Psychiatry* 57:178–198.

Mahler, M. (1975). *The Psychological Birth of the Human Infant*. New York: Basic Books.

Modell, A. (1975). Narcissistic defense against affects: The illusion of self-sufficiency. *International Journal of Psycho-Analysis* 56:275–282.

Novick, K. K., and Novick, J. (1987). The essence of narcissism. *Psychoanalytic Study of the Child* 42:335–385. New Haven, CT: Yale University Press.

Pine, F. (1985). *The Developmental Theory and Clinical Process*. New Haven, CT:Yale University Press.

Pumpian-Mindlin, E. (1969). Vicissitudes of infantile omnipotence. *Psychoanalytic Study of the Child* 24:213–226. New York: International Universities Press.

Renik, O. (1993). Analytic interaction: conceptualizing technique in light of the analyst's irreducible subjectivity. *Psychoanalytic Quarterly* 62:553–571.

Shengold, L. (1988). *Halo in the Sky*. New York: Guilford.

Stern, D. (1985). *The Interpersonal World of the Infant*. New York: Basic Books.

Weiss, J., and Sampson, H. (1986). *The Psychoanalytic Process*. New York: Guilford.

White, R. (1963). Ego and reality in psychoanalytic theory. *Psychological Issues* 11. New York: International Universities Press.

Winnicott, D. W. (1960). The theory of the parent–infant relationship. *International Journal of Psycho-Analysis* 41:585–595.

——— (1965). *The Maturational Process and the Facilitating Environment*. London: Hogarth.

2

Omnipotence: Pathology and Resistance

Jack Novick, Ph.D. and Kerry Kelly Novick

Editors' Comments

Jack Novick and Kerry Kelly Novick continue their work on the importance of fantasies of omnipotence in every area of pathology. They have not found (as Freud, Ferenczi, Mahler, and Winnicott did) that omnipotence plays a role in normal development; rather they describe the contrast between pathological omnipotence and the development of healthy and realistic sources of competence and self-regard.

The Novicks trace the way in which sadomasochistic systems are created from birth through toddlerhood, then through the oedipal period, the latency period, and adolescence, and add much to their other work by specifying what they see as the developmental tasks of each period. Starting with infancy and the helplessness of the baby, they describe in great detail failures in reality (in terms of parental care) that can lead the infant to start using pain as the basis of all relationships. In descriptions of each stage, the Novicks highlight the complex interaction throughout development between past and present, between psychic reality and failures of external reality, which lead the child to increasing dependence on omnipotent fantasies in order to handle the narcissistic challenges of each period.

The Novicks take a broad developmental point of view and show how the defense of omnipotence can be woven from the strands of each developmental level and become organized in adolescence into an implacable system. Their views on the treatment of these patients and issues of termination are particularly valuable.

In our work with severely disturbed children, adolescents, and adults, and in our infant and toddler observations, we were drawn to explore sadomasochism, the beating fantasy as its essence, and externalization as a major mechanism in the development and functioning of this pathology. However, in working with the sadomasochism of these patients, we found, as have others from Freud on (Freud 1909, 1940, Meyers 1988), that the analyses were long and arduous because of the self-destructive character of the pathology, its roots at every level of development, and the intense countertransference reactions evoked. This led us to wonder about the nature of the resistance. In 1988, we presented a paper that said:

> [I]n our studies of masochistic patients, we have found derivatives of each phase, but, like a thread linking knots of fixation points at oral, anal, and phallic-oedipal phases, there is a delusion of omnipotence which infuses the patients' past and current functioning. [Novick and Novick 1991, p. 309]

Up to that point we had more or less accepted and worked with the classical formulation of the development of omnipotence and its role in normality and pathology as described by Freud (1911, 1915, 1917) and Ferenczi (1913). That view was that the child is born feeling omnipotent and only gradually and reluctantly, under the impact of failure of the omnipotent system, turns to and accepts reality. Most psychoanalysts speak of infantile omnipotence as a state of mind characteristic of the first eighteen months of life, the period Piaget (1952, 1954) called the *sensorimotor period*.

There is a curious discrepancy between the omnipotence attributed to the infant in these theories and the adult clinical manifestations attributed to omnipotent fantasies. And yet analysts have continued to posit a direct relationship between the adult fantasies and so-called "normal infantile omnipotence." Current authors follow this thinking as we did. But in the course of our work on sadomasochism we came to feel that there are inherent difficulties in the traditional formulation, and these led us to describe the development of omnipotence rather differently. In an earlier paper, we said: "The classical view is that the failure of omnipotence forces the child to turn to reality. In our view it is the failure of reality that forces the child to turn to omnipotent solutions" (Novick and Novick 1991, p. 320).

Looking at the development of the delusion of omnipotence in that way implied a separate pathway of pathological development, in contrast to the development of a normal system of self-esteem regulation based on an economy of pleasure from competence at each phase. In that paper, we described two systems of self-esteem regulation, the competent and the omnipotent. We now think that these are aspects of distinct paths of development that may be traced through the life span and may help us to understand the overdetermination of pathology at any point in development. This is different from the formulation that pathology represents a solution to conflict that involves regression to an earlier normal state. The traditional approach has been to view pathology as either an exaggeration of normal traits or the persistence or reemergence of normal infantile behavior in a later phase when it is no longer appropriate. Many widely accepted terms and concepts exemplify this way of thinking, for example, the autistic and symbiotic phases, the schizoid and paranoid positions, infantile omnipotence, the anal-sadistic phase, normal feminine masochism, adolescence as a normal phase of disturbance, and so on. To generalize from pathology to normality can be seen as an epistemological stance, one that has proven its value, but, like all positions, also has its drawbacks.

A major thrust of our current work is to consider the possibility that there are two different pathways in development, two distinct solutions to conflict. We assume that conflict and conflict resolution are universal but that neurosis is not. Neurosis is one of numerous possible solutions to conflict. It would follow, then, that the normal mother–infant bond is not necessarily symbiotic, the anal phase is not in itself sadistic, the oedipal period need not be experienced as a trauma, latency is not a period of arid repression, masochism may be pervasive but is not normal, and normal adolescence is not a period of emotional turbulence akin to a severe emotional disorder. Our formulation assumes a developmental path in which "healthy" or "adaptive" solutions to conflict may be achieved throughout life. We suggest that omnipotence does not play a role in normal development. Rather, the presence of omnipotent functioning is a sign of pathological solution to conflict.

We may summarize this view by pointing, on the one hand, to an omnipotent sadomasochistic system of self-regulation, based on the active search for pain with the change throughout development of the experience of helplessness into a hostile omnipotent defense. On the other hand, there is a competent system based on mutually respectful and growth-promoting relationships formed through realistic perceptions of separate autonomous individuals. These two distinct systems of self-regulation do not differentiate people, that is, they are not diagnostic categories. Rather they describe potential choices of adaptation within each individual at any point in development and allow for a metapsychological, or multidimensional, description of the components of the individual's relation to himself and others. The treatment goal of restoration to the path of progressive development refers to restoration to the path of reality-rooted competence, pleasure, and self-esteem.

We have extensively studied the sadomasochistic solution to conflict and have concluded that sadomasochism is not a diagnostic category, but is an integral part of all pathology. Omnipotence is a hostile defensive component of sadomasochism. Most simply, in all pathology there is sadomasochism; in all sadomasochism, there is an omnipotent fantasy. It is like a Russian doll, with the largest one representing psychopathology. Inside, the next one is sadomasochism, the next is omnipotence, and inside that is a helpless, traumatized child. The decorations, patterns, and designs painted on the dolls could represent different diagnoses. In this chapter, we are concentrating on one of the smaller dolls in the set. Zeroing in on a single aspect of a large field has the drawback that the reader may forget that we are discussing only a part, and assume that our thoughts are meant to explicate the whole. The advantage of a close focus, however, is that we may isolate significant elements that otherwise go unnoticed, but that can gravely disrupt clinical work. The aim of zeroing in on omnipotence is to add to our technical repertoire, not to replace or subtract. In empathy with the patient's defenses, therapists may be reluctant to label phenomena as pathological. We do not do ourselves or the patient a service by avoiding an accurate perception of pathology. But we must also be aware that what we see as pathological may be experienced entirely differently by the patient, who has made the best possible adaptation he can to his inner and outer circumstances. The technical problem is to encompass both points of view in a way that advances the treatment.

In this presentation we would like to explore the technical implications of a detailed examination of omnipotent fantasies. We will use a developmental approach, as we have done in the past, to describe the life history of omnipotent fantasy functioning, and to see what amplification of our ideas may result. Each developmental phase highlights a different aspect of omnipotence and adds a strand to the rope.

Development of Omnipotence

Pregnancy

We have not heretofore formally included pregnancy in descriptions of the development of the individual, but it is well known, although not well explained, that pathology is transmitted across generations. There is a growing literature (Brody 1956, Fonagy et al. 1993, Piontelli 1992) that documents psychological factors in the mother as crucial influences on the development of psychopathology in the infant. There are many aspects of the mother's personality that could be isolated for study. Here our focus on omnipotence points to the role of maternal fantasies in the unfolding psychological development of the child. We would extend Anna Freud's remark that the mother's fantasies create the child's reality to include maternal fantasies during pregnancy.

Fantasies during pregnancy are central to the mother's preparation for parenthood. Wishes for a healthy baby do not violate anything known about the unborn baby and can relate to normal maintenance of the mother's self-esteem: she wants to feel like a healthy woman who can produce a healthy baby. Anxieties that the baby may not be healthy can relate to the mother's preparation for tolerating the anxiety involved in protecting her child from real dangers. This exposes the mother to her own vulnerabilities in the area of maintenance of her own feelings of safety; this necessary empathic identification with her child's vulnerability evokes either a constructive adaptive use of her ego capacities to protect herself and her child or recourse to omnipotent fantasy solutions. In our earlier paper on masochism and omnipotence we distinguished between realistic fantasies, which enhance the self, and unrealistic omnipotent fantasies, which have as their goal the control of others. The manifest content of the fantasy or anxiety cannot tell us which it is; this can only be discerned in clinical exploration.

As we look at the life cycle, highlighting issues around omnipotence, we find in examining phenomena in pregnancy that omnipotent fantasies are a defense against feelings of helplessness. With support, most mothers who turn to the omnipotent response to their actual helplessness can relinquish it and shift their energies to the realities they can enjoy and control. Without support, or when the omnipotent defense is embedded in more severe pathology, the omnipotent defense may persist through the pregnancy and cross the generational barrier to have impact on the newborn child.

We started with pregnancy because it is the beginning of the life cycle for the individual; the mother's psychic state during pregnancy affects the unfolding of the infant's early experience. What we can take away from an initial look at the role of omnipotent fantasies during pregnancy is that the strand of defense against helplessness will persist throughout development. Even in adulthood, when the omnipotent fantasy has undergone changes through many layers of development, the most minor manifestations of omnipotent defense, such as "knock wood," or "Thank God," or "Gesundheit," contain the strand of helplessness.

Infancy

All phases can be described from a variety of vantage points: in relation to omnipotence, the important dimension to highlight in infancy is the pleasure economy and its corruption. We have described the operation of the pleasure economy in normal mother–infant pairs as follows:

> Ordinarily, the child's real capacity to elicit the appropriate response from the caregiver is the root of feelings of competence, effectance, and reality-based self-esteem. The capacity of the mother–infant couple to repair inevitable breaches in the empathic tie is an equally important source of feelings of competence and positive self-regard. A range of positive feelings from contentment to joy becomes associated with these competent interactions and comes to instigate, reinforce, and signify empathic interaction. Thus pleasure is dependent on and regulated by the capacity of each partner for realistic percep-

> tion and interaction with the other, which leads in turn to the experience of having an actual effect on the other. [Novick and Novick 1991, p. 312]

There can be outside interferences with the unfolding of this normal development, for instance, from harsh circumstances or medical problems in either mother or child. If there is no support for the normal development of pleasure in competence, or there is pathology in the mother such as we referred to in the section on pregnancy, or there is experience in infancy such as we have reconstructed in the treatments of sadomasochistic patients, the infant is at risk for corruption and deformation of the pleasure economy. Instead of repeated and accumulating experiences of pleasure in getting his needs attended to, the infant's inborn capacities to elicit needed responses are ineffectual. The infant's experience of cause and effect is then formed and formulated in relation to painful feelings. If a mother does not smile in response to the child's smile, but only on emergence from a depressed or anxious state, when she feels like it, the only constant in an unpredictable life will become the range of dysphoric feelings. Mothers become associated with pain, indeed, the currency of existence becomes pain. Pain is central to sadomasochistic pathology and is a trigger for the omnipotent defense, as the infant is helpless to effect change without the intervention of parents or caregivers attuned to his needs. In later years, when sadomasochistic pathology is entrenched at all levels of development, the central element of pain can be understood to hark back to infantile experience, to this early layer of the magical use of pain for safety, comfort, and control. The basic needs of attachment, good self-feeling, and predictability become connected with feelings of helplessness to secure their gratification; what ought to be pleasurable is transformed into pain. Pain then becomes the affect that triggers the defense of omnipotence, pain is the magical means by which all wishes can be gratified, and pain justifies the omnipotent hostility and revenge contained in the sadomasochistic fantasy. Because the infant's developing sense of power is not rooted in actual experiences of effectance, there is no reality to contradict his illusion of control through dysphoric feelings and counteract the development of an encompassing delusion, that is, an omnipotent fantasy.

For the last ten years, we have been part of a research program with Drs. Donald Silver and B. Kay Campbell, studying the development of relationships between adolescent mothers and their babies. We have followed eighty-five pairs through their two-year stay in a residential center, which provided schooling, therapy, and medical and social support for the mothers, and medical and day-care services for the babies. Research data included periodic videotaping as a developmental record, therapy notes, cottage observations, medical and social history records, and case information discussions.

In the videotapes of adolescent mothers feeding, bathing, or playing with their babies, we may track the development of dysphoric interactions between parent and child that become a source of pain the baby learns to control in the effort to defend against helplessness. For instance, Kathy and her 2-week-old daughter were seen in a film enjoying a feeding, with the infant gazing into her mother's eyes. Kathy was a sweet, warm young mother whose functioning was compromised by a strong defensive identification with an apparently narcoleptic grandmother who had been her primary caretaker. Kathy could engage with her baby, but also withdrew her attention intermittently, tuning out abruptly and unpredictably. Four weeks later, when the baby was 6 weeks old, a dramatic change in their interaction showed in a feeding videotape. The baby's affect had been transformed from pleasurable expectation and involvement to distinct aversion and unhappiness. Her expression was fretful, she resolutely avoided meeting her mother's eyes, averting her gaze despite mother's efforts to engage her attention, and she held her hands as far away from contact with her mother as she could.

In a film of Nicole feeding at 2½ months we saw Nicole's attempt to engage her mother in effective interactions. Her mother's developmental level and depression inhibited her appropriate responsiveness and gradually Nicole's smiles changed to an habitual frown. Nicole's mother began to make clear her displeasure and disgust with the baby. Observations recorded her attribution of failure to Nicole. The mother externalized unacceptable aspects of herself onto the child. At 4 months Nicole was diagnosed failure-to-thrive, coincident with her mother's deepening depression. Nicole turned to self-comfort, in particular to hair-pulling. This symptom represented an early attachment via pain, the first strand in a sadomasochistic development and the first attempt to control the object.

This is the foundation of the repetitive search for painful relationships, in which the patient in later life seeks a magical omnipotent way to restore early controls and meet his legitimate needs. Highlighted in infancy is the transformation of the pain of helplessness into pain as an affect associated with attachment, safety, and control. Pain is transformed from a passive experience of helplessness into an illusory sign of safety and eventually will be part of an omnipotent delusion that gratification of these basic needs can be achieved only in a painful relationship. We suggest that a painful relationship during infancy, whatever the source, needs intervention to prevent the development of later pathology. Technical interventions in therapies at all later phases can be enhanced by the awareness that a painful treatment relationship may partially be serving functions of maintaining attachment and safety that were disrupted by an early mother–child relationship characterized predominantly by pain.

Toddlerhood

For most children toddlerhood is a time of exponential expansion of possibilities. The flowering of motor and cognitive capacities allows for rapid development and elaboration of competence in regulating tension states, feeding, dressing, and protecting oneself, and establishing bowel and bladder mastery. Parents' capacities to channel assertive impulses appropriately and "absorb aggression" (Furman 1985, Orgel 1974) are crucial to the toddler's growing confidence and pleasure in his new skills. The toddler's libidinal investment in his excretory functions and the associated sensations and his gratification in asserting his wishes and effecting their satisfaction are sources of both instinctual gratification and ego nurturance. Seen from this perspective, toddlerhood is not intrinsically a time of sadism, nor of the rageful disruption of "normal omnipotence," as formulated in current mainstream theory. Splitting, projective identification, and defensive externalization are not necessary and usual elements of this developmental phase. When we attempt to distinguish normal toddler development from pathological, either during toddlerhood itself, or in the derivatives apparent in the treatment of older patients, we look for the antecedents in this phase of reactions to experiences of helplessness. Accidents of fate, like illness or bereavement, may inflict helplessness and pain on a child. When these appear in a history, the question is the patient's choice of solution, and his environment's provision of possibilities. Has he chosen an omnipotent fantasy solution or a realistic adaptation to adversity? What are the roots in the anal phase of such a choice?

Problems in the toddler period do not usually arise spontaneously, because of the "terrible twos." And the solution is not to wait for the child to outgrow them. Sadism is created in the context of a sadomasochistic relationship. If the mother and father are not sadomasochistic, assertion will be appreciated and enjoyed, aggression will be absorbed and channeled, and fusion promoted. In our observational research, we have not seen spontaneously arising sadism in very young children. Visible, active assertion of needs and wishes is accompanied by strong affects of pleasure associated with effectance. When this is blocked, aggression swiftly follows and amplifies all other affects.

This still does not constitute sadism. The permutation of assertion to aggression to sadism depends on what happens next. In our view the crucial shift occurs when the child feels helpless to deal with the internal experience of his anger, and the outside world offers inappropriate or inadequate assistance. When adaptive solutions are unavailable, the child turns to omnipotence. Omnipotence is the additional quality that turns aggressive and assertive impulses into sadism. Internal changes have taken place in the child; this is evident when he becomes the aggressor and initiator of sadomasochistic interactions with others. This may be seen in some of the children we have followed in our research on adolescent mothers and their babies.

As we tried to discern the next strand in the development of omnipotent functioning, we could see in films of play taken at intervals through her toddlerhood how Nicole's normal exploratory impulses, curiosity, and creativity in her play were continually blocked and thwarted, leaving her helpless to predict what would happen next. Without help from her mother, indeed with her mother the source of the interference with experiences of realistic cause and effect, proportional stimulus and response, and accurate learning of meaning in the results of her actions, Nicole turned to sadistic control of her mother. Omnipotent pathology was set in motion. Similar patterns were discerned in other children's play.

In our work with sadomasochistic patients, it has become clear that they entered the toddler period with little confidence in their own capacities, and further opportunities for competent interaction were blocked and frustrated. Assertions were experienced and labelled by parents as aggressive; channels for appropriate discharge were not made available, so the frustrated child did indeed become aggressive. Attempts at effective steps toward self-reliance were experienced by their mothers as stubborn battles for control; through their mothers' externalization and physical intrusiveness, the children were never allowed to be in charge of and own their bodies. Aversive or angry responses to mother's lack of empathy occasioned increasing spirals of rage, guilt, and blame so that the patients as toddlers had been made to feel responsible for their mothers' pain, anger, helplessness, and inadequacy. The continuing failure of the caretaking person to meet the child's appropriate need for competent interactions created a feeling of intense helpless rage that was defended against by omnipotent fantasies of control, rescue, and potential destructiveness.

The development of omnipotence in the toddler period is fuelled by the continued blocking of pleasurable experiences of competence and the development of greater specificity in object relations, leading to the transformation of generalized frustration into object-directed rage. But we must also explain the development of the fixed quality of omnipotent fantasy, the delusional conviction, apparent in the functioning of patients of all ages who suffer this pathology, that they can *really* destroy another. We think the source lies in the external confirmation of the notion that anger really is destructively powerful and can overwhelm, damage, or kill the parent. The child's functioning is responded to as omnipotently destructive or omnipotently reparative: through externalization of responsibility the child is told "You're killing me," "You'll be the death of me," and so on or "Mommy has a headache, be a good boy and Mommy will feel better." The child, searching for a solution to his helplessness, is offered the idea that his mother's feelings and well-being depend on him. The wish to feel effective is granted in the illusory form of a message from the arbiter of reality, the parent, that the child's anger and aggressive behavior is the best way to have his wishes fulfilled. The stage is set for the development of a full-blown sadomasochistic relationship with the quality of omnipotence an essential component of the child's narcissistic economy; already his self-esteem depends on proving his power to control the object.

Further corruption of the pleasure economy results from furious parental reactions to normal assertion and growing independent functioning. The caretaking person reacts as if the toddler is capable of destroying with his activity. Parents of toddlers seen in childcare or clinical consultations frequently give descriptions of their children that sound like Godzilla, instead of someone two feet tall. This is a clue to the presence of parental omnipotent fantasies, in which the need is for total control. Anything less threatens anarchy and so the fantasy must be violently protected.

The development of sadomasochistic patterns of relating between adults and toddlers demands intervention to prevent further consolidation of omnipotent thinking and erosion of pleasure from competent functioning. Various symptom pictures can include these elements, with children presenting as wild, uncontrolled, and impulsive, or depressed, withdrawn, and inhibited.

Edward, a boy whose joyful and competent ball playing at 9

months was interfered with by his mother's uncontrolled sadism, was filmed having a snack at 15 months. By that time he was a competent self-feeder. When his mother tried to make him eat, Edward resisted, the tension between them increased, he turned away from his mother, looked right through her, and gazed at the ceiling, while she sighed in helpless frustration and rage. Nicole, whom we filmed in early toddlerhood, was bewildered by interference with her developing competence in play, and began to plague her mother with stubborn defiance, in small and large matters. We recorded her at nearly two in a film with her mother, trying to use her dolly to master feelings. When her mother interfered with the game, directing it according to her own needs instead of Nicole's, the toddler turned to escalating provocation and successfully generated a fight with her mother.

Without intervention, toddlerhood supplies significant strands to the rope of omnipotent fantasy functioning in adulthood, as we may see clinically with adult patients. The clinical manifestations of omnipotent fantasies are many, for example, Mrs. T., who asserted that she could indeed throw the analytic couch through the window, or Mr. D., who refrained from telling his sexual fantasies so the analyst would not be uncontrollably excited by them, or Miss J., who expected daily that the analyst would eject her from treatment. Many defenses against breakthroughs of aggressive impulses are involved, such as reaction formations, splitting of ambivalence, inhibition, negation, and so on, but interpretation of these alone may not lead to therapeutic progress. The patient's concern about the impact of his aggressive impulses is excessive and persists, leading to the hypothesis that the defenses are a secondary formation, built upon an omnipotent fantasy and designed to protect the fantasy rather than the object. Work must be directed toward confronting the delusional component of this formation, for instance, the patient's idea that the analyst is so fragile or so uncontrolled that only the patient's efforts can make a difference.

To the infantile strand of the transformation of helplessness into the control of attachment through pain the toddler period adds the strands of object-directed rage and reality confirmation for the later delusional conviction of the power of feelings for hostile omnipotent control of others.

Phallic-Oedipal

In our developmental delineation of the epigenesis of masochism (Novick and Novick 1987) we said that a crucial transformation occurs during the phallic-oedipal phase. In our paper on masochism and omnipotence we noted that in our sample of sadomasochistic patients the oedipal period presented them with realities they could not integrate, realities that carried potential traumatic impact. In classical libido theory, the phallic-oedipal phase relates to a shift of libido from oral and anal zones to the phallic. There is a concomitant shift in object relationship from a dyadic to a triadic constellation. An important distinction, sometimes overlooked, is the one between phallic assertion and a perversion of this development that takes the form of phallic sadism, which is not a necessary part of normal development. Difficulties in including all three people in the libidinal milieu become part of a pathological experience of the impulses of this phase. The child's assessment of his impulses depends on his parents' reactions; they define the acceptability and nature of his wishes and will contribute to the self-assessment that is internalized in the superego toward the end of this phase. The contrast between normal and pathological development can be marked on many dimensions. Joy is an expression of self-esteem that springs from inside, a self-confidence and unselfconsciousness that comes with safe, uncritical appreciation of the child's real self and capacities. Manic excitement, on the other hand, relates to pathological narcissism, in which self-esteem is vested in unstable outside sources; it represents also an omnipotent compensation for humiliation. The child who is laughed at, teased, or shamed has his self-respect attacked, feels helpless in the face of hostility from powerful adults, and turns to unrealistic solutions. The connection of humiliation with aggression at this level has profound implications: instead of experiencing oedipal defeat as frustration of libidinal desire that actually meshes with physical realities, the child equates the humiliation with annihilation, obliteration, emptiness, and complete helplessness. This will affect all later situations that demand taking a risk of narcissistic failure; all later libidinal impulses can trigger this reaction and include such deep anxieties, creating ever more powerful motives for massive defense.

If parents respond to exuberance as if it is hostile or actually a threat, the child begins to experience his own enjoyment as sadistic. He can no longer take pleasure in his own achievement without seeking further gratification in triumph over the other. During a recent World Cup soccer tournament, an Italian supporter declared before the Ireland–Italy match, "Two things are going to happen: Italy's going to win and Ireland's going to lose!"

Perhaps underemphasized in psychoanalytic theory is that the period of late toddlerhood is especially marked by flowering and consolidation of ego functions, including the cognitive capacity to make comparisons along numerous dimensions. We often see this skill make its first appearance in the charged comparison between the self and the new baby, with the toddler insisting that the bawling, burping, smelly one is the baby, while he *himself* is not. Comparisons continue and intensify; they are always affect-laden rather than neutral ascriptions of adjectival qualifiers. The older toddler notices who has more cake or more toys. Rather than thinking in terms of continuous increments, he is likely to use all-or-nothing categories. If his brother has more cookies, he is apt to react as if the other has all the cookies and he has none. This affect-laden capacity to measure and compare feeds into the potential envy, jealousy, and drama of the phallic-oedipal phase.

In relation to omnipotence, the phallic-oedipal period provides a new possibility of reality contradiction to an illusion of power, attachment, and control of the object through pain, suffering, or aggression. The main threat to the child's pathological form of self-esteem regulation (Reich 1960) is his own growing cognitive capacities, what Mahon has called the child's cognitive revolution (1991). Each comparison of self with others and of parents with others threatens the illusion of attachment through pain, of power and equality through sadomasochistic internalization. The growth of reality-testing and the increase in experience of the real world offer the child the opportunity to take pleasure and pride in his real achievements. Oedipal exclusion and rejection are actually potentially progressive experiences, as they mandate an acceptance of and turn to reality. The child with a cushion of reality-based self-esteem can bear the narcissistic hurt. For the child with an inadequate narcissistic base, however, the experience is one of overwhelming attack and rejection and so the child constructs a *delusion* of omnipotence, a fantasy of power maintained by denial of reality and idealization of self and object. This decisive turn away from fulfillment of cognitive potential and the pleasure of a reality-based engagement with the world is reinforced by parental collusion with denial and idealization. Bach (1994) has written about two types of narcissism, subjective and objective; in his terms we see omnipotence in this phase as constituting a strenuous resistance to objective narcissism and the blocking of those ego capacities that support reality-based self-esteem or objective narcissism. In 1987 we wrote:

> A crucial transformation occurs during this phase, when the painful experiences in the pre-oedipal parent–child interaction become libidinized and represent for the child participation in parental intercourse. To the powerful motives for masochism of the earlier phases is added the circumvention of the normal oedipal exclusion, humiliation, and rage. [p. 371]

Such a pathological resolution of the oedipus complex leads to two outcomes in relation to omnipotence. First, omnipotence is reinforced as an apparently viable solution to conflict. Secondly, there is no genuine resolution of the Oedipus complex and thus no internalization and consolidation of the superego. The child is constrained to return to omnipotent fantasy as a control and a regulator of thoughts and actions. The original objects are not relinquished, and so the child will have difficulty turning to new objects in a genuine way later. And, without a viable superego, none of his achievements and accomplishments may be used as occasions for praise of the self, for satisfaction mediated internally.

A further significant aspect of omnipotent fantasies is added during this period. As we described it in our earlier paper:

> [P]arental collusion with the child's need to deny oedipal exclusion not only confirms the feeling of omnipotent power but adds a quality to omnipotence which will become a standard by which all achievements are measured. The omnipotent oedipal triumph feels quick and effortless; henceforth any achievement which requires time and effort is devalued. The conviction that things should come easily becomes a significant element in the formation of the ego ideal and forms a kernel of reality in the latency fantasy that there really was a time when all wishes were instantly gratified, that mother and child were really a "purified pleasure dyad." [Novick and Novick 1991, p. 316]

The point we are emphasizing here is how an illusion becomes a delusion, how the fixative is applied to an idea or a wish that is available to anyone but in certain people takes on a permanent quality that affects all their thinking and functioning. Our clinical and observational experience indicates that the development of the delusion of omnipotence always involves a distortion that is confirmed and contributed to from the outside. The child's attempts to change reality are given the stamp of verisimilitude by those whose proper task is to present and dose the characteristics of the real world in such a way that the child may internalize and integrate its characteristics and develop accurate reality testing. Thus omnipotent thinking cannot persist only as a force from inside the child, but needs the contribution of the environment to become the fixed delusion and distortion of reality testing we see in our patients at later stages.

Many authors working from an adult clinical base emphasize the patient's denial of painful realities about himself. We would add and put equal emphasis on the patient's need to deny parental weakness, inadequacy, and pathology. The child's denial of these realities is also reinforced by parental collusion and defensive externalization. Shengold's (1991) observations about the impact of parental weakness on the development of narcissistic pathology are relevant here. The oedipal child's capacity to observe differences does not only include comparison of himself with others, but is applied acutely to comparisons of his parents with other adults. As the child enters a wider world of school and friendships, he is exposed to teachers and the parents of his friends and begins to build a real basis for assessment of his own parents. Such comparisons can be intensely painful.

This brings us to the subject of idealization of self and object, which plays an important role during the phallic-oedipal phase in interplay with denial and the delusion of omnipotence. The concept of idealization has a long history in psychoanalysis, dating back at least to Freud's formulation of a normal state of infantile narcissism and omnipotence. The shattering of this hypothesized state of normal omnipotence, or what Bach (1994) has most recently termed "psychobiological omnipotence" (p. 167), by the realization of the reality of separateness and helplessness, was said to force the child to attribute omnipotence to his parents through idealization. This has been described by many theorists as a normal stage in object relations. The dynamic interaction between idealization of the self and of the object has been reconstructed or reiterated by most modern analysts from clinical material seen in the light of a fundamental assumption of a normal stage of infantile omnipotence that when shattered by ordinary reality, usually at the stage of separation-individuation, leads to a lifelong attempt to regain the infantile state.

Various therapeutic goals and techniques follow from this assumption, as in Kohut's (1971, 1977) ideas concerning the idealizing transference as a means of repair, Balint's (1968) idea of a new beginning, and the position of many that the aim of treatment is to accomplish mourning for lost omnipotence of self and object. This view is implied in Melanie Klein's (1950) developmental positions, in Winnicott's work (1965), and in Kernberg's (1975, 1980) formulations, and is well described by Bach (1994). The idea of mourning lost omnipotence as a therapeutic goal is predicated on the classical view that the only reason the child turns to reality is the failure of omnipotence.

We wrote earlier that, "it is the failure of reality that forces the child to turn to omnipotent solutions" (1991, p. 320). It follows that with this perspective we have a somewhat different view of idealization than the classical. We suggest that idealization represents a defensive attempt to transform the real and overwhelming inadequacies, weakness, or pathology of the primary object. We distinguish idealization from reality-based admiration, appreciation, respect, or love. The good-enough parent, the good-enough teacher, the good-enough friend, and later the good-enough lover or mate does not need to be idealized. From the phallic-oedipal phase, when cognitive capacities to compare and contrast and so be realistically critical become consolidated, the child whose parent falls outside the limits of the good-enough range may deal with his overwhelming anxiety from perception of parental failure by changing his reality and creating an omnipotent delusion of idealized self- and object-representations. Usually in such situations the inadequate parenting has been present from long before and the idealizing, reality-altering solution builds upon those of the previous phases. Many elements of phallic-oedipal functioning and development are combined to form a hostile defensive fantasy of forcing the parent to fit an idealized image. We may see this clearly in the formation of the beating fantasy, which contains an idealization both of the object and of the means to achieve the desired goal (Novick and Novick 1972, 1987). The struggle to maintain the idealized image of the parent can appear in treatment in the form of a negative therapeutic motivation (Novick 1980), that is, a need to enter treatment in order to displace the representation of the inadequate parent onto the analyst, turn the analyst into a failure by leaving, and return to the newly purified parent–child dyad.

From the phallic-oedipal phase we are highlighting the way in which an illusion of attachment and control through pain from early infancy becomes a fixed delusional element of the individual's defensive functioning and interferes significantly with reality-testing. The role of the environment is crucial to the formation of the delusion of omnipotence and this delusion may appear in many guises, for instance, in the form of idealization. The vicissitudes of omnipotent thinking in the phallic-oedipal phase demonstrate, in our view, its inherent pathology and support our rejection of the concept of normal omnipotence.

Latency

> Latency is the time when the [normal] child becomes firmly established in enjoying the endless possibilities of competent interactions in the real world. Still smarting from the oedipal defeat the normal child will have fantasies of glory and fame to fill the gap between his real and his ideal self. Such daydreams lead the child back to competence as a source for pleasure and self-esteem. [Novick and Novick 1991, p. 316]

We think there is an important distinction to be made between such daydreams, which are often casually termed "grandiose," but really represent the child's ambition, and pathological omnipotent fantasies. Ambitious daydreams may be farfetched, but they contain a germ of reality potential. Not every little boy can turn out to be Babe Ruth, but there is no way of knowing which 7-year-old, with application and years of batting practice, will end up in the majors. It is in the realm of possibility; such ambitious daydreams turn the child toward work and the transformation of self that result from it and carry true pleasure and self-esteem. There is no element of coercion or hostility in the effort or the goal. For children with such fantasies,

> pleasure is experienced not only in achievements but also in the exercise of those ego functions leading to achievement, that is, work becomes as much pleasure as the prize. It is through these competent

> interactions that the child forms sublimations, the most adaptive and gratifying defense available. [Novick and Novick 1991, p. 316]

The complexity of latency development itself has been understated in our classical theoretical descriptions; similarly, the significant contributions of latency development to later functioning have been undervalued. This also applies to an understanding of the development of omnipotence. Hostile defensive omnipotent fantasies of latency are built upon the foundation of pathological earlier developments from pre-oedipal and oedipal phases, but there are crucial elements added in this phase. It is in latency that the characteristics of the omnipotent fantasy are consolidated, its aims and methods fixed.

We have found a point of entry into the phenomena of omnipotent pathology in problems of treating sadomasochistic patients. There is a particular interest in relation to latency, as the sadomasochistic patients we have studied had no genuine latency to consolidate ego development and no realistic sources of self-esteem that could be internalized in the superego.

> For these children, the gap was not between the real and the ideal self but between the real and the ideal mother–child relationship. Fantasies were aimed not at enhancing the real capacities of the self but at denying and transforming the pain and inadequacy of the mother–child relationship. Unable to make use of real capacities to elicit appropriate responses from mother, these children fell back on omnipotent fantasies of control to maintain their self-esteem. [Novick and Novick 1991, p. 317]

The omnipotent fantasies of latency demand immediate effects, with no work; indeed, they always partake of magical means of implementation. Their goal is to change the object, not the self. The magic of thought, word, and deed is felt to be all-powerful and comes to be invested with all the force of idealizations developed in earlier phases.

As long as the fantasies remain internal secret means of mental control, they are not troublesome to the environment and so may often go unchallenged, but they persist underground, with reality-testing more and more distorted in the search for confirmation. The major loss is the child's pleasure in his real accomplishments. Usually, however, omnipotent fantasies bring with them further anxieties. When they spill over into life and relationships, children in the school years are often given medication to control their worrying or the restlessness that may result from it. Medication only compounds the problem, as it confirms to the child his helplessness to grapple with his difficulties and reinforces the notion of a magical solution, external to the child. There is also a tremendous secondary gain, in that the child's anxiety, fears, phobic symptoms, and so on really do become a means of controlling the others in his family. Thus a loop is established, in which the child's painful experience again is felt, with reality confirmation, to be a means to control the object and to force compliance with his wishes.

This experience of feelings as overwhelming to the self and as a means to overwhelm others is a consequence of the bypassing of normal oedipal resolution. Without a consolidated superego for dependable internal control, affects do not develop their appropriate signal function, but are defended against with accumulating anxiety. Patients who present with extreme anxiety about the impact of any emotions may be protecting the fantasy that their feelings are omnipotent. When we are buffeted by the affect storms of the adult hysteric or borderline, we may consider whether there are roots in an omnipotent latency fantasy of overwhelming the object with feelings.

Central to the normal developmental task of latency is the growth of the relation to reality and the expansion of the ego by integration of new experiences. How the child comes to know the world, himself, and others in latency has a profound effect on all his later functioning. During this phase the child learns to relate to and negotiate with separate real objects who have their own needs and wishes. Normal latency play progressively includes elements of fairness, sharing, and rules that take into account the separate reality of the other.

Experience filtered through the lens of omnipotent fantasy contains inherent distortions. One of these is the construction of a self-representation that contains externalizations imposed by parents and is perpetuated by the child's identification with them. The self-representation of latency is the one that persists into adulthood, particularly when it is bound up with an omnipotent defense structure. Thus omnipotence and externalization are intimately linked, and are usually both found in the context of sadomasochistic pathology. The play of the disturbed school-aged child quickly reveals these elements. In treatment such children immediately develop a sadomasochistic interaction with the analyst and the toys, establishing an externalizing transference. The child bosses and attempts to control the therapist or obsessively organizes the toys, instead of using them in a dynamic displacement of affectively-informed themes. This pattern may also contain initial manifestations of masturbation fantasies of hostile self-sufficiency, in which objects are interchangeable and are used mainly for externalization. The sexualization of hostile fantasies of control that has turned narcissistic and aggressive pathology into true sadomasochism provides the additional motive of libidinal gratification for clinging to omnipotent fantasies. The schoolchild's self-esteem regulation and sources of instinctual gratification become ever more bound up in omnipotence.

Gabbard and Twemlow (1994) and Ogden (1989) point out the difficulties that ensue in treatment when there is difficulty in separating fantasy from reality on the part of the patient. We suggest that the propensity to seek fantasy solutions under stress becomes fixed in latency and undermines later possible choices of alternative solutions. The multiple motives for maintaining the quality of omnipotence in fantasy life and the functioning of the structured personality combine in latency to become part of character and are thus increasingly resistant to change from experience or analysis. Derivatives of such developments in latency appear in adult treatments in the quality of, and resistance to, the therapeutic alliance.

Adolescence

The youngster who has had a latency that has consolidated and enhanced skills, talents, and pleasure in competent interactions welcomes the growing capacities of mind and body that come with adolescence and open further opportunities for engagement and the increase of self-esteem. This is not to deny that adolescence, like all of life, contains disappointment, hurt, failure, and painful realizations of limitations. But the teenager who had a good-enough latency, which includes good-enough parents and environment, can surmount, and may even be strengthened by grappling with, the ordinary obstacles encountered.

On the other hand, the adolescent who has lived in a sadomasochistic world, with its destructive omnipotent fantasies of easy, quick, hostile triumph over others, will be unable to integrate those fantasies with the reality of a changing body and changing external demands. The internal and external realities of adolescence challenge the omnipotent fantasies of the latency child. Adolescent growth, with the capacity to put wishes into action, demands transformation of earlier fantasy solutions.

> The accomplishment of the adolescent task of taking ownership of the mature body requires relinquishment of the fantasy that one can be both a man and a woman. The experience of genital pleasure renders untenable the notion of oedipal equality, and requires acknowledgement of generational differences. Coalescence of a separate identity contradicts the fantasy of indispensability to the primary object. Acceptance of the realities of time, choice, and person limitations necessitates abandoning the fantasies that one need never grow up, grow old, die, have to choose, or give up anything. All of the developmental tasks of adolescence require a transformation of the relation to reality and fantasy, as part of the integration of the mature body and self. [K. K. Novick and J. Novick 1994, pp. 62–63]

The normal adolescent, in the course of integrating his mature body and self, achieves a new integration of the pleasure and reality principles. For the disturbed adolescent the two remain in opposition, so that what is real is not pleasurable, and pleasure resides in unreal magical fantasies. The major task of early adolescence is the integration of the maturing body with childhood self-representation and fantasies. Late adolescents have the task of identity formation with its attendant choices, goals, and commitments. None of the phase-appropriate tasks can be accomplished while simultaneously maintaining an omnipotent delusion. The resolution of the contradiction between the reality demands of adolescence and an omnipotent fantasy determines the outcome of adolescent development and sets the course for adult health or pathology. The normal adolescent opts for the pleasures of reality and sets aside a past or recently formed omnipotent fantasy solution. Clinging to the omnipotent solution can lead to avoidance of adolescence—Freud's own adolescent trauma is a good example of that outcome (Novick 1994)—or an escalating series of actions designed to deny reality, attribute responsibility and guilt to others, make others feel helpless and anxious, and indeed, enact an omnipotent fantasy of hostile control over the actions and reactions of others.

We suggest that adolescence is the period when a perverse sadomasochistic solution to conflict, with its omnipotent core fantasy, is consolidated as feeling essential to the individual's survival. The choice of an omnipotent solution becomes a built-in response of the personality and is experienced as increasingly inevitable. Each of the strands from earlier levels can be intensified under the impact of the real changes of adolescence. As the adolescent moves or is pushed toward autonomy and independence, and anxiety about issues of attachment, separateness, loneliness, and loss intensifies, so the strand of pain as an omnipotent means of attachment is reinforced. Toddler fears about rage, death, and destruction are revived in the light of the adolescent's real ability to put his killing wishes into action, and so the strand of omnipotent conviction of the capacity to murder can also be intensified. Adolescent sexuality can heighten oedipal feelings of rejection, humiliation, envy, and jealousy, and thus the strand of delusional belief in the power and irresistibility of sexual urges is further strengthened. The latency need to externalize the superego and avoid responsibility and guilt is intensified by adolescent incestuous and perverse wishes; the strand of quick, externally imposed, immediate gratifications is also thereby thickened.

A further important factor in the development of adolescent health or pathology is the influence of parents and culture in counteracting or fostering and maintaining omnipotent fantasies of hostile control over others. Omnipotence of thought or deed is a potential response to any experienced helplessness, but as a *fixed* fantasy it is usually embedded in a lifelong interaction with parents who deal with their own anxieties by the imposition of their omnipotent fantasies in enactments with their children. To be the object of someone else's omnipotent fantasy is to be stripped of selfhood, thus rendered helpless and perhaps driven to the construction of omnipotent defense both in reaction and identification. We have referred to externalization as the dynamic underpinning of abuse (J. Novick and K. K. Novick 1994). It is relevant here in that externalization represents the enactment of an omnipotent fantasy, an attempt to force the other to conform to a particular, need-driven image. It is what Goethe and Shengold have called "soul murder." A patient who clings to an omnipotent defense has often been the target of someone else's omnipotent manipulation. Such interactions are not, however, restricted to early life. Just as the teenager may respond to the changes of adolescence with an intensification of the omnipotent defense, so too may his parents. Adolescent separateness, autonomy, sexuality, strength, and youth pose serious threats to parental omnipotent defenses against their helplessness in the face of advancing years and accelerating decline. Like Snow White's stepmother, who could not accept the reality that she was no longer the "fairest of them all," and who responded as if Snow White's beauty threatened her very existence, some parents react to the adolescent's burgeoning with destructive rage.

In adolescence the strands from all the prior developmental phases become braided into an unbreakable rope of omnipotent fantasy clung to as a defense against the danger of experienced threats of annihilation, abandonment, humiliation, castration, rage, jealousy, and guilt. It is during adolescence that the omnipotent fantasy is either superseded by reality-based modes of self-esteem regulation or becomes fixed as a delusional core of a diverse range of adolescent and adult pathology, from the apparently normally functioning obsessional neurotic to the perverse, addicted, impulse-driven, narcissistically damaged borderline personality disorder.

Looking at omnipotence from a developmental perspective, we have suggested that the fantasy of omnipotence is not a normal infantile state, but rather a defense woven of strands from each developmental level that become organized in adolescence into a pervasive, implacable resistance to external influences, often including therapy. In adult work, omnipotence becomes manifest as a resistance to change at all phases of treatment.

Omnipotence, Resistance, and the Therapeutic Alliance

Our interest in the concept of omnipotence arose from our work on the sadomasochism of our patients and the fact, recognized by Freud at the very beginning of his clinical work and by all analysts since, that sadomasochism presents the most severe resistance to change and the most frequent cause of failure in therapy (Freud 1909). In our earlier work we suggested that "In adult patients, the omnipotent derivatives from all levels of development . . . are a major source of resistance throughout analysis" (Novick and Novick 1991, p. 323). In that article we touched on resistances due to omnipotent fantasies at the beginning, middle, and end phases of treatment; here we will expand on the opposition between resistance from the delusion of omnipotence in sadomasochism and the forward progression implied in addressing the therapeutic alliance tasks of each phase of treatment.

Many theorists have described omnipotent fantasies as a part of borderline disorders. Borderline patients were first described in 1884 in the journal *Alienist and Neurologist* by C. H. Hughes (cited in

Novick 1985). He referred to such patients, however, as *borderland patients*, which clinically seems very apt. We, too, feel more comfortable describing a place than labeling a person. When a patient is called *borderline* there is an implication of difference from us, with an assumed superiority scale from normal down to neurotic to borderline and then psychotic. But when a person is operating in a borderland we can join him if we have the bravery, skill, and desire to do so. If we are secure in our original identity, we may safely travel and explore, trying to see the other place through his eyes. The sadomasochistic aspect of pathology, imbued with the quality of omnipotence, resides in the borderland. We have suggested that experiences of helplessness, that is, traumatic experiences that overwhelm the ego, can lead anyone to take up residence in the borderland, choosing an omnipotent solution in the absence of a sense of alternative possibilities. When we choose to join a patient in his magical borderland, we may do so safely only if equipped with numerous ties to reality and the support of colleagues, institutions, training, and experience (Novick 1985, Panel 1987). Our theories, too, provide us with conceptual tools and techniques to stay anchored in reality while ranging through foreign territory. The clinical landscape may be surveyed through a number of lenses; it is the same field whether we look at it through the lens of transference, defense, object relations, or the lens of the therapeutic alliance. We have found it particularly useful to consider the opposition of omnipotent functioning to those tasks of the therapeutic alliance highlighted at different phases of treatment.

From the beginnings of psychotherapeutic work, changes in technique came about in response to problems engaging patients. The therapeutic relationship cannot be taken for granted at the start of treatment nor at any time during its course. Patients come to treatment because they are unable to use their capacities to be with others or work together. The more impaired their capacities, the more important becomes a focus on the therapeutic alliance as we hope to reformulate it, as a dynamic, integrated, and fluctuating component of the whole therapeutic process.

The crucial importance of a therapeutic alliance for the successful conduct of a treatment was stressed in technical discussions during the 1960s and 1970s, but the concept has undergone such drastic changes in fashion that recently it has sometimes been described as actually harmful to the establishment of a proper treatment. Yet we have found that we cannot do without some attention to the techniques needed to get a person into treatment, get him to stay and work, and help him leave when it is appropriate; therefore, we continue to find the therapeutic alliance a significant concept for all age groups. We have come to some general principles regarding our revised understanding of the therapeutic alliance, which we summarize as follows:

1. The therapeutic alliance is not separate from other technical perspectives, or lenses, such as transference, resistance, defense analysis, and so on.
2. All patients have the capacities necessary for a therapeutic alliance. Individual differences among patients lie in the motivational sphere. Our experience with severely disturbed patients of all ages has been that they are able to build and maintain an alliance when that is made an integral part of the therapeutic work.
3. The various motives for the alliance may be rational or irrational, conscious or unconscious.
4. The therapeutic alliance is not stable, but varies at different stages of treatment and, more microscopically, with each successive emergence of a conflict and its object, drive, and affective components. The fluctuations of the alliance enable the therapist to see, share, and interpret conflict, defense, anxiety, and transference in a way the patient, even a young child, can understand. Fluctuations in the alliance may be used as a barometer of conflict, resistance, and change.
5. The therapeutic alliance is a relational concept and thus requires input to it from all parties. Minimally (and usually) this includes patient, therapist, parents, or significant others, each of whom has complementary phase-appropriate therapeutic

alliance tasks. The therapeutic alliance tasks of each phase of treatment persist through all subsequent phases, but the primary task highlighted in each phase relates to the progression of the therapeutic work and provides a measure of that progress.

6. The concept of the therapeutic alliance can serve to bridge the gap between the therapist's knowledge and the patient's experience by providing for an understandable shared formulation of goals and ways to measure progress towards them.
7. We find it useful to distinguish between two fundamental therapeutic modes, the mode of active intervention and that of receptivity. The therapist's receptivity operates throughout the treatment to put him in touch with the deep current of the patient's unconscious wishes and feelings. We think that this knowledge may best be used for interpretation when the analyst has actively engaged the patient around the therapeutic alliance issues.
8. It follows that the initiative for creating a therapeutic alliance lies with the therapist and not the patient.

The consequence of this approach is to shift the locus of problems from outside to inside the therapeutic setting. It is our view that the greatest danger in treatment, even greater than premature termination, is the patient's submission to an authoritarian system of unfounded statements, interpretations that carry the weight of irrational authority rather than a shared evidentiary base. In work with patients whose main way of relating is to try to engage the analyst in a sadomasochistic interaction, it is particularly important to focus joint attention on fluctuations around a baseline of mutually agreed phase-specific therapeutic alliance tasks that serve as a barometer of dynamic issues. Attention to the therapeutic alliance allows us to create a field within which valid interpretations may be made, heard, and used.

There is understandable reluctance in analysts to categorizing of patients or schematizing of phase of treatment. Each patient forms a unique relationship with each analyst, who in turn changes with and is changed by each patient. The course of each analysis is also unique, unpredictable, and perhaps more amenable to chaos theory than two-dimensional linear regression coefficients. At the same time, from Freud's (1895) early distinction between passive and active seductions and his recommendations to analysts for the beginning of analysis, the heuristic value of categorization has been accepted. Freud discussed the beginning phase of analysis and referred to the middle and end phases, but it was Glover (1955) who explicitly expounded a tripartite form of analysis into beginning, middle, and termination phases. If we keep in mind that the phases of treatment are not mutually exclusive, nor are they mechanical checkpoints in a sequence, then they can be useful for highlighting certain tasks, resistance, and techniques.

The specific task of the therapeutic alliance during the evaluation phase is the initiating of several transformations. Transformation starts with the assumption that things can and do change. The patient's omnipotent defense opposes any change and so the tasks of the evaluation phase meet with more or less intense resistances from the omnipotent system.

In the beginning phase of treatment the patient's therapeutic alliance task is to *be with* the analyst; the analyst strives to *feel with* the patient. Disruptions and deviations in being with are our first indicators of resistance to engaging in the therapeutic process and direct our attention to describing the conditions under which the patient can be with the analyst. The model for this attunement is the early mother–child relationship. Fluctuations in attunement draw upon and relate to issues of mother–child attachment during infancy and toddlerhood. Even before we know the full history or dynamics of the pathological relationship, we may quickly engage the patient in noticing feelings about being with and what he does to make himself comfortable, and begin to wonder together what he gives up in the service of maintaining a sadomasochistic interaction, with its omnipotent core. For the middle phase of treatment the therapeutic alliance task is *working together.* Both analyst and patient work to effect the beginning transformations of the evaluation phase and to elucidate the conditions for being together at the start of the treatment process. Increasingly, working together becomes central and we begin to track its fluctuations and the patient's willingness to engage in the work. During the middle phase of analysis the multidetermined levels and functions of his sadomasochism and its omnipotent fantasy could be more clearly elucidated.

Genuinely non-exploitative, joint work threatens a stable sadomasochistic character organization that seeks to turn analysis into a never-ending perverse gratification. Sadomasochism has determinants from all levels of development, serves multiple functions, and is a most difficult pathology to deal with. Hostile omnipotent fantasies are a triumphant, self-protective shell of sadomasochistic disorders, and patients may go to extreme lengths, even to suicide, rather than relinquish them. The therapeutic alliance and its several tasks provide an alternative to this omnipotent way of relating. As such, the alliance is a major means for helping people battle with perversions, but it also constitutes a major threat to the omnipotent system of mental functioning. This is the reason that the therapeutic alliance tasks appear so centrally in conflict at each stage of treatment.

The pretermination phase of treatment is seldom discussed or delineated, but recent intensive study of termination has made it clear that there is a distinct set of tasks to be addressed before a termination phase can be started. The tasks for the patient are to *maintain progressive momentum, take increasing responsibility for the joint work, and translate insights into effective actions.* Each of these tasks may arouse intense resistance, as they clash directly with features of an omnipotent system of defense and self-regulation.

The pretermination phase is marked by a clinical sense that termination has become a genuine rather than a fantasied possibility. The real possibility of readiness to end is based on the reestablishment of progressive momentum in the patient's life in and out of treatment (Novick and Novick 1991). This impels a departure from the timelessness of the middle phase and actively imports the reality dimensions of time and change. But the reality of time challenges the omnipotent denial of change, growth, generational differences, and mortality, and triggers resistances to forward development. The patient's increased involvement in working together, which was the focus of the middle phase, has led to recovered capacity to take responsibility. But this runs counter to the old way of relating in which the other/analyst appears to be all-powerful, while the patient presents himself as a helpless or passive or compliant victim. Such a sadomasochistic relationship has been an important organizer of otherwise unintegrated experience for the patient, functioning rather like a religion in which the analyst plays the role of omnipotent God, but the patient secretly retains the ability, through the power of prayer, to get God to do or be exactly what he wants.

Putting insight into action directly challenges the omnipotent assumption of the magical power of thought. The patient who manages to achieve brilliant insights, but never changes, is denying the pleasure of achievement and reality for the sake of maintaining a delusion of the power of his thoughts and wishes. He will never want to move on to setting a termination date, because any action implies the distinction between fantasy and reality.

The therapeutic alliance tasks of each phase persist throughout treatment, overlapping and interacting with each other. So the highlighted tasks of the previous phase lead into and inform the termination phase. Similarly, the patient's tasks in the termination phase, *relinquishing infantile fantasies, mourning, and internalization of the alliance,* are not new, indeed have been part of all the work of the treatment, but take on new prominence and character in the light of the reality of ending. During the pretermination phase process of choosing the date, the analyst has been entirely flexible, stipulating only that the date stand alone and that the patient and analyst take time to explore the connotations of any particular date proposed by the patient. In contrast, once the date has been jointly determined, we are firm about holding to it. This implies including reality in the treatment process in a somewhat new way. The reactions of both people elucidate conflicts over the integration of reality and the role of the ego function of reality testing in the overall working of the patient's personality. There is an opportunity to examine hitherto hidden pockets of fantasy functioning and to test the therapeutic alliance in new directions. Particular aspects of omnipotent fantasy functioning inform resistances to alliance tasks in this phase.

Internalization is the outcome of an adaptive process of mourning the loss of real valued relationships, feelings, or experiences. Treatment includes a unique way of working, specific to the relationship created by particular individuals, and productive of its own satisfactions. When it ends, there is a real loss, accompanied by sadness. A normal grieving process, with mourning and eventual internalization, allows the patient to keep the positive aspects of the therapeutic alliance inside, available for his own use.

Throughout treatment there has been a struggle within the patient between the wish to hold onto past infantile solutions with the hope of magical gratification and the progressive forces that represent realistic relations with others and the world, mediated by competent functioning and yielding genuine, predictable pleasure. Relinquishing infantile wishes from all levels of development, including magical omnipotent images of the self and others, seems a frightening and painful loss for the patient. But the work of the earlier phases has allowed for the establishment of alternative sources of security and self-esteem in realistic achievements and representations. Much of the work of the termination phase involves drawing the distinction between the illusory loss of unreal fantasy gains and the real loss of the setting, the analyst, and the special therapeutic relationship. This contrast was first drawn during earlier explorations of the patient's fantasy fears that the end of therapy means total loss of the therapist, that the therapist will die or disappear into a black hole. The hostile wishes contained in these fears and the assumption of omnipotence of thought demand continued and repeated work at each phase of treatment. We differentiate between fear of abandonment, which implies hostility, and sadness and missing, which come from loving feelings and are intrinsically part of them. The intensity of fantasies of omnipotence becomes evident in the termination phase when the patient persists in thoughts that the therapist will cease to exist after the end of treatment, or that patient and analyst will become friends, colleagues, or lovers. This in turn gives rise to material about what will or should happen after termination. We are careful to explore these thoughts in detail, as they often contain the hidden remnants of defensive fantasies and other conflicts underlying them.

The reality of the imminent ending adds a special intensity to these conflicts. Denial bolstered by fantasies of omnipotence is a common response to the experience of helplessness in the face of reality. When the patient has in fact been traumatized in the past by cruel and overwhelming reality events, there is an even greater likelihood that all aspects of reality, such as the passage of time, change, loss, and death, are experienced as hostile personal attacks to be resisted with all possible psychic power, including delusional fantasies of omnipotence.

Children, adolescents, and adults should finish good-enough treatment with the potential for adaptive transformation in response to the vicissitudes of life. From the alliance task of being with comes confidence in the capacity to be alone with oneself, to value oneself, and to cooperate in a trusting, mutually enhancing relationship with others. The new level and range of ego functions used to work together in alliance with the analyst can be used for living and for self-analysis whenever necessary. The explicit inclusion of self-analysis as a goal arises in the context of pretermination phase focus on issues around independent therapeutic work; thus self-analysis may be seen as one of the tools for living that will be available to the patient after finishing. Each therapeutic alliance task accomplished and internalized equips the patient in specific ways.

The internalization of the therapeutic alliance tasks of being with, working together, relinquishing magical fantasies, and carrying on adaptive transformations throughout life strengthens the competent, reality-attuned mode of self-regulation and so equalizes the forces in the lifelong struggle against developmentally determined and culturally reinforced hostile omnipotent solutions to the vicissitudes of life.

References

Bach, S. (1994). *The Language of Perversion and the Language of Love.* Northvale, NJ: Jason Aronson.

Balint, M. (1968). *The Basic Fault.* London: Tavistock.

Brody, S. (1956). *Patterns of Mothering: A Study of Maternal Influence during Infancy.* New York: International Universities Press.

Ferenczi, S. (1913). Stages in the development of the sense of reality. In *First Contributions to Psycho-Analysis*, pp. 213–239. New York: Brunner/Mazel, 1980.

Fonagy, P., Steele, M., Moran, G. S., et al. (1993). Measuring the ghost in the nursery: an empirical study of the relation between parents' mental representations of childhood experiences and their infants' security of attachment. *Journal of the American Psychoanalytic Association* 41:957–989.

Freud, S. (1895). Studies in hysteria. *Standard Edition* 2.

——— (1909). Notes upon a case of obsessional neurosis. *Standard Edition* 10:153–250.

——— (1911). Formulations on the two principles of mental functioning. *Standard Edition* 12:215–226.

——— (1915). Instincts and their vicissitudes. *Standard Edition* 14:117–140.

——— (1917). A metapsychological supplement to the theory of dreams. *Standard Edition* 14:217–235.

——— (1940). An outline of psycho-analysis. *Standard Edition* 23:141–207.

Furman, E. (1985). On fusion, integration, and feeling good. *Psychoanalytic Study of the Child* 40:81–110. New Haven, CT: Yale University Press.

Gabbard, G. O., and Twemlow, S. W. (1994). Mother–son incest in the pathogenesis of narcissistic personality disorder. *Journal of the American Psychoanalytic Association* 42:171–189.

Glover, E. (1955). *The Technique of Psychoanalysis.* New York: International Universities Press.

Kernberg, O. (1975). *Borderline Conditions and Pathological Narcissism.* New York: Jason Aronson.

——— (1980). *Internal World and External Reality: Object Relations Theory Applied.* New York: Jason Aronson.

Klein, M. (1950). On the criteria for the termination of a psycho-analysis. In

Envy and Gratitude and Other Works 1946–1963, pp. 43–47. London: Virago, 1988.

Kohut, H. (1971). *The Analysis of the Self.* New York: International Universities Press.

——— (1977). *The Restoration of the Self.* New York: International Universities Press.

Mahon, E. J. (1991). The "dissolution" of the Oedipus complex: a neglected cognitive factor. *Psychoanalytic Quarterly* 60:628–634.

Meyers, H. (1988). A consideration of treatment techniques in relation to the functions of masochism. In *Masochism: Current Psychoanalytic Perspectives*, ed. R. Glick and D. I. Meyers, pp. 175–189. Hillsdale, NJ: Analytic Press.

Novick, J. (1980). Negative therapeutic motivation and negative therapeutic alliance. *Psychoanalytic Study of the Child* 35:299–320. New Haven, CT: Yale University Press.

——— (1985). Discussion of *Treatment of a borderline/severely neurotic child.* Panel presented at the annual meeting of the American Psychoanalytic Association, Denver, CO, May.

——— (1994). *Deferred action: the transformation of memory in the reality of adolescence.* Paper presented at the Workshop Series of the American Psychoanalytic Association, Miami, FL and Houston, TX, 1994, 1995.

Novick, J., and Novick, K. K. (1972). Beating fantasies in children. *International Journal of Psycho-Analysis* 53:237–242.

——— (1991). Some comments on masochism and the delusion of omnipotence from a developmental perspective. *Journal of the American Psychoanalytic Association* 39:307–331.

——— (1994). Externalization: the dynamic underpinnings of abuse. In *Victims of Abuse: The Emotional Impact of Child and Adult Trauma*, ed. A. Sugarman, pp. 45–68. Madison, CT: International Universities Press.

Novick, K. K., and Novick, J. (1987). The essence of masochism. *Psychoanalytic Study of the Child* 42:353–384. New Haven,CT: Yale University Press.

——— (1994). Postoedipal transformations: latency, adolescence and pathogenesis. *Journal of the American Psychoanalytic Association* 42:143–169.

Ogden, T. H. (1989). The threshold of the male Oedipus complex. *Bulletin of the Menninger Clinic* 53:394–413.

Orgel, S. (1974). Fusion with the victim and suicide. *International Journal of Psycho-Analysis* 55:532–538.

Panel (1987). Issues in psychoanalytic treatment of a borderline/severely neurotic child. *Journal of the American Psychoanalytic Association* 35:727–737.

Piaget, J. (1952). *The Origins of Intelligence in Children.* New York: International Universities Press.

——— (1954). *The Construction of Reality in the Child.* New York: Basic Books.

Piontelli, A. (1992). *From Fetus to Child: An Observational and Psychoanalytic Study.* London and New York: Tavistock/Routledge.

Reich, A. (1960). Pathologic forms of self-esteem regulation. *Psychoanalytic Study of the Child* 15:215–232. New York: International Universities Press.

Shengold, L. (1991). A variety of narcissistic pathology stemming from parental weakness. *Psychoanalytic Quarterly* 60:86–89.

Winnicott, D. W. (1965). *The Maturational Process and the Facilitating Environment.* New York: International Universities Press.

3

Omnipotence in the Transference and in the Countertransference*

Otto F. Kernberg, M.D.

Editors' Comments

Otto F. Kernberg, a leading authority on borderline and narcissistic pathology, once again describes the difficulties in working with very disturbed patients and their issues around control. He describes various uses of omnipotence (both as fantasy and defense) and he details developmentally how control of the object becomes central when the pathology revolves around aggression. He is particularly interested in the issue of omnipotent control, because he feels battles over control often lead to strong countertransference reactions.

Kernberg's formulations on the etiology of this need for omnipotent control are particularly interesting. His discussion of the transformation of the aggressive drive into hatred (a complex, structured, derivative of the affect rage that expresses several wishes: to destroy

*A modified version of this chapter was published in the *Scandinavian Psychoanalytic Review* 18:2–21, copyright © 1995, and is reprinted here with permission.

the bad object, to make it suffer, and ultimately to control it) is fundamental in understanding his theories of aggression and borderline behavior. Central to Kernberg's ideas of treatment are his ideas about projective identification and their relationship to pathological hate.

Kernberg presents three clinical vignettes that illustrate omnipotence and omnipotent control. These vignettes are particularly illuminating as they represent three different manifestations of omnipotence (as exemplified in a borderline patient, a neurotic patient with narcissistic personality problems, and a patient with an obsessive personality). He shows how in each case a technical problem revolves around dealing with an enactment of "omnipotent control." Kernberg points out how it is "practically unavoidable that in response to the expression of omnipotent control in the transference, the therapist will be forced to reassess and reassure the boundaries of the relationship . . . in order to protect the situation from destructive aggression." Kernberg gives detailed descriptions of how he managed the potential enactment in each case. Kernberg's ideas of how to set limits and manage the countertransference form the essence of his presentation.

Omnipotence was first described by Freud (1913, 1921) as a characteristic of the magical thinking of primitive cultures and of infantile thinking. He linked it with the state of primary narcissism and the hallucinatory gratification of desire under conditions of frustration. This primitive mode of thinking might then reappear as omnipotence in psychopathology, particularly in obsessive thinking (Freud 1909). Later, both ego psychologists and object relations theorists described omnipotence as a defensive operation in the psychoses, one manifestation of the permanence of magical thinking when there is a loss of reality testing.

Edith Jacobson (1967, 1971), for example, described the omnipotent implications of psychotic identifications, in which refusion of self and object representations in idealized or ecstatic states recreates an omnipotence of thought that serves an important defensive function, together with denial of reality, thus preserving an idealized state as a defense against severe depression and even schizophrenic fragmentation.

Melanie Klein's (1946) description of primitive defenses and object relations linked to the early struggles between the life and death instincts included omnipotence of thought as an early defensive operation. This defense, she proposed, was related to the defenses against envy by means of a fantasy of fusion between self and object that denied separation and dependence, and an omnipotent control of the object by means of projective identification. Herbert Rosenfeld's (1964, 1971) development of Klein's thinking stressed the behavioral aspects of omnipotent control as a major defense in narcissistic personalities, thus shifting the emphasis from omnipotence of thought to omnipotent control as a crucial clinical manifestation of narcissistic pathology.

Winnicott (1960a,b), describing the original undifferentiated dyad of baby and mother, focused on the baby's sense of omnipotence when all his needs are met, in contrast to the sense of impingement when frustration of his desires shows him the limits of his control of reality, and leads to the establishment of a transitional object on the child's road to acknowledging frustration and dependency.

As psychoanalytic exploration of severe character pathology, borderline conditions, and the psychoses evolved (Jacobson 1967, Mahler and Furer 1968, Searles 1965, Rosenfeld 1987), observations of the defensive functions of delusional grandiosity and omnipotence in schizophrenic, manic-depressive, and paranoid psychosis were noted, and later on, the importance of omnipotent control in the psychoanalytic treatment of the borderline conditions and pathological narcissism (Kernberg 1975).

Omnipotence therefore is at once a primitive fantasy, a mechanism of defense, and a pathological psychic structure. All three of these are present in many clinical situations.

I propose that omnipotence as an early fantasy constitutes one aspect of the "all good" gratifying fused or undifferentiated selfobject representation, related to what Freud (1930) described as the "oceanic feeling," and potentially reactivated as an early defense whenever a regressive idealized fusional state emerges as a defense against the threat of frustration, trauma, pain, or aggression. This original function of omnipotence as fantasy and defense is replicated during the stage of separation-individuation (Mahler et al. 1975) in the fantasy of reunion between the "good self" and the "ideal object," the basis both of actual, secure dependency on a good object and of a satisfactory relation of the ego to the early ego ideal. The pathological transformation of this development during manic and hypomanic states reflects the regressive refusion of these ideal relationships. The pathological construction involved in a pathological grandiose self (Kernberg 1984) also implies the defensive aspect of omnipotence in a denial of all negative, split-off, and projected aspects of the self, denial of dependency on other objects, and fantasied undisturbed self-gratification.

What I have described is the defensive utilization of early omnipotent fantasies in the segment of libidinal internalized object relations. A parallel process may be described regarding the development of aggressive object relations. Here omnipotence evolves out of intense frustration, trauma, or pain as activators of aggressive affect and early defensive operations to deal with such affect (Kernberg 1992). In contrast to the function of omnipotence to assure an illusional pleasure and grandiosity in the libidinal segment, the aspect of control of the object becomes central, and omnipotent fantasies are transformed into the defensive operation of omnipotent control.

Under pathological conditions, the aggressive drive dominates the early development of the psychic apparatus so powerfully that it leads to the psychopathological structures that we observe in psychosis, borderline personality organization, the severe types of perversion, and some psychosomatic disorders. This dominance of aggression has its roots in the excessive activation of aggressive affects. I have proposed in an earlier work (Kernberg 1992) that affects are instinctive components of human behavior, that is, inborn dispositions common to all individuals of the human species and that they emerge in the earliest stages of development and are gradually organized as part of early object relations into gratifying, rewarding, pleasurable affects or *libido* as an overarching drive, and painful, aversive, negative affects that, in turn, are organized into *aggression* as an overarching drive. Within this conceptualization, affects are the inborn, constitutionally, and genetically determined modes of reaction that are triggered first by various physiological and bodily experiences and then by the development of object relations from the beginning of life on.

Rage, within this conceptualization, represents the basic affect of aggression as a drive, and the vicissitudes of rage explain, in my view, the origin of hatred and envy, as well as anger and irritability as moods. Similarly, the affect of sexual excitement constitutes the core affect of libido, which slowly and gradually evolves out of the primitive affect of elation. Elation is produced by the infant's early sensual responses to intimate bodily contact with mother. Aggression as a drive develops out of the primitive crying response that evolves first into the affect of rage, and later into the crying response as part of sadness. Hatred, the core affect of aggression as a drive is an even later, structuralized aspect of rage, as is envy, a particular structural development of hatred.

Developmentally, the earliest function of rage is the effort to eliminate a sense of frustration; rage is thus always in response to frustration or pain, although the intensity of the rage response may depend upon temperament. A little later in development, rage is in response to an obstacle or barrier to gratification and aims to eliminate the obstacle. Still later, at a third developmental stage, the rage aims at elimination of a bad object, that is, at what is seen as a deliberate source of frustration standing between the self and the gratification of a need.

Later yet, the wish is no longer to destroy the bad object, but to make it suffer: we are now definitely in the complex developmental area in which pleasure and pain combine, sadism expresses a condensation of aggression and pleasure, and the original affect of rage is transformed into hatred with new, stable structural characteristics.

At a further stage of development, the wish to make the bad object suffer shifts into the wish to dominate and control that object in order to avoid fears of persecution from it; now obsessive mechanisms of control may psychopathologically regulate the suppression or repression of aggression. Finally, aggression may be sublimated in the search for autonomy, self-affirmation, and freedom from external control, reflecting characteristics of the original, self-affirmative aspects of rage.

Hatred, then, is a complex, structured derivative of the affect rage that expresses several wishes: to destroy a bad object, to make it suffer, and to control it. In contrast to the acute, transitory, and disruptive quality of rage, hatred is chronic, stable, and usually characterologically anchored or structured. The object relationship framing this affect expresses concretely the desire to destroy or dominate the object. An almost unavoidable consequence of hatred is its justification as revenge against the frustrating object; the wish for revenge is typical of hatred. Paranoid fears of retaliation are also usually unavoidable accompaniments of intense hatred, so that paranoid features, a wish for revenge, and sadism go hand in hand.

If we examine this progressive series of manifestations of the psychopathology of aggression, it becomes evident that a major transformation of the dominant affect of aggression evolves throughout. At the most primitive level of experience, the aggressive reaction centers around rage, and in the clinical situation aggression of any stage of development eventually leads to primitive rageful affect states in the transference. The crystallization of an external, bad object—in other words, the separation of self and object representation in the sector of aggression—transforms rage into hatred (and the intimately related affect of envy). It is here that omnipotence emerges in the form of an effort to control the bad object.

I have suggested in an earlier work (1984) that projective identification may have an important early developmental function in fostering separation in primitive persecutory, "all bad" states, reflecting an effort to attribute the aggression to an external source, in order to maintain a purified idealized self and object representation as a core self experience and to protect the ideal self from the feared attack from the bad object. Clinically, projective identification (the attribution to the object of an intolerable internal impulse, maintenance of empathy with that dangerous, projected impulse, an unconscious tendency to induce the corresponding impulse in the object, and the need to control the object under the effect of the projected impulse) goes hand in hand with efforts at omnipotent control. We might also say that omnipotent control combines the fantasy of omnipotence with the aspect of control implied in the mechanism of projective identification. In short, omnipotent control evolves together with the psychopathology of hatred.

At still later stages of development, sadistic enjoyment of power replaces primitive hatred. As I mentioned before, at this stage the wish is no longer to destroy the object but to make it suffer, or, in less primitive ways, to maintain it under one's own control. Omnipotent control now becomes a powerful defense involved with the expression of sadistic power and the maintenance of power as an essential condition for feeling psychologically secure. At a still more advanced stage of development, the internalization of sadistic or sadistically perceived objects as part of the oedipal phase of superego development transforms the conflict into sadistic superego pressures and secondary characterological identifications with the sadistic superego typical of obsessive-compulsive personalities. Here the defensive operation of omnipotent control is transformed into the unconscious omnipotent fantasies of obsessive conditions.

In describing the typical constellation of primitive defenses centering around splitting that characterize borderline personality organization I mentioned omnipotence and omnipotent control together with protective identification, primitive idealization, devaluation, and denial (Kernberg 1975). The mutual relationships between omnipotence and omnipotent control, and these other defenses now may become clearer. Both omnipotent fantasies and omnipotence as a defense in the libidinal sector, and omnipotent control in the aggressive sector, aim at protecting the splitting of idealized and persecutory segments of psychic experience. In narcissistic personalities, omnipotence and omnipotent control protect the patient from dreaded separation, dependency, and envy, maintaining the idealized concept of the pathologic grandiose self.

I have already mentioned how projective identification and omnipotent control are indissolubly linked and reinforce each other in the context of intense, primitive hatred, for example, in patients who have experienced severe physical or sexual abuse. Omnipotence goes hand in hand with denial in manic and hypomanic conditions, and it is the counterpart of devaluation of significant others in schizoid, narcissistic, and hypomanic states. Primitive idealization of the self and omnipotence also are intimately linked. Thus, omnipotence and omnipotent control are essentially primitive defensive operations that are typically part of severe character pathology and psychosis.

Clinical Illustrations

What follows are three clinical vignettes that illustrate omnipotence and omnipotent control. The first is a psychotherapy session of a patient presenting borderline personality organization and a narcissistic personality functioning on an overt borderline level. This session took place in the middle of an extended enactment of sadomasochistic acting out in the transference.

> The patient was a college student in her early twenties. I already knew that she had experienced her mother as withholding love and interest from all her children in order to encourage rivalry among them. The patient started the session by asking me why I was not able to see her later the same day because this particular hour was very inconvenient. I told her I had received her request through my secretary and I had left a message for her that I would not be able to see her later that day because of other commitments. The patient angrily interrupted me to say that she had mentioned some time ago that she wanted to see me at a later time on that day, if it was possible, and that I obviously had given preference to

other patients regarding her hour. I replied that I realized she was angry because she felt that I was giving preference to other patients and neglecting her. She ignored this statement and repeated her demand for another time. When I said that she was having her session even as we were speaking, she ignored that effort to focus on the here and now and repeated what she had already said. I commented that her demand for additional time—with the affirmation that this hour would be lost anyway—indicated her wish to punish me for not doing what she wanted and also to punish me by destroying her own opportunity to experience me as somebody available to help her understand what was going on now. But the patient persisted in her demand that I accede to her request. I tried again, saying that what I considered most important at this point was her perception of me as uninterested and neglectful and her effort to transform me, by force if necessary, into a good therapist again by giving her an extra session. My interventions had no observable effect; her rage continued to mount, and every time I tried to say something she interrupted me. Finally I fell silent. After she furiously repeated her various accusations, I intervened with the remark that she was repeating herself, and I asked what the function of that could be. Then she fell silent. After a few minutes, I asked if the venomous look on her face and her silence were serving the same purpose as her accusations, namely, to maintain an intensely adversarial atmosphere that would preclude our looking further into what was stimulating this rage.

The patient said contemptuously that if I wanted, I could go on saying whatever nonsense came to my mind. I said that her accusations against me reminded me of the way she had described her mother's attacking her in her childhood, leaving the patient to experience herself as the helpless victim of that assault, and that enacting this role of mother in relation to me gave her a sense of strength and power. I also said that that seemed more important to me than her efforts to obtain an additional session. (This interpretation was not new: we had been exploring her tendency to enact relations with mother as torturer and patient as victim, with frequent role reversals in the transference, throughout this entire period of her treatment.)

After some minutes of silence the patient said that she was aware of what I was saying, but that I had provoked this situation. I said that if she really had not been able to come at this time, I would have evaluated whether we could find a better time to meet, but she had engineered the situation in a way that precluded such a solution. I also reminded her of how often we had seen that she was expert at provoking situations in which she could feel that I had mistreated her. The patient replied that while she was angry, she could still listen to what I was saying, and I wondered aloud whether this meant that she really was experiencing what I was saying as thoughts that changed her view about herself, or whether she was now experiencing me as a powerful mother and herself as the naughty little girl who had to make amends. She said she didn't feel she had to make any amends, and the hour ended a short time later.

The next illustration is of a psychoanalytic session with a neurotic patient presenting a narcissistic personality disorder. Mr. B., a business man who consulted me because of sexual promiscuity and marital problems, had presented, in early stages of his treatment, a typical manifestation of omnipotent control in relation to my interpretations. He would listen attentively to what I said, slowly repeat part of it, muse about it, and finally give his nod of approval. When he felt my interpretations were not meeting his expectations, he might express disappointment and disgust by telling me, in a bantering way, that I should do more preliminary work before making interpretations or review the basic texts of psychoanalysis; at other times, he would say despondently that he had nothing to expect from me. At the same time, if my interpretations did not fit with his own view of the material, he became anxious and questioned me: Where did I get this interpretation from? What did it really mean? He could not, in other words, accept something that he himself had not thought of before or could not immediately make his. This effort to control the analyst, to assure himself that I was neither better than he (which would generate intolerable envy), nor worse (which would generate an intolerable devaluation of the analyst) had by now been sufficiently worked through in the transference for the patient to begin to establish a dependent relationship with me.

Three years into analysis, Mr. B., for the first time in his life, had replicated his childhood sadomasochistic relation with his mother with a new girlfriend, the first extended relation he had had after the termination of his third marriage. At the same time, a subtle change occurred in the transference in the direction of its "emptying out." I sensed that Mr. B. was so absorbed in his daily life with his girlfriend that it was largely replacing his world of fantasy. I also felt that he seemed increasingly "unreal" in his behavior toward me. He seemed more and more an "as if" personality in the sense that my interpretations would become so cleverly integrated in his association that I could no longer assess their effect. When I told him that I experienced an enormous distance in our relationship, Mr. B. freely acknowledged that he felt independent from me, and that this must indicate that he was now much healthier than before.

His ongoing compliance, his attention to everything I was saying, and an apparent uninhibited flow of free associations only reinforced my feeling that our relationship was completely phony, yet I felt strangely reluctant to confront Mr. B. with my feeling, as if it would be hopeless even to try. I sensed that either he would not understand what I was saying and think I was being paranoid, or accuse me of making impossible demands on him—he who was so obviously a "good" patient who was improving in his understanding and in his life.

Only gradually did I realize that my sense of impotence resulted from identifying with Mr. B. as he had related to his "crazy" mother: I was submitting to the patient (mother) like a submissive son who was carrying out a pseudo-analysis as prescribed by mother. I thought that the patient was unconsciously identifying with his mother, pretending to be caring but treating me like a son who had to be manipulated into obedience. And in my efforts to break out of this situation, I was tempted to act like an impatient, controlling mother who pretended to know exactly what was going on in her child without listening to him, then overpowered him, forcing him either to protest in rage or obligingly submit.

Here is a description of a session in which I attempted to transform my countertransference reaction, which on reflection seemed to express my identification with the patient as an impotent child, into an interpretation of the dominant issues in the transference.

> The session started with Mr. B. saying that he had had an uncanny experience. He had proposed a major business deal to a firm connected with a foreign country and then had become afraid that the deal would be resented by a competitor attempting to do a similar deal with another country. The patient had suddenly become afraid that agents working for his competitor in that other country might try to steal technical information from him. While telling me that he knew this was a paranoid reaction, he was nonetheless uneasy and thought that two men were following him that afternoon and evening. He said he had become very anxious and was oscillating between this anxiety and a sense that he was exaggerating. The patient said he felt genuinely anxious even as he was telling me this.
>
> At the same time, as he had done frequently in recent months, Mr. B. turned toward me smiling, as if to say, "I know this is crazy, and I know you understand that I know it." I said that I realized he was oscillating between fear and a sense that the fear was absurd, and that he was looking at me as if to reassure me that he was aware of that, but perhaps also to reassure himself, to check if I was still on his side or if I was silently concluding that he was crazy. The patient immediately said he didn't think I would think he was crazy. When I said I felt he was giving me a reassuring smile, as if some danger had to be avoided, he remarked lightly that the only danger could be that I might be aligned with the foreign country with whom his competitor was colluding. I now realized that the patient had not named the foreign country, and I sug-

gested to him that that was a further indication of his fearfulness of me. My unspoken fantasy was that the foreign competitor was from my country of origin. He then became uneasy and reluctantly admitted that he had wondered if my office was wired, and if it wouldn't be easy for me to obtain confidential information from him that I could use for my own purposes. He went on to associate about the possibility of break-ins into psychiatrists' offices and linked it with Watergate and several films in which psychiatrists had been involved in shady, dangerous deals. I said he might be trying to defend himself against a vision of me as dangerously spying on him by substituting the enemies as foreign agents.

Mr. B. again smiling, said somewhat ironically that I might need protection, rather than being dangerous, and he remembered an incident from several months ago. What he considered (realistically) to be a psychotic woman had appeared in my waiting room and tried to enter the office ahead of him. On that occasion, he had become intensely fearful that she might reappear later in the session with a gun, and in attempting to shoot me would shoot him. He said, half jokingly, "That woman might reappear any day and stab you in the back." I said I wondered whether he was trying to make a joke out of a fantasy that otherwise might be very frightening to him, namely, that I might stab him in the back by betraying his technical innovations to a competitor.

As I was saying this, I had two contradictory feelings: that I was on the right path in interpreting his pseudo-compliance as defensive omnipotent control against an underlying paranoid relationship in the transference; at the same time, I experienced myself as forcefully invading the patient with interpretations beyond his capacity, "brainwashing" him, as it were, and acting like a paranoid mother. For a few fleeting moments, I felt "paranoid" in interpreting a primitive persecution fantasy to this smiling, relaxed patient. But then I felt that my fantasy reflected my fear of asserting myself as a father who could transcend this madness and transform what seemed a "violent" interpretation into a "reasonable" one.

Mr. B. remained silent. I said, "You suddenly appear very tense." He said he had just had an image of himself stabbing his mother. After a few minutes, continuing to look tense, he said he was very upset and he would never do such a thing. I said I thought he was trying to reassure me and himself and that he was afraid that his wish to stab her might be the same as actually stabbing her. I also wondered whether his fear and wish might be connected with his fear of my stabbing him in the back: I interpreted that he was projecting his own rage onto me, and I said that I wouldn't be surprised if his immediate response would include some effort to transform this into a humorous situation in order to take the edge off the frightening feeling we were exploring.

The patient said he wasn't surprised that I should say that, but that he had been thinking very seriously of how enraged he had become at his mother in their last extended telephone conversation. He proceeded to speak with great emotion about something she said that seemed to him totally crazy but that he felt impotent to puncture. I said I wondered whether he had been putting into me this sense of impotence while he enacted his mother's role in the session. I elaborated on my interpretation, referring to his reassuring smiles, the frightening fantasies, and so forth. I pointed out that his friendly smile and his comments might have easily derailed my awareness of the violence or made me appear to be "crazy" when I noted the madness going on in fantasy in this room, namely, the danger that I might stab him like an impotent enraged boy would stab a crazy mother. After a long silence, Mr. B. said it was true he tried always to keep things on an even keel with me, and in fact, that had been his usual behavior with women, except with his new girlfriend, and he realized how enraged he was at all women.

The third example is a psychoanalytic session with a patient presenting an obsessive personality. Mr. C., a business man in his middle thirties, had consulted me because of obsessive doubts that interfered severely with his business decisions, chronic anxiety, depression, and sexual inhibition in relations with his wife. He also became easily involved in power struggles with business associates and clients, which had been damaging to his business enterprise. The following session occurred in the third year of his psychoanalysis.

> The last session before a week-long separation, during which the patient had a commitment out of town that coincided with my own absence, started with Mr. C.'s obsessively discussing whether he should give in to the financial demands of a provider whose product he wanted to acquire or stand firm on his counterproposal. Gradually, his anger at the provider became stronger. He complained bitterly about the lack of gratitude of this young man, whom the patient had helped in the past, and he expressed indignation at the defiant and inconsiderate ways in which the man was treating him. I asked whether, in the middle of this disappointment, there might also be disappointment with me for not helping him to make a decision. Mr. C. responded with irritation that I was wrong; he wasn't expecting anything from me, and this analysis was proving to be completely useless.
>
> I wondered aloud whether his disappointment with me might have something to do with the forthcoming separation. I reminded him that I had wondered whether he had set up a business trip at the time of my absence in order to avoid feeling being left behind and alone. He responded that, on the contrary, he would have to cancel an additional hour at the time of his return because of flight complications. As he said this, I remembered that I had a similar flight problem, and said that I had planned to suggest to him a later time on the day of our first appointment.
>
> The patient then exploded with rage at me. Why was I bringing up a change in his schedule in the middle of a session when my usual practice was to convey new information of any kind only at the beginning of a session? I was disrupting his flow of free association, he went on, showing how distracted I was by raising

issues that concerned only me, and totally neglecting his needs—the last thing he would have expected at the final session before the one-week separation!

As the patient's anger increased over the next few minutes, I experienced a rapidly changing set of feelings. First I felt guilty for not having remembered to make my suggestion at the beginning of the session, and felt I had indeed been neglectful. I wondered what might have influenced me in this regard. I remembered I had had a fleeting sense of guilt before the session for having to make a last-minute change in the patient's schedule, and wondered to myself whether I was acting like Mr. C.'s mother, that is, pretending to be interested and concerned for him. Then I became irritated, feeling he was making a mountain out of a molehill. I thought I had fairly acknowledged my mistake. Finally, while the patient raged on over my unreliability, I thought that I was now in a relationship to him similar to the one he had experienced when confronted with his father's dissatisfaction with his performance. The patient was now enacting the role of his father and projecting his "unreliable self" onto me, replicating, at the same time, his problem in the relationship to the young provider.

I commented on his disappointment and its transformation into rage at me, and on his sense that I was unreliable because I was not helping him with his problem with the young provider and I was neglecting the particular intensity of his need to be understood and cared for when a coming separation brought about the feeling of being abandoned. I interpreted that I was like an unreliable mother who only pretended to care for him, a most painful experience against which he could protect himself by making me an unreliable son and enacting his father's demands in relation to me. To be an angry father scolding an unreliable son was preferable to being an abandoned son relating to an unreliable mother.

Mr. C. said he had felt the provider was like an unreliable, unloving son, and that it was true that he had been treating both him and me in ways that reminded him of what he hated in his father. He then added that he did not feel as fearful as he had in the past about some forthcoming important meetings, and that he felt more like an equal with his colleagues. After a silence, I said that I sensed a change in his emotional disposition. He said he was no longer angry and actually felt sad thinking of our separation for a week. I said that insofar as it was less frightening to him to identify himself with his father, in spite of the father's traits that he was so critical of, he was also less afraid to acknowledge his wishes for my concern and dedication to him, without experiencing that as a sexual threat. The patient then remembered that he had felt less inhibited in having sex with his wife the previous night. The session ended shortly afterward.

I should add that Mr. C.'s angry response to my changing the time of his first session after the one week separation was a relatively mild reaction compared to his need for consistency at the beginning of the treatment. The fact that this aspect of his pathology had already been worked through over an extended period of time shows the relative ease with which my interpretation helped to resolve this defensive operation and shift the emotional reaction in the transference. In general, however, the analysis of omnipotent control in the transference of obsessive personalities is easier to accomplish and requires less time than is usually necessary in cases of the severe psychopathology reflected in the two earlier examples.

Discussion

The activation of omnipotence as a defense in the transference usually takes the form of omnipotent control. The uncovering of unconscious omnipotence as part of an obsessive personality structure, in schizoid personalities, and in other personality disorders is much less of a technical problem than is dealing with the enactment of omnipotent control, which usually occurs in the context of the simultaneous activation of several of the primitive defensive operations. The activation of advanced defensive operations accompanying omnipotent control in obsessive personalities is less of a problem than that of primitive ones: usually intellectualization, rationalization, and reaction-formations present together with omnipotent control in neurotic personality organization. In contrast, omnipotent fantasies and enactments in psychotic conditions are the most difficult to approach with a psychoanalytic perspective.

For practical purposes, then, management of omnipotent control in severe personality disorders represents the most frequent clinical situation we have to deal with. The main problem under conditions of enactment of this defensive operation is how to maintain a position of technical neutrality without being manipulated into a rigidity that lends itself to an enactment of projective counteridentification, that is, a contertransference identification with the same tendency toward omnipotent control that the patient is trying to avoid recognizing in himself. Obviously, an alternative danger is to comply with the patient's pressure and demands. The therapist's masochistic submission to a patient's enactment of sadistic control may temporarily appear to improve the therapeutic relationship and to reduce the expression of overt aggression in the transference. This "improvement," however, comes at the cost of driving the relevant conflict underground and may lead to the splitting off of the negative transference from a protective idealization of the therapist. If, for example, I had agreed to my first patient's demand that I give her an additional appointment that evening, she might have relaxed immediately and shifted to telling me about new developments in her daily life, but the underlying identification with her sadistic mother would then no longer have been emotionally available for analytic work.

In my experience, it is practically unavoidable that in response to the expression of omnipotent control in the transference, the therapist will be forced to reassess and reassure the boundaries of the psychoanalytic relationship. In other words, the analyst will need to reaffirm the overall treatment frame, and, if acting out in the transference seems potentially dangerous, the therapist must set limits to protect the treatment and the patient. A clearly established understanding of time and other limits to protect the patient, the therapist, and the space in which they work together from destructive aggression also protects the therapist from countertransference acting out and provides the space for his or her countertransference analysis as a preliminary step to continue transference interpretation.

I refrained from including countertransference developments in my first clinical example because previous experiences when the patient's demands were not met had created an internal sense of clarity and security regarding the limits to which acting out in the sessions could be expressed, permitting me to maintain relative equanimity. In the second example, however, the enormous difficulty in resolving Mr. B.'s massive combination of omnipotent control and denial in the transference was affecting my countertransference disposition and required significant work outside the treatment hours before I became able to interpret that defensive operation as I illustrated.

I have found the most difficult cases in management of omnipotent control are severely traumatized borderline patients who enact a victim–victimizer dyad in the therapeutic interaction, with an intensity and rapidity of role reversals that create a maximum risk for intense countertransference developments and countertransference acting out, which may contribute to repetitive vicious circles of transference acting out.

The combination of the patient's intense hatred, omnipotent control, and projective identification in the transference and the therapist's need to establish and maintain firm boundaries of the treatment situation in order to continue an analytic approach often make it almost impossible, in the short run, to distinguish the therapist's firmness, technical neutrality, and holding and containing patterns from his or her acting out of omnipotent control in a projective counteridentification, that is, in the countertransference. Such a difficulty may temporarily feed into the therapist's masochistic potential and lead to a dangerous, guilt-motivated submission to the patient's acting out, followed by an internal or actual rejection of the patient.

If, however, the therapist can tolerate this ambiguity while maintaining an ongoing analysis of transference and countertransference outside as well as during the sessions, it is usually possible to clarify the patient's transference. At the same time the analyst's capacity to absorb the aggression without reacting with counteraggression, abandonment of the patient, or masochistic surrender is facilitated. The analyst's consistency and firmness will, in turn, permit the patient to realize that his aggression is not as dangerous and intolerable as he feared. In identifying with the observing function of the therapist, the patient may thus develop the potential for accepting and elaborating his or her own aggression. The result will reduce the splitting that separates idealized and persecutory internalized object relationships and lead to the integration of self and object representations, the tolerance of ambivalence, and the deepening and maturing of internalized and actual object relationships.

References

Freud, S. (1909). Notes upon a case of obsessional neurosis. *Standard Edition* 10:151–249.

——— (1913). Totem and taboo. *Standard Edition* 13:1–164.

——— (1921). Group psychology. *Standard Edition* 18:67–143.

——— (1930). Civilization and its discontents. *Standard Edition* 21:59–243.

Jacobson, E. (1967). *Psychotic Conflict and Reality*. New York: International Universities Press.

——— (1971). *Depression*. New York: International Universities Press.

Kernberg, O. F. (1975). *Borderline Conditions and Pathological Narcissism*. New York: Jason Aronson.

——— (1984). *Severe Personality Disorders*. New Haven, CT: Yale University Press.

——— (1992). *Aggression in Personality Disorders and Perversions*. New Haven, CT: Yale University Press.

Klein, M. (1946). Notes on some schizoid mechanisms. In *Developments in Psycho-Analysis*, ed. J. Riviere, pp. 292–320. London: Hogarth, 1952.

——— (1957). *Envy and Gratitude*. New York: Basic Books.

Mahler, M., and Furer, M. (1968). *On Human Symbiosis and the Vicissitudes of Individuation*. New York: International Universities Press.

Mahler, M., Pine, F., and Bergman, A. (1975). *The Psychological Birth of the Human Infant*. New York: Basic Books.

Rosenfeld, H. (1964). On the psychopathology of narcissism: a clinical approach. *International Journal of Psycho-Analysis* 45:332–337.

——— (1971). A clinical approach to the psychoanalytic theory of the life and death instincts: an investigation into the aggressive aspects of narcissism. *International Journal of Psycho-Analysis* 52:169–178.

——— (1987). *Impasse and Interpretation*. New York: Tavistock.

Searles, H. (1965). *Collected Papers on Schizophrenia and Related Subjects*. New York: International Universities Press.

Winnicott, D. (1960a). Ego distortion in terms of true and false self. In *The Maturational Processes and the Facilitating Environment*, pp. 140–152. New York: International Universities Press, 1965.

——— (1960b). The theory of the parent–infant relationship. In *The Maturational Processes and the Facilitating Environment*, pp. 37–55. New York: International Universities Press, 1965.

Discussion

Steven J. Ellman, Ph.D.

Editors' Comments

Dr. Ellman provides a thorough and richly articulated discussion of Dr. Kernberg's contribution, not only in terms of his thoughts about handling omnipotent control in the transference but also regarding Kernberg's developmental model of affects as the central organizing unit of human behavior. Drawing upon a previous chapter he had written with Monica Carsky, Dr. Ellman elaborates some of his criticisms of Kernberg's ideas and shows how, even though Kernberg's concept of envy and projective identification stem from Kleinian thought, they are neither Kleinian nor Freudian. He offers a very interesting discussion of what Klein really meant by the infant's destructive wishes toward the breast and raises the question of whether Kernberg's ideas of hatred are really developmentally the same. He shows how difficult it is to build a theory when we change some of the concepts.

Ellman's discussion also focuses on how Kernberg's model of development influences his treatment and interventions. In discussing Kernberg's suggestions regarding the setting of boundaries, Ellman provides a clinical example from a patient who set his own boundaries in the treatment. He describes a different model of omnipotence than Kernberg's and a different view of analytic trust. Ellman points out that "the theory we choose for ourselves necessarily implies certain countertransference and enactment potentials." While Kernberg's views of omnipotence lead him to focus on the destructive potential of omnipotent fantasies and omnipotent control, Ellman's views lead him to focus on the patient's vulnerability and fragmentation. Ellman describes how he has been able to integrate Winnicott's ideas into his treatment of borderline patients. Although he agrees that the expression of omnipotent control inevitably arises in the analytic treatment of narcissistic and borderline patients, he presents a different view of how important it is to "manage" them.

I am honored to discuss Dr. Kernberg's typically rich (typically for him, that is) and thoughtful presentation. When I was asked to discuss his paper I felt particularly pleased until my wife and Dr. Anni Bergman informed me that I had not been chosen for any special clinical or intellectual expertise, but rather I had been selected for what they termed "characterological reasons" relating, they said, to certain traits that Dr. Kernberg would be discussing. Given this somewhat narrower role, I hope readers and Dr. Kernberg will understand that at some points in my discussion I might seem defensive or even mildly upset as I write about issues relating to the topic of omnipotence. This might be hard to empathize with or even understand for those of you who come to this topic with an objective attitude motivated only by scientific curiosity.

My discussion will be broken up into four brief sections. I will first go over aspects of the developmental model that Dr. Kernberg has so succinctly summarized for us. My focus will be to look at one aspect of this model that I believe relates directly to the clinical approach that has been advocated. After this discussion I will briefly go over an alternative view of omnipotence and then discuss a therapeutic stance that differs from the one that has been articulated. I will then go over one session and try to discuss it in detail. After going over these three points I will discuss how one's theoretical view dictates the boundaries of an analyst's therapeutic stance.

Although I have written a chapter with Dr. Monica Carsky (Carsky and Ellman 1985) on Dr. Kernberg's theoretical and clinical work, I am still left with certain questions about his developmental assumptions that I am not able to answer. The developmental model that he has schematically outlined is complex enough that a serious discussion would require a full paper. Kernberg has moved to a model where affect is a central aspect in the development of self-object-affect (S-O-A) units. His S-O units are colored by affect states and gradually coalesce (during passive splitting) into libidinal (good) and aggressive (bad) units, which eventually must be brought together for true self and object differentiation as well as for the formation of identity. Affects are instinctive components of human behavior: inborn dispositions that are gradually organized "into pleasurable affects, or libido, as an overarching drive, and painful, aversive, negative affects that, in turn, are organized into aggression as an overarching drive." As I understand this assertion, Dr. Kernberg is placing affect as the central motivating concept in his theoretical matrix and what he calls drive seems to be the coalescing of similar affects into central behavioral, emotional tendencies with accompanying mental representations (not necessarily in that causal way). For him rage is the ontogenetic precursor of hatred and "hatred is a chronic stable, . . . usually structured affect." There are several concomitants of hatred—one may wish to destroy an object, dominate an object, and almost always revenge oneself upon the object. Not surprisingly a person consumed with hatred is usually filled with paranoid retaliatory anxieties. In describing the vicissitudes of hatred, Kernberg utilizes Klein's concept of envy.

Here we get into some of the difficulty that I find with how Dr. Kernberg combines concepts from different theories. He utilizes affective states and inborn affective or temperamental differences to get to a place that is quite similar to a Kleinian position. Klein's concept is invoked when he states that her "explanation is of envy as a major manifestation of human aggression." This, however, is not quite Klein's concept for she talks not of aggression but rather of destructiveness when she says, "The struggle between life and death instincts and the ensuing threat of annihilation of the self and of the object by destructive impulses are fundamentals in the infant's initial relation to his mother" (1957). Clearly when the infant envies the good breast the infant does not project aggression into the breast, but rather projects destructive tendencies into the breast (mother). In fact the projection of aggression doesn't fully make sense since part of the reason for projecting into the mother is to rid oneself of internal destructive tendencies. One can tolerate aggressive feelings toward the other but not destructive feelings both because of the internal danger of destructiveness and the danger these feelings constitute to the good breast. It seems to me that Dr. Kernberg then hedges his subsequent distinction between aggression and destructiveness when he blends Kleinian theory into his own writing. The breast that aggressively withholds itself is, in turn, hated, and its fantasized contents are spoiled and destroyed. This is a typically mixed concept that Dr. Kernberg presents. A Kleinian breast isn't aggressive; it threatens survival, and the infant's destructive impulses threaten its survival. A vicious cycle may ensue, in which the destroyed and destructive breast is experienced as a persecutory object. Here lies the origin of envy, the need to spoil and destroy the object that is also needed for survival and is in the end the object of love.

Kernberg links the clinical study of patients with narcissistic personality disorders to both conscious and unconscious sources of envy "as a *major* affective expression of aggression." The theory of aggression would not have taken him to this conclusion as rapidly or with the certainty that he assumes. Thus I conclude that however he maintains he reached these conclusions, Dr. Kernberg must still share Klein's views of the importance of destructive states in early development. If envy has the early and central importance that Kernberg posits then he must either use the concept of a destructive drive or show how the breast aggressively presented is a typical experience in human development. Klein's theory of envy is part of a normal development sequence; Kernberg has not as yet shown how his concepts form the basis of a normal developmental schema.

In a previous publication Carsky and Ellman (1985) noted that while Dr. Kernberg still talks about the drives, the theory that he is proposing uses drives in a substantially different way than does psychoanalytic theory. In brief, when Freud utilizes the concept of drive he is referring to endogenous stimulation that is present regardless of the external conditions. Kernberg's use of affect refers to states that are reactive to external stimulation. This is a fundamentally different concept and the type of predictions that these two concepts yield are quite different. I have attempted to explore some of these differences (Ellman 1991, 1992). It may be that Kernberg is using affect as a central concept because of the analytic community's reluctance to accept the implications of Freudian and Kleinian drive theory. Part of the difficulty in our theory building has been that we have not paid enough attention to what happens to our theoretical structure when we eliminate a central concept but act as if nothing has been altered in our theories. Thus the focus on temperament and affect states may be all to the good but not if these changes lead to theories that are unintegrated, without implicit or explicit rules of correspondence. As an aside, I must state that I believe an updated version of drive, or what I have called endogenous stimulation, is needed where we offer an explanation for temperamental differences and issues of bonding and attunement as well as activity levels and various types of stimulation thresholds (Ellman 1992).

Brief Remarks about Other Developmental Perspectives

It is important to stop here and note that I believe Dr. Kernberg has the most complete integration of different theoretical perspectives that has so far been attempted in psychoanalysis. Despite this we can see some of the difficulties inherent in such an integration. In his introduction he mentions a number of views related to omnipotence and gently glides among and between these views. I would argue that some of the views he mentions are incompatible in tone and perhaps logically incompatible with his positions on omnipotence.

Let me assume for a moment that I am incorrect in my evaluation of the present state of Dr. Kernberg's theoretical integrations. I would still have to state that Freud's (in what I have called his object relations period) and Winnicott's (or probably Mahler's) view of omnipotence leads to a different view of the infant and the borderline and narcissistic adult than the one Dr. Kernberg is discussing. Freud's view of omnipotence in the purified pleasure ego (1915) led him to assume the infant splits the world to retain the good object and be at one with it. Dr. Kernberg's theory leads him to an emphasis on the destructive potential of omnipotent fantasies; Winnicott's perspective leads him to focus on issues of vulnerability and patients' difficulties in experiencing themselves as whole objects. Not surprisingly Winnicott stands the problem on its ear and maintains that the experience of omnipotence is not possible in a person who cannot tolerate himself as a whole object. In a previous publication (Ellman 1992) I have introduced a model that integrates Winnicott's and Klein's views on development and tries to show under what conditions an infant would look more Kleinian and under what conditions Winnicott's views of absolute and relative dependence would obtain. At the end of this discussion I will burden you with an aspect of his model.

Clinical Perspectives

I see McLaughlin's (1991) and Jacobs' (1986) continuing efforts to describe the nature of enactments in the clinical situation as an interesting tool with which to look at the clinical implications of different positions. It is my view that each perspective (Klein and Winnicott) will lead to different types of enactment and if we are to have convergent positions that are not empty ones it is crucial to look at the implications of divergent positions. From my perspective, Dr. Kernberg's overall position does not consider in sufficient detail the issues of what I have called analytic trust (Ellman 1991).

With this concept I seek to understand the conditions under which it is possible to enter the patient's world without being experienced as an object that is impinging on a patient's sense of self. In my theoretical matrix it is important in the treatment of narcissistic or nonclassical patients to be included initially within the patient's world rather than being seen as a fully external object. Analytic trust is begun by demonstrating that you are prepared and able to experience the patient's world in a way that shows that you know and at times can feel what they are experiencing. This concept assumes that particularly at the beginning of the treatment (but in cycles throughout the treatment) the analyst will be a safe container for the analysand's aggressive and destructive fantasies and behavior until this material is ready to be interpreted. Bach (1985, 1994) and in a different way Modell (1984) talk about a process that allows for the analyst to enter the patient's world, be utilized, and still be intact enough to emerge eventually as a separate object.

What are the implications of this position? Interpretive efforts should be undertaken only when the patient has developed sufficient trust to (on occasion) allow the analyst to exist as a separate object. Interpretations should be undertaken early in the treatment only when the patient's sadism threatens to disrupt and/or destroy the therapeutic situation. When this occurs it is still important to include the need this behavior served in the past as well as the wish, or in other words, to include the adaptive aspects of their response. (Why they feel forced to respond in particular ways.) In addition I would not go outside the therapeutic field if possible. Resorting frequently to reconstructive statements (while soothing) in my view promotes a certain type of splitting that is dangerous for real therapeutic growth. How does this position relate to one of Dr. Kernberg's sessions?

Session: The College Student

She begins with a complaint that Dr. K. was not able to see her later in the day. Dr. Kernberg responds realistically by referring to his communication with the patient through his secretary but this does not mollify the patient, and she angrily accuses him of giving preference to other patients. At this point he makes a remark that is difficult to classify. He points out that he realized that she was angry because she felt that he was neglecting her and showing preference for other patients. One might be tempted to call this a reflective statement depending of course on the tone that was used. From my point of view, what may have been absent is some indication that the analyst knows how disruptive it is for the patient when she feels neglected.

Why do I indicate that this may not have been an appropriate response? Because I am not certain why the patient is in an extended sadomasochistic transference to the analyst. It may be that the patient has reached a point where she trusts the treatment situation enough so that she is able to display the aspects of her inner life that are most problematic to her. There is no way I can determine the state of the patient except to say that the reading of the dialogue between patient and analyst causes me to wonder about Dr. Kernberg's equanimity in the face of her demands. The patient continued to ask Dr. Kernberg to give her another session at the end of the day. The analyst responded by saying that she was having her session right now. Clearly the patient knew this, so again from another perspective, I would have inquired what was preventing her from utilizing the present session. She again repeats her demand. At this point Dr. Kernberg provides an interpretation. It did not feel to me that she was in a position to utilize this multilayered interpretation. ("Her demand for additional time affirmed that the hour would be lost anyway; this indicated her wishes on the surface to punish me for not doing what she wanted and at a deeper level to punish me by destroying her own opportunity to experience me as somebody available to help her understand what was going on in this hour.") After several angry interchanges (that is, the patient was angry) Dr. Kernberg commented that she was repeating the same statements again and again, wondered what the function of that could be. For me this would indicate that my interpretative efforts had not been effective (perhaps filling me with the same feeling of helplessness and uselessness that the patient was experiencing in her rage) and belief of mine that analytic trust had not been established would come rushing to my mind. If the patient responds in the same stereotyped manner to your interpretative efforts (by not responding with any self-awareness), something must be amiss with an element of your communication.

After her (hateful) silence Dr. Kernberg, it seems to me, takes a slightly different tact. He asks what the function of silence is and says that if it is to repeat the previous statements, then he and the patient will remain as adversaries, and that precludes "our looking further into what was stimulating this rage." This is the first time in the session that either patient or analyst uses a pronoun other than *I* or *me*. The patient then seemingly takes a mocking stance (and sarcastically becomes Dr. Kernberg): "You can go on saying whatever nonsense comes to mind." Dr. Kernberg then brings in the patient's mother in an interpretation that combines reconstructive and transference elements. He again tries to enlist her efforts by reminding her of an element they had explored (it was not a new interpretation) to resolve the fight that had taken place in the beginning of the session. This enabled Dr. Kernberg to make another interpretation at the end of the session, when he wondered, "whether the patient was really experiencing what I was saying as thoughts that changed her view about herself, or whether she was now experiencing me as a powerful mother and her as the naughty little girl who had to make amends."

The main issue that is commented on has to with the "management of omnipotent control in severe personality disorders." He tells us that, "if I had agreed to my first patient's demand that I give her an additional hour she would have relaxed immediately but the underlying identification with her sadistic mother would no longer have been emotionally available for analytic work at that time." The accent on management of the patient leaves out what for me is the more important issue of the patient's being overwhelmed by interpretive efforts. Nevertheless, it is important to consider Dr. Kernberg's assertion that if had acceded to the patient's demands she would not have been available for analytic work. We can ask:

1) Whether or not (or to what extent) we agree with this assertion.
2) The extent to which the patient was available for analytic work anyway.
3) Is the management of the case the central issue with which we are usually concerned with borderline patients?

Let me give a short clinical vignette. A lawyer I was seeing was initially described to me as a vicious litigator who was charming but impossible and extraordinarily narcissistic. He continually complained about a number of the boundary conditions of our treatment situation. (I think that this vague description in no way compromises a litigator's confidentiality.) The boundary issue that eventually remained for him (after he reconciled himself to coming four times a week) was my policy of charging for missed sessions. He explained that he himself did not bill for missed sessions and despite the fact that he was able to point out a variety of things that were different between our situations, it remained a point about which he would periodically become enraged. He felt that his rages were pointless, for he was only wasting his time and "shooting himself in the foot while hopefully trying at the same time to fatally hit me." Although after three years he had made some progress in treatment, he was disrupted whenever this issue came to the fore. At one point I decided that he seemed unable to develop trust in the process in a full manner and his conflicts focused (in a paranoid persecuted manner) around this issue. At a session when he was relatively calm I told him that we did not seem able to understand why this issue so enraged him and that at this time I thought perhaps we should have a policy we could both agree on. He set up a relatively complicated policy that I will not attempt to describe (it would be something like Freud's attempts to describe the rat man's obsessive journey). I decided I could be relatively comfortable with this policy and decided to see how it worked out. When the time came to institute this new policy because he was going on a business trip, he asked me if he could make up his sessions. My policy is that if I have cancellations I am willing to switch a patient's sessions when necessary. His request surprised me, however, since previously his schedule never allowed him to take any but his scheduled sessions. After we discussed this issue I asked him to review our new policy on missed sessions so that we had the same understanding. After attempting to articulate the policy he decided to give up on it saying that it was too complicated. I wondered if after winning the battle he was worrying about damaging me any further and needed to restore me to the role of the authority who set unfair standards that I forced him to live up to. In short he was reinstating me as a punitive figure who forced him to do things that he hated to do.

This incident began a period of intense, at times split, at times extremely ambivalent, homosexual transference manifestations. The patient's paranoia during this period was intense but somehow tolerable to him (and even to me at times) and mostly contained within the transference. This period was followed by what I think might be described as a transference reaction that came from what Klein (1928) described at one point in her career as the femininity phase of development. Within the transference he was able to slowly unravel what I would consider to be the primary issues of envy that were embedded in his intense anal sadistic fantasies and character structure.

This brief example is brought up to illustrate this point: if the patient is unable to utilize the analyst in the transference (and in the beginning of the treatment in other ways as well), then the analyst, it seems to me, should attempt to alter conditions to allow narcissistic and borderline patients to feel that they are participating in certain types of boundary issues that may allow them to utilize the analytic situation. This patient was unable to explore this particular boundary, and I felt relatively safe in relinquishing control of this aspect of the treatment because I did not feel manipulated. Rather, I thought such intense issues were embedded in this boundary that my willingness to set his boundary mutually enhanced his realistic representation of me (his trust in the situation, the process, and its boundaries) so that he could explore his deeper narcissistic conflicts. (Here I would agree with Dr. Kernberg that patients with narcissistic disorders usually have sadomasochistic conflicts and always have strongly conscious and unconscious fantasies that have at the center issues of envy.)

I would also agree that the expression of omnipotent control inevitably arises in the analytic treatment of narcissistic and borderline patients. But issues of vulnerability and fragmentation come up with even greater frequency, and if these issues are met concurrently or at the beginning of the treatment, then the rage reactions that Dr. Kernberg experienced are, in my view, better contained within the transference.

Before I conclude let me go back to the session of the college student that we were considering. From McLaughlin's (1991) point of view the session was an example of enactment. Both analyst and patient felt that they were acting in a certain way because of how the other had influenced them. Toward the end of the session the patient said that she was aware of Dr. Kernberg's interpretation but felt that he had provoked the situation. Dr. Kernberg answered, "If she really had not been able to come at this time, I would have evaluated whether we could find a better time to meet, but she had engineered the situation in a way that precluded such a solution." Thus the analyst, while feeling safe and secure and not that susceptible to the patient's blantly manipulative efforts, also interpreted from a distance that allowed him to be interpreted realistically as an omnipotent and sadistic figure. Is there any way out of this conundrum?

Rather then answering this question I will circle around to the brief example that I provided. While I reported or implied a successful analytic result, it seems to me in retrospect that I masochistically surrendered to the analysand pressure that both frightened him and forced him to surrender some of his valuable contents lest he destroy what was proving valuable to him (his analysis) and what felt to him like his last chance to be related to the object world (he had been in several other treatments). This was something that I gradually and painfully struggled with and generally was able to maintain in my analytic attitude for most of his analysis. (It lasted seven years.)

Clearly I am maintaining that the theory we choose for ourselves (or rather our theoretical niche) necessarily implies certain countertransference and enactment potentials. All of our theoretical positions are, by and large, partial attempts and it may surprise readers to learn that, by and large, I find Dr. Kernberg's and certain of the Neo-Kleinian approaches to be among the most complete in psychoanalysis. However, I will end with a paragraph that takes us back to some developmental hypotheses and perhaps give some indications of the types of theoretical integrations I am attempting.

I will hastily attempt to describe a line of research that I was involved in from 1969 to 1985 (Ellman and Weinstein 1991, Ellman 1992). This research was aimed at elucidating the role of REM sleep in mammalian development. From this research I have postulated that REM sleeplike mechanisms fire throughout the 24-hour cycle and may be considered one candidate for what Freud called *drive*. We have demonstrated in animals that REM mechanisms are correlated with pleasure centers (Spielman et al. 1973, Steiner and Ellman 1972). These pleasure centers are important motivational pathways for all mammals but particularly for primates, who depend on more flexible drive systems. I have postulated that the large amounts of REM sleep in human and other mammalian infants are present to facilitate drive (or endogenous stimulation) mechanisms that are necessary for survival. It is my view that human infants differ in the amount of endogenous stimulation or drive, and that high-drive infants present quite a different picture to the aspiring good-enough mother than normal or low-drive infants. I will end this section by showing how I view Winnicott in terms of some of the issues that I have raised.

To paraphrase Winnicott (1965): he postulates that after a phase of absolute dependence the infant achieves what might be called unit status. The infant is becoming a person in his own right. Associated with this attainment is the infant's psychosomatic existence, which begins to take on a personal pattern; Winnicott has called this the psyche indwelling in the soma. The basis for this indwelling is a linkage of motor sensory and functional experiences with the infant's new state of being a person. As a subsequent development there comes into being what he calls a limiting membrane, which to some extent (if the baby is healthy) is equated with the surface of the skin, and has a position between the infant's me and his not-me (representations). So the infant begins to have an inside and an outside and a body-scheme. In this way, psyche meaning comes into one's fantasy life in terms of taking in and shutting out; moreover, after a period of time it gradually makes sense to postulate a personal or inner psychic reality for the infant. I would add to this that the strength of the drives and how well the drives unite into a consolidated state (walking and sleeping) will be a powerful determiner of how well formed this membrane will become in the infant's developing body ego. If the mother is not able to understand the intensity and the restrictive range of certain high-drive infants, than this membrane will at best be a highly permeable one or, alternatively, one that is so impermeable as to render object relations unable to give life or sustenance to the child. I believe we are at a point of being able to study this process. In a similar vein I would say that the analyst who encounters such a patient in adult life has to wait until the patient can utilize the analyst and then has confidence that the analyst will not break through (or impinge upon) this membrane. It is here that we respect the analysand's sense of self and fragility of ego until the patient can own their own drive states, fantasies, and object relationships. This can be done in a variety of ways. What is the best way always depends on the analyst's sense of clarity about his boundaries, beliefs, endogenous states, and how his own sense of self and being impinges on the analytic process.

References

Bach, S. (1985). *Narcissistic States and the Therapeutic Process*. Northvale, NJ: Jason Aronson.

——— (1994). *The Language of Perversion and the Language of Love*. Northvale, NJ: Jason Aronson.

Carsky, M., and Ellman, S. J. (1985). Otto Kernberg: psychoanalysis and object relations theory; the beginnings of an integrative approach. In *Beyond Freud*, ed. J. Reppen, pp. 257–296. Hillsdale, NJ: Analytic Press.

Ellman, S. J. (1991). *Freud's Technique Papers: A Contemporary Perspective*. Northvale, NJ: Jason Aronson.

——— (1992). Psychoanalytic theory, dream formation and REM sleep. In *Interface of Psychoanalysis and Psychology*, ed. J. W. Barron, M. N. Eagle, and D. L. Wolitzky, pp. 357–374. Washington, DC: American Psychological Association.

Ellman, S. J., and Weinstein, L. N. (1991). REM sleep and dream formation: a theoretical integration. In *The Mind in Sleep*, ed. S. J. Ellman and J. S. Antrobus, pp. 466–488. New York: Wiley.

Freud, S. (1915). Instincts and their vicissitudes. *Standard Edition* 14:111–140.

Jacobs, T. J. (1986). On countertransference enactments. *Journal of the American Psychoanalytic Association* 34(2):289–307.

Klein, M. (1928). Early stages of the Oedipus conflict. In *The Writings of Melanie Klein, vol. 1: Love, Guilt, and Reparation*, pp. 186–198. London: Hogarth, 1975.

——— (1957). Envy and gratitude. In *The Writings of Melanie Klein, vol. 3: Envy and Gratitude and Other Works*, pp. 176–235. London: Hogarth, 1975.

McLaughlin, J. T. (1991). Clinical and theoretical aspects of enactment. *Journal of the American Psychoanalytic Association* 39(3):591–614.

Modell, A. (1984). *Psychoanalysis in a New Context*. Madison, CT: International Universities Press.

Spielman, A. J., Ellman, S. J., and Steiner, S. S. (1973). The effects of varying amounts of intracranial self-stimulation on the normal sleep cycle of the rat. *Psychophysiology* 11:171–174.

Steiner, S. S., and Ellman, S. J. (1972). Relation between REM sleep and intracranial self-stimulation. *Science* 177:1122–1124.

Winnicott, D. W. (1965). *The Maturational Processes and the Facilitating Environment*. New York: International Universities Press.

4

Omnipotence in Health and Illness

Paul H. Ornstein, M.D.

Editors' Comments

In a charmingly written paper, Dr. Ornstein, a prominent exponent of self psychology, views infantile and child omnipotence that are part of the grandiose self and the idealized parent imago primarily as examples of health and only secondarily as expressions of pathology. Ornstein's paper is a unique contribution, differing because of his theoretical orientation from other papers in this collection.

He presents a moving picture of a personal nightmarish experience in which he audaciously escaped being a slave worker for the Germans during the later stages of World War II. Omnipotent fantasies, one of which included a fantasy of rescue by a farmer's daughter, sustained him in his search for a way to escape. Ornstein sees his rescue fantasies as averring that omnipotence can never be viewed in isolation but only within a larger context, and he argues further for the adaptive value of omnipotent fantasies.

Ornstein elaborates on the developmental vicissitudes of omnipotence, relying heavily, of course, on Kohut's theoretical teachings. He shows that there are transformations from archaic grandiosity into psychic structures as a result of a wide range of positive caretaker functions, that a lack of mirroring will undermine the possibility of these transformations, and that omnipotent fantasies thus produced will have a more archaic quality. Omnipotence is embedded in the grandiose self and borrowed from the idealized parent or imago and thus can be an aspect of healthy self-esteem. Ornstein describes the essential elements of a self psychologically informed psychoanalytic treatment as well as the essential curative factors in treatment and the nature of cure.

He relates the fascinating case of Mr. I., demonstrating many of the principles of self psychological treatment. In the course of treatment Mr. I. retreated from grandiose and omnipotent fantasies as well as from feelings of helplessness. Ornstein presents a poignant example of his own empathic failure and demonstrates the working through of an idealized transference. The focus on interpretation was not necessarily on content but on those aspects of the vulnerable self from which those contents arose. In the case of Mr. I. Ornstein demonstrates a movement from grandiosity and omnipotence to reliable self-esteem.

Introduction

In this chapter I wish to make a basic tenet of self psychology more explicit, namely, that infantile and childhood omnipotence (as a content of the constellation of the grandiose self and of the idealized parent imago) are first and foremost the nucleus of health and only secondarily may become the expression of illness.

We all have experiences of one sort or another that form the core elements of our *Weltanschauung*, our outlook on the human condition. Our view of the world and our own place in it begins to be formed very early in infancy and childhood (cf. Arlow 1982). Parental responses, the gleam in the mother's eye along with the father's pride in his offspring, are powerful contributors to the final shape of our Weltanschauung prior to our choosing psychoanalysis as a career. Only later reflections and a personal analysis, then life after analysis, will bring some of those influences to our conscious awareness. Whether its varied early sources are explicitly known or only dimly perceived, our Weltanschauung has a powerful hold on us, much more powerful than we generally realize. I submit that it is this highly personal outlook on life that determines the kind of psychoanalysis we gravitate toward and how we forge it into an intensely absorbing profession. In fact, no matter what brand of psychoanalysis we have chosen, the way we later practice it and the way we later absorb or exclude certain alternative approaches from the one we have ultimately chosen depends, to a large extent, on our outlook on life—although it might seem that it is entirely a well-reasoned scientific choice. Our Weltanschauung and our psychoanalytic theoretical and technical outlook are so thoroughly intertwined and often seamlessly amalgamated that we cannot really tell where the one ends and the other begins (P. H. Ornstein 1993, 1995, in press).

It is therefore fitting, I believe, that I introduce myself and my topic by offering a glimpse of what in my own background and experiences predisposed me to see infantile and childhood omnipotence through the lens of self psychology (after a thorough prior grounding in ego psychology and Balintian object relations theory) as the core of health rather than of illness, although we know that it frequently becomes a part of psychopathology, and we then encounter it in the psychoanalytic treatment process.

Although I shall first exemplify the adaptive value of omnipotence, my presentation will remain focused on omnipotence as an ideational content of the "grandiose self," which is a developmental nucleus of health. We should differentiate between health and adaptation, which are not synonymous. Very likely, omnipotence as an aspect of an archaic grandiose self would not have shown the necessary flexibility for adaptive use in the circumstances I shall describe.

My presentation consists of two parts. Part I offers a perspective on omnipotence in everyday life (although in this instance a highly atypical one) and describes its developmental vicissitudes. Part II offers a perspective on omnipotence from the psychoanalytic treatment process as embedded in archaic grandiosity and becoming available for analysis in a mirror transference and as omnipotence borrowed from an archaic idealized other, becoming available for analysis in an idealizing transference.

Part I

Omnipotence in Everyday Life

For the sake of propriety as well as brevity, I shall telescope earlier forms and contents of some of my omnipotent fantasies into their much later derivatives.

I was 20 years old, almost to the day, living in Budapest, when the Germans suddenly and unexpectedly invaded and occupied Hungary on March 19, 1944. Our fate was sealed, but we did not know it. Three months later I found myself in a forced labor camp, building roads and airport landing-strips, before being transported to the Eastern front to work for the Hungarian army between Russia and German-Hungarian front lines, in Poland. The details are irrelevant except to say that after the Russians broke through the front-lines one Sunday morning in September of 1944, the Hungarians retreated into the Carpathian Mountain Range and were determined—so it seemed—to camp out there for the winter and hold up the Russian invasion. The other prisoners and I were herded along on this retreat; many died and those who survived were exhausted and considerably weakened. The optimists among us were hoping that the Hungarians would not succeed and that with the next wave of retreat we would all be thrown back to Hungary, where there might be a chance to escape. As September wore on, however, the optimists, myself among them, were beginning to lose hope. The Russians remained idle; in fact, as we now know, they later broke through at a point further north and were only pretending to threaten the part of the front where we were building roads and fortifications. As you may realize, winter starts early in the Carpathian Mountains; therefore, my skimpy, tattered clothing, the inadequate food, and the flimsy shelter convinced me that I would soon freeze to death or die of hunger, and I became obsessed with plotting my escape.

It was during this endless, obsessive plotting that some of my omnipotent fantasies came to my aid. Of course, I would not have called them "omnipotent fantasies" then; I did not even know the term. I thought only, in desperation, under the threat of freezing to death, that I had to and that I could and would outfox the Hungarian army and find some devious way to return to Hungry. And once on Hungarian territory, where I knew the language, I would escape. A farmer's daughter—I imagined—would hide me until it was safe to emerge.

It was truly a preposterous plan, fueled by omnipotent fantasies. Preposterous, but not totally impossible. The important point is that I kept thinking only about its not being impossible, never of its being preposterous, otherwise I would not have been able to put my plans into action. After each failure (and there were many along the way), instead of seeing the ridiculousness and utter stupidity of my plans, I thought only of forging better ones.

Before continuing my narrative, let me pause here and reflect for a moment, with clear hindsight, on my situation in the Carpathian Mountains.

In that stressful situation it was extremely important that my omnipotent fantasies fuel my actions, in order for me to dare to undertake the considerable risks. But this influence of archaic omnipotence had to occur outside my awareness, since I needed to feel that my plans were well laid and so inordinately clever and reality-based that nobody could find me out. I had to be convinced that I was fully rational and acting on carefully garnered knowledge about my circumstances in order to make the necessary preparations and predictions for a felicitous outcome. Needless to say, most of my predictions were off the mark; most of my plans backfired, and only unexpected improvisations and accidental encounters with helpful people saved me.

To return to my story: I finally feigned appendicitis in the hope that I would be sent to a hospital on the Hungarian side of the border, where I could plot my further escape. I succeeded, with many near misses and many new and clever plans along the way (all of which, in retrospect, were utterly foolish, some even dangerous). Only accidental turns of events saved me. But meanwhile—and this is the significant point—I could feel that I took my fate into my own hands and that somehow it was up to me whether I survived or not. This unrealistic feeling of confidence, at a time when many of my fellow inmates fell into apathy, depression, and a degree of listlessness, helped me remain alert and vigilant and therefore able to take advantage of accidentally arising opportunities to escape. The fantasy that a Hungarian farmer's daughter would save me—in spite of mounting evidence that this would not happen—sustained my efforts to search for some means of escape, because, if there was nowhere to go, escaping was entirely futile. Getting caught meant certain death.

To underscore the unbroken continuity of my survival fantasies with archaic omnipotence, the kind that might certainly be more dangerous to have under similar circumstances, I shall conclude my story with a fantasy that propelled me to the brink of disaster.

As luck would have it—although I believed it was in part due to my own cunning and, as one of my friends remarked, luck was necessary, but not sufficient—I did ultimately escape. I made my way to Budapest and succeeded in sneaking into the city without being caught. I arrived there feeling a mixture of triumph and fear about my future. But my triumphant feelings suppressed my fears. I recall having had the omnipotent fantasy that, "If I came back this far from where I was, nothing could happen to me now!" I thought I was invulnerable. This feeling of invulnerability made me expose myself to situations, one in particular, where I could easily have lost my life. It is inexplicable that it did not happen. But this near-fatal experience instantly jolted me back to reality—which could only happen in the relative safety of my new situation. At this point I had to acknowledge my vulnerability in order to plan more safely for survival.

What do these experiences illustrate? First, and foremost, they illustrate that the nature of omnipotence cannot be considered separately from its matrix; omnipotence cannot be viewed in isolation, but only in its embeddedness in the total structure of the personality and more specifically, in its embeddedness in archaic grandiosity as one of its contents (along with omniscience and omnipotent control). The adaptive value of omnipotent fantasies and the actions they generate depend on how freely and flexibly the archaic layers are available to the person, who has one foot in these fantasies and has the other, simultaneously or in rapid succession, in current reality. In the planning stage of my escape, the idea that a farmer's daughter would hide me until the Russian troops occupied that part of Hungary played a prominent role. It does point to the early origins of the fantasy, although the rest of the specific features of the fantasy of escape exemplify only the adaptive use of its transformed, later derivatives. The last part of my example shows that certain experiences that confirm the power of one's omnipotence and the effectiveness of one's actions based on it, can stimulate even more archaic layers of omnipotent fantasies. These can lead to dangerous actions. It is then the capacity to contain them, to be able to refocus on what the new circumstances demand to achieve one's goals, that separates the adaptive from the maladaptive use of omnipotent fantasies. The containment of this last fantasy was contingent on the relative safety of my new situation, which no longer demanded risky exposure for a successful escape. It demanded the opposite: a calm, nonheroic hiding. An inflexible, compelling dominance of archaic fantasies pushing for action would have precluded my channeling them into reality-oriented activities.

To put this into more abstract theoretical language, I wish to remind you of the image Kohut presented to us as he refined Hartmann's view of the structure of the psyche in the early 1960s (Kohut and Seitz 1963). On one side, in response to traumatic frustration, the repression barrier divided the psyche. On this divided side of the psyche conflict reigned and only transferences across the repression barrier could give us access to what was repressed. There could be no conflict-free access to walled-off experiences. On the other, in response to optimum frustration, there was no repression barrier; progressive neutralization (we would not say as a result of the impact of felicitous responses form the environment) transformed early infantile, archaic experiences into a conflict-free sphere of the psyche, which could be smoothly integrated into the adult personality. In this nondivided area there could be relatively free access to early experiences, because they did not have to be walled off.

As is well known, for Freud (1914, 1915) and Ferenczi (1913) a direct line led from omnipotence to reality; once the latter was reached, the former had to disappear; omnipotence was a mark of infantilism. We have given up this linear sequencing, which smuggled a "maturational morality" (Kohut and Seitz 1963) into psychoanalysis under the guise of a scientific approach. We can now appreciate that what was decried as infantile, could be—in fact, needs to be—available to us in adulthood to provide not only the necessary fuel for the varied expressions of creativity but also to lend our personality its richness in depth.

We should now take a closer look at the developmental role and function self psychology attributes to omnipotent fantasies, omniscience, and omnipotent control. We all use these terms within our own systems of thought, where they each have a different developmental and theoretical position, inviting a different therapeutic approach. Unfortunately, giving these concepts Latin names often makes well-delineated pseudo-entities out of them, when in fact, they simply refer to fantasies of "virtually unlimited power and influence," fantasies of "unlimited knowledge," and "unlimited power to control others." Expressed in plain English (or in plain German, as Freud had done), these fantasies seem more naturally a part of early life, rather than expressions of psychopathology. Bowing to general usage for the sake of easier communication, we almost have no choice but to retain these Latin (or Greek) technical terms.

Developmental Vicissitudes of Omnipotence

Kohut once raised this question:

> Under what circumstances and in what way is an old unrealistic fantasy from childhood helpful to the individual, driving him forward, leading to achievement, becoming part and parcel of his sustaining self-esteem, and under what circumstances is it a grave hindrance, leading to inhibitions, to withdrawal from life, becoming a block? In general, and keeping the average in mind, the answer is not difficult to get. It depends on the gradualness of the integration of the early fantasy into the totality of the personality. The original fantasy may have been unrealistic, and undoubtedly it always is: the demand for baby worship later in life is obviously unrealistic. As an adult one cannot expect to be the center of attention in the way one can expect, and has the right to expect, when one is a newborn baby. Even early fantasies can be verbalized, which as daydreams continue to exist and are to some extent helpful, and part and parcel of normal human equipment. They belong to the resilience of the human [mind] capable of reacting to disappointments with wish-fulfilling fantasies. [Elson 1987, p. 242]

Kohut conceived of the vicissitudes of archaic omnipotence on the basis of his reconstruction of early development from the working through of the selfobject transferences. For our present purpose it should suffice to recall that Kohut conceived of "subject-bound omnipotence" as an ideational content of the grandiose self and "object-bound omnipotence" as an ideational content of the idealized parent imago. (These terms have the unfortunate connotation of representing severe psychopathology. Kohut defended his usage by saying that new ideas needed evocative terms for their successful communication and they may be changed later on. Perhaps the time has arrived to change them, but no attractive substitutes have as yet been presented.)

There is widespread agreement among clinicians and researchers alike (irrespective of their theoretical persuasions) that the human infant is born "hard-wired" with the capacity to elicit the empathic responses from its surround—empathic responses that are necessary for its psychological survival and healthy emotional development. Whether as a part of that hard wiring, or as a consequence of the experience that the infant can elicit the physical and emotional care it needs, the feeling of virtually unlimited power, influence, and control over others, that is, the feeling of omnipotence, will naturally be a part of early psychic life.

Kohut postulated that the infant's early needs cluster around three major constellations. I can only sketch this very schematically in the present context. (1) With its "grandiose self" the infant expresses its needs for *mirroring*, an umbrella term for a wide range of caretaker functions such as unconditional acceptance, admiration, affirmation, validation, the gleam in the mother's eye, and so on. Their predictable, steady availability and phase-appropriate adjustment to the infant's and child's changing needs will ultimately transform them into sturdy self-esteem and reliable self-esteem regulation; into a capacity for the enjoyment of physical and mental activities; and into an unhindered pursuit of goals and purposes. These transformations of archaic grandiosity into abiding psychic functions ("psychic structures") simultaneously include the transformation of omnipotent fantasies that belong into this cluster. Lack of adequate mirroring or their unreliable or otherwise faulty availability will thwart these transformations and will lead to what Kohut called the deficits or defects in the self. In such instances omnipotent fantasies will retain their archaic nature and remain unintegrated into the adult personality. Whether repressed or disavowed, they may become prominent features of the patient's psychopathology (See also Novick and Novick 1991, 1994). (2) With its "idealized parent imago" the infant (and growing child) expresses the need for a perfect, all-powerful, and all-knowing (omnipotent and omniscient) other, with whom it can merge, to whom it can attach itself, in order to partake of all the power and knowledge. This idealization—and all it entails—is again a phase-appropriate developmental need. To have an idealizable parent or caretaker is necessary for the child's acquisition of internalized values and ideals, capacities that serve self-soothing and self-calming functions, contain and channel affects, and allow for enthusiastic participation in human activities that enlarge the self. The slow and tolerable, but inevitable, disappointments lead to the consolidation of these functions (structure building) in this sector of the personality. Massive, traumatic, phase-inappropriate disillusionments lead to the specific deficits or defects in the whole area of tension and affect regulation, the capacity for enthusiasm, and, again, to a wide array of defensive sexualization and aggressivization (in the form of perversions, delinquency, and drug abuse). (3) With its twinship or alter-ego needs the infant (and growing child) searches for an echo of affirmation, for its own likeness or like-minded others, kindred spirits, in relation to whom the unfolding of skills and talents occur and who confirm its belonging to the human community. No one has linked these experiences to omnipotence, but there may be an indirect link in the sense that increasingly free use of one's talents and skills may contribute to successful performance, enhancing healthy self-esteem, which "belonging" also buttresses. These, in turn, make the use of archaic omnipotent fantasies for self-esteem regulation unnecessary. The sense of competence generates "I can do" feelings, bolstering self-esteem.

There are two lessons to be learned. One, a quick glance at this highly abbreviated outline indicates that omnipotence is embedded in the grandiose self and is "borrowed" from the idealized parent imago—the two healthy nuclei of the developing personality. It follows, therefore, that omnipotence, with its contribution to the development of stabile self-esteem, is also an aspect of these healthy nuclei; it is their ideational content. They are certainly necessary features of infancy and childhood, a sine qua non for the phase-appropriate "structuralization" of the self. Two, the outline also indicates the fact that Kohut replaced the psychosexual schema of development with a schema of his own, deriving the development of the self from the three archaic nuclear constellations just described. With this proposition he offered a different view of the nature of psychopathology, which then led directly to a different set of psychoanalytic treatment principles.

It is to these treatment principles, exemplifying the interpretive process with some clinical examples, that I wish to turn in the remainder of this paper, after a few general remarks in response to two questions: (1) What are the essential elements of the self psychologically informed psychoanalytic treatment approach to omnipotence as a frequently encountered ideational content of usually complex and often difficult-to-treat forms of psychopathology? (2) What are the essential curative factors and what is the nature of cure in the approach to grandiosity and omnipotence suggested by self psychology?

Neither the patient's psychopathology, nor the curative process as conceived by self psychology, can be fully understood without the recognition of the central position of the empathic vantage point of observation in the clinical process (P. H. Ornstein 1979). Simply put, this means that we always attempt to grasp the patient's subjective experience (which includes the way the patient experiences us), from his or her own perspective, as consistently as we are able to do so. Not that we exclude other observational modalites—they are inevitably present—but they remain subordinated to the effort we have to make in order to grasp the patient's own idiosyncratic subjectivity. Our primary goal is not to assess and point out the discrepancy between the patient's inner experiences and current reality, but to capture and put into words (understanding and explaining) the archaic logic of that inner experience, without judging it from the perspective of our own reality. The patient's own conflict, however, between archaic needs and adult reality is of legitimate analytic concern.

Whatever the specific form of the patient's psychopathology, or any of its dominant features, such as grandiosity and omnipotence, sadomasochism or narcissistic rage, it is the matrix of the archaic constellation of the self into which these are embedded that commands our analytic attention. In other words, it is the mobilization of a sustained, cohesive selfobject transference, within which aspects of the patient's psychopathology become activated, that determines the nature of our interpretive participation in the treatment process. In addition, it should be noted that whereas the concept of the classical transference focuses on repetition and distortion, the selfobject transferences also contain the striving for a new beginning. Repetition—undoubtedly present—is here seen as functioning in the service of finding a better solution to derailed or thwarted development, as the patient revives the interrupted process of structure building and strives to complete this in the analysis (see Kohut 1970). It is this analytic focus on the patient's unextinguished hope and push for belated acquisition of missing psychic structures, in which vestiges of infantile grandiosity and omnipotence participate, that is a prominent feature of the working through of selfobject transferences. Nonjudgmental acceptance of archaic needs and longings, their understanding and explanation, are the analytic vehicles that bring about structure building through the bit by bit accretion of new structures ("transmuting internalization"), slowly transforming grandiosity and omnipotence into healthy self-esteem. Perhaps it is more accurate to say that "structure building," which occurs via transmuting internalization, strengthens the self, its cohesiveness and vitality. This makes the use of archaic grandiose and omnipotent fantasies unnecessary or much less necessary, but they do not disappear once and for all. The important point about transmuting internalization is that "internalization" is conceived here as the bit-by-bit change of what is originally within the infant and need not be taken inside from without, as this is conceived to occur via identification or introjection.

The way some of this appears in the analytic process will now be illustrated from the analysis of Mr. I.*

---

*The clinical vignettes that follow were culled from my lengthy report about the entire analysis of Mr. I. (see P. H. Ornstein 1978), adapted here by permission of International Universities Press.

Part II

Archaic Grandiosity in the Idealizing Transference

Mr. I. was in his middle-twenties and single when he came for analysis with a variety of diffuse complaints about not being able to perform adequately on his new job, and being too preoccupied with his unhappiness with himself and with the lack of direction in his life. He was tall, handsome, carefully dressed and soft-spoken; he was extremely anxious and spoke rapidly and in somewhat rambling fashion during our initial contact.

Mr. I. began his analysis by wishing to give a detailed, chronological history of his life experiences, which he thought might take several months to accomplish. He carefully planned and controlled what he would say and at what pace in order not to be overwhelmed. However, he was soon derailed because of the intensity of his day-to-day analytic experience. The early phase was dominated by his detailed focus on his continuous, compulsive, sadomasochistic sexual exploits. As we later understood these, they were in the service of either calming himself, exciting himself, or regaining lost self-esteem in his daily encounters at work.

He later told me that he said to the analyst whom he consulted for a referral: "I needed somebody who was an all-around he-man because he would give me credit for this"—meaning his sexual exploits. "Someone who would think it was wild, great, and who would really appreciate it." He thus introduced his need to be admired by someone whom he could put on a pedestal. Both the mirror transference as well as the idealizing transference were thus quickly foreshadowed, which determined the functions he unconsciously assigned to his analyst.

During the initial phase of his analysis Mr. I. became aware of how much he needed center stage, but it was no longer unconscious, and that was what was so embarrassing about it. He wanted to be the best analysand there ever was. He hated to admit that he needed somebody else to do the job; he thought he could do his analysis himself and become famous. "Maybe I am on the verge of it now, and you are going to get the credit for it. My case has to be the greatest!"

Mr. I. slowly retreated from these grandiose, omnipotent fantasies, and his helplessness, powerlessness, and feelings of insignificance moved into the center of his analytic experience, establishing a more sustained idealizing transference. This became quite clear when he once asked thoughtfully, with some despair in his voice: "Why do I have to have you acknowledge that I feel good before I know I feel good?" His own further reflections were of considerable significance: He felt that he was

> a splat on the wall. When you throw hot rubber against the wall, it hardens and is like an octopus with suckers on it, clinging to the wall. Then nothing matters, only the clinging like the splat. It can't tolerate the rumbling of the wall. Any disconnection is a threat to the survival of the splat. That's how I am with T. [his girl friend] and with you. I want you to be the wall—shut up and listen! If I would no longer have to be a splat on the wall, it would be a major accomplishment.

But at this point he could feel strong, powerful, and important only in his attachment to the idealized analyst. Whatever disrupted this attachment—weekend separations, vacations, or even slight unempathic rebuffs—all felt like the "rumbling of the wall," endangering the splat. As long as he felt this oneness with me, as long as the idealizing transference was not disrupted, Mr. I.'s sadomasochistic, sexual exploits decreased considerably and finally abated, only to return as emergency measures, related to specific disruptions in the idealizing transference. It was important to discover the intra-analytic precipitants for these disruptions, to understand their meaning and origin in order to reestablish the analytic bond, which reinfused Mr. I. with borrowed strength and power, until much later, bit by bit, he could establish his own.

I want to introduce a sample intervention, representative of what I had done to facilitate the repair of the frequent, inevitable disruptions during this phase of the analysis. Mr. I. spoke with some urgency in his voice about wanting to marry his girlfriend. I mistakenly rushed in to prevent a "rash acting-out"—a premature marriage—by focusing on the urgency, without any real indication that Mr. I. contemplated immediate action. In a dream that followed, Mr. I. was nasty and derogatory to an old man. His father criticized him for it and reminded him that his grandfather knew this man. Whereupon Mr. I. felt overwhelmed with kindly, warm feelings and wanted to go up and hug the old man. He couldn't hug him, and then he just wanted to be able to talk to him.

Mr. I.'s associations and the broader context in which this dream occurred revealed his intense longing for the idealized analyst-father. I acknowledged that it pained him whenever his admiring and loving feelings were not accepted, but seen only (mistakenly) as "the other side of the ambivalence." He was tearful in response and, for the first time, said with emotion: "I am really ready to love the old man, but he couldn't take it, he'd brush it off!" I was then also able to clarify that my earlier focusing on the "urgency" in connection with his marriage plans, rather than on the urgency with which he presented it, must have contributed "to the rift in here, to my not accepting your admiring and loving feelings. This must have added to your anguished retreat and made you turn to T. for consolation." Invariably, such interventions, whenever I could appropriately introduce them, even if often somewhat belatedly, with concrete and specific references to the events within the analytic experience, quickly reestablished the disrupted transference and regularly brought forth some relevant, hitherto unavailable memories.

The working through of the idealizing transference led to a decisive improvement of Mr. I.'s life outside of the analysis, at work and in his relationships, but his vulnerability in the analytic situation increased as a prelude to the remobilization of his archaic grandiose self. An example from this transitional stage will illustrate my contention that there is no need for confronting the patient with what he himself is not yet able to introduce into the analytic dialogue. An acceptance and understanding of the meaning of what he does bring in to his sessions will open up otherwise unavailable parts of himself.

Additionally, Mr. I.'s oscillations between his idealization of me and his need for mirroring affirmation of his greatness and uniqueness provide us with an opportunity to witness his object-bound as well as subject-bound grandiosity and omnipotence. These vignettes also show his subtle and not so subtle efforts at controlling the analyst and the analytic situation in order to forestall being retraumatized by the analyst's responses.

An abrupt cancellation of his session on Washington's birthday infuriated Mr. I., and he warned me to give him considerable notice before termination when the time came. He then announced in a celebratory tone that this was his 400th session. "A special occasion, yet it gives me an empty feeling." I referred to the abrupt cancellation and said that it must again have felt arbitrary to Mr. I.; he must have felt at my mercy since I could cut him off any time. "I don't want to be at your mercy," he responded angrily. "I associate it with being a damned fool. I take it seriously [meaning his analytic experience] and somebody else doesn't [meaning his analyst]." Not being taken seriously was the most painful treatment anyone could accord him. He recognized that in response he felt "depressed, lonely, empty, and dead inside" on Washington's birthday. He needed "some exciting sensations, some kicks, to get me out of it." The hot shower was not enough and then he fell asleep, exhausted. After a brief silence he added: "If I perceive you as uninterested I lose my complete sense of wholeness; then I need more stimulation to make up for it." For the next few days Mr. I.'s feeling of emptiness continued, further intensified by the fact that I did not celebrate the 400th session with him. As Mr. I. berated me for this, he felt dizzy on the couch. I responded by saying: "It must have seemed to you a very insensitive rejection that I did not share your mood to celebrate, or at least recognize your mood; you acknowledged the anniversary, I didn't, so it was all the more painful." Mr. I. replied: "I almost cried when you recalled all the feelings for me. If I felt rejected here last Wednesday I must have felt it lots of times elsewhere. How much I must demand someone's 100 percent constant attention."

In a reflective mood he described himself as a globe with a defect on it like the Grand Canyon. "In analysis you try to work on it, excavate the surface of it so it can heal in. It's comforting that somebody, your analyst, knows how sick you are and he is not alarmed, not scared, not discouraged, but optimistic of what can be done about it." Then he became more anxious: "What if I suspect that even deeper defects are there and my analyst does not know they are there? I can't tell him because even he might get discouraged. But I don't want to conceal that."

Archaic Grandiosity in the Mirror Transference

During the arduous working-through process of Mr. I.'s mirror transference, he saw a replay of Fellini's movie *8 ½*, about which he spoke during the first week of his analysis. He was then strongly identified with the provocative, arrogant director of the movie—these are his words—who collected all past important figures around himself and controlled and manipulated them; he was in complete charge. Now, as he saw the movie again, he recognized the flashing back and forth between reality and fantasy, present and past. "I could not understand it some years ago," he said. He was still identified with the movie director.

> Now I see it as the eventual death of infantile sexuality, in a man: omnipotence, grandiosity, thousands of girls with no real relationship to them, narcissistically having the center stage, conducting. It's all neurotic, infantile, oedipal, Catholic church versus the whores. Shooting himself is giving up all that stuff—that is what analysis has been for me. It's difficult to give up all these infantile things.

He was wondering how it all happened in the analysis that he could give up so much.

> One reason, I tell you, one reason, you are a good analyst; you have always consistently maintained your confidence in the potential of my health. Whatever I said—even when I argued with you about the

> twenty dollars extra charge when I missed a session—even when I said I was psychotic, you reacted as if I were capable of responding in a healthy way. Having gone through this time with you, it was a real therapeutic experience for me. If you had ever given me back the twenty dollars, deciding you were wrong, I would have resented it for the rest of my life; it was so solid, you would have destroyed it by undoing.

Near termination he repeatedly reflected on what he accomplished. He said at one point that what he achieved

> isn't mostly insight, but ego-capacities, different functioning. Every minute of the day I am different from what I used to be. The underlying force was the stability of this relationship. Once it got me stabilized then I was able to develop a stable relationship with others—with myself too. Now I can leave with more stability and transfer my ties to others.

Conclusion

In the present context, I could offer only three quick psychological biopsies from the analysis of a young man, in whose psychology and psychopathology grandiosity and omnipotence, including omnipotent control, played a central role. Working within the selfobject transferences entailed a focus on the function the patient unconsciously assigned to me, his analyst-selfobject, thus it was vicissitudes of the state of his self, its enfeeblement, depletion, frequent entanglement in conflicts, fragmentation, and other identifiable states (such as rage and revengefulness) that claimed interpretive attention. The function the patient assigned to me demanded a focus on the here-and-now of the transference, which replicated his lifelong thwarted needs as well as his habitual ways of attempting to satisfy them. The transference also offered us numerous hints regarding the earliest psychogenetic precursors of the patient's psychopathology and reflected his efforts to acquire the missing psychic structures, the so-called "structural deficits" beneath the often elaborate, maladaptive, distorted "defensive structures," that gave rise to these transferences.

The focus of interpretation was not on this or that specific content (e.g., omnipotence) but on the matrix (the vulnerable self) from which the contents arose. Nor was the focus ever on confronting the patient with external reality as a way to prove the omnipotent fantasy an illusion or a remnant of an infantile delusion. Instead, an analytic climate of *acceptance* was created, in which the therapeutic reactivation of the original need for the selfobject's responses could safely be expressed. In this climate, the consistent application of the two steps in the interpretive process, *understanding* and *explaining*, then led to a thorough working-through process. This resulted in the gradual lessening of grandiosity, omnipotence, and omnipotent, sadistic control, accompanied by a gradual return to healthy assertiveness and reliable self-esteem regulation.

Our analytic aim with regard to these archaic fantasies, emotions, and behaviors is always the gradual transformation of the archaic matrix from which they arise and are concomitantly integrated into the adult self. It is this transformation and integration that make their maladaptive use ultimately unnecessary.

References

Arlow, J. A. (1982). Scientific cosmogony, mythology and immortality. *Psycholanalytic Quarterly* 51:177–195.

Elson, M., ed. (1987). *The Kohut Seminars on Self Psychology and Psychotherapy with Adolescents and Young Adults*. New York: Norton.

Ferenczi, S. (1913). Stages in the development of the sense of reality. In *First Contributions to Psychoanalysis*, pp. 213–239. New York: Brunner/Mazel, 1980.

Freud, S. (1914). On narcissism: An introduction. *Standard Edition* 14:69–102.

——— (1915). Instincts and their vicissitudes. *Standard Edition* 14:111–140.

Kernberg, O. (1994). *Omnipotence in the transference and in the countertransference.* Paper presented to the New York Freudian Society, New York.

Kohut, H. (1970). Narcissism as a resistance and as driving force in psychoanalysis. In *The Search for the Self,* vol. 1, ed. P. H. Ornstein, pp. 547–561. New York: International Universities Press, 1978.

——— (1971). *The Analysis of the Self.* New York: International Universities Press.

——— (1977). *The Restoration of the Self.* New York: International Universities Press.

——— (1984). *How Does Analysis Cure?* Chicago: University of Chicago Press.

Kohut, H., and Seitz, P. F. D. (1963). Concepts and theories in psychoanalysis. In *Concepts of Personality,* ed. J. M. Wepman and R. W. Heine. Chicago: Aldine.

Levin, R. (1986). Infantile omnipotence and grandiosity. *Psychoanalytic Review* 73:57–76.

Novick, J., and Novick, K. K. (1991). Some comments on masochism and the delusion of omnipotence from a developmental perspective. *Journal of the American Psychoanalytic Association* 39:307–331.

——— (1994). *Omnipotence: pathology and resistance.* Paper presented to the New York Freudian Society, New York.

Ornstein, A. (1974). The dread to repeat and the new beginning: a contribution to the psychoanalytic treatment of narcissistic personality disorders. In *The Annual of Psychoanalysis,* ed. Chicago Institute for Psychoanalysis, vol. 2, pp. 231–248. New York: International Universities Press.

——— (1991). The dread to repeat: comments on the working through process in psychoanalysis. *Journal of the American Psychoanalytic Association* 39:377–398.

——— (1992). *A psychoanalytic developmental perspective on the sense of power, self-esteem, and arrogance.* Paper presented to a conference on Power, Empowerment and Abuse in Clinical Practice and in Everyday Life at the Boston Psychoanalytic Society and Institute, Boston, MA.

Ornstein, P. H. (1978). The resolution of a mirror transference: clinical emphasis on the termination phase. In *Psychology of the Self: A Case*

Book, ed. A. Goldberg, pp. 13–120. New York: International Universities Press.

——— (1979). Remarks on the central position of empathy in psychoanalysis. *Bulletin: Association for Psychoanalytic Medicine* 18:95–109.

——— (1993). The clinical impact of the psychotherapist's view of human nature. *Journal of Psychotherapy Practice and Research* 2:193–204.

——— (1995). Heinz Kohut's vision of the essence of humanness. In *Psychoanalytic Versions of the Human Condition and Clinical Practice*, ed. P. Marcus and A. Rosenberg. New York: New York University Press, in press.

Discussion

William M. Greenstadt, Ph.D.

Editors' Comments

Dr. Greenstadt expresses his gratitude for having the opportunity to discuss a paper written from a self psychological perspective and feels that he increased his knowledge of self psychology. Greenstadt contrasts self psychological theory with ego psychology, arguing that what seems to distinguish the two is the presence of sexual and aggressive drive in the former, whereas in self psychology the view of early development involves a "drive" that is the impetus for self-actualization. He wonders whether this drive–deficit dichotomy may represent an unbridgeable gap between the theories but hopes that this idea may not be pessimistic and that schools will one day coalesce in a useful search for common ground. Greenstadt discusses Ornstein's analysis of Mr. I., questioning some of Ornstein's technical interventions in a rich and searching discussion.

In Arthur Conan Doyle's story "The Yellow Face" (1930), Sherlock Holmes listens with concentration to a long and elaborate story, told with intense anguish by a client from the London district of Norbury. He had consulted Holmes about a personal problem that was causing him constant pain and puzzlement. After the client had concluded his account of the problem and left their rooms, Holmes offers Watson a detailed and complete explanation of the mystery. It is one of his *tours de force* of inferential logic, following which, Holmes asks Watson, "What do you think of my theory?"

Watson answers rather dryly, "It is all surmise."

Holmes, seemingly undismayed, replies, "But at least it covers the facts. When new facts come to our knowledge which cannot be covered by it, it will be time enough to reconsider it."

As the rest of the narrative unfolds, it turns out that the true explanation—that is, the correct theory—is indeed completely different from Holmes's original idea.

The story ends with Holmes saying to his friend, "Watson, if it should ever strike you that I am getting a little overconfident in my powers, or giving less pains to a case than it deserves, kindly whisper, 'Norbury' in my ear, and I shall be infinitely obliged to you."

I suspect that in my remarks I may be indulging myself in a little "Norburying" of my own. I hope I will be forgiven.

Stimulated by Dr. Ornstein's article, it soon seemed clear to me that the subject and concept of omnipotence is central to self psychology. Omnipotent and grandiose fantasies and feelings are core factors in the self psychological theory of development. They represent the primary matrix of experiences that stabilizes the infant physiologically and produces the self as a psychic structure. In addition, self psychology seems always to assume that *absences* of structure rather than maladaptive or distorted structures may be produced by experiential deprivation. The vicissitudes of pre-programmed maturation, interacting with a *less* than "average expectable environment" (Hartman 1939) does not necessarily ensure that some array of adaptations and mental structures, whether healthy or distorted, will *always* occur. The emphasis in the self psychology developmental theory is rather on the idea that primary identifications, or in the newer terminology, selfobject interactions and experiences, have not been consistently present throughout the growth of the child, and that this has led to the failure to internalize the selfobject experiences into healthy, optimally adaptive psychic structure. The happy outcome of these experiences also assures that such "internal" feelings, like self-confidence and optimism, will evolve into their adult forms. self psychology is heavily weighted toward the environment as the "casual agent," and the concept of trauma is also de-emphasized in favor of deprivations of self and object interactions. The whole sweep of development seems motivated by tendencies of self-assertions, creativity, and joyful experience (Kohut 1977). Further, it is, as Dr. Ornstein states it, "the patient's unextinguished hope and push for belated acquisition of *missing* psychic structures" (p. 16, italics mine) that propels the analytic process, not the sexual and aggressive drives. It is insufficient to account for the construction of the self and its healthy attributes by invoking the formulation that it is built up out of "libidinal cathexes" of the bodily and functional attributes in infancy (Hartmann 1950). Thus, the self in self psychology is formed, apparently, by means of a conceptually independent trend that is *superordinate* to the sexual and aggressive tendencies also present. Is it correct to say, then, that the drive concept is actually alive and well in self psychology, but that the superordinate drive is an object relations version of Freud's (1914, 1915) self-preservative instinct?

I take it from Dr. Ornstein's paper that the "true" subject matter of a treatment, the analysis of which produced intrapsychic change, is the vicissitudes of narcissism. For self psychology, narcissism is not merely the libidinal cathexis of the self as defined by Hartmann, but represents a different way of describing mental development, one that is independent of the instinctual drives. Instead, sexual and aggressive drive manifestations are "breakdown products" of failed narcissistic integrations or already existing integrated narcissistic structures. The "stuff" that binds narcissistic integrations together—at least at the time of their formation—is empathic attunement. In analytic treatment, the analyst's empathic attunement, as expressed in the form and manner of his interpretations, are the mutative agents. The content of the interpretations refer to "failures" in the acquisition and transformation of selfobject experiences with the result that lacunae in the fabric of the self appear. Attunement and empathy place the accent on communication by means of affects, supported or framed by words.

The aim in self psychological therapy, consequently, is ultimately to *provide* the missing selfobject events through the analyst's empathic attunement to the patient's experiences while involved in forms of mirror and idealizing transference. This is supplemented by the absence of a judgmental stance by the analyst toward those experiences. These are the events in the therapeutic process that are mutative. The self-elimination of the analyst—that is, of the mirroring and idealizing transferences—is accomplished by the invoking of the concept of *transmuting internalizations*, through which healthy forms of omnipotence and self-assertion may be restored or created anew. The internalizations of selfobject experiences and identifications are different processes. The former represents age-appropriate structure building that seamlessly forms a part of the child's self, while identifications are internalizations of age-*inappropriate* characteristics of the adult that are basically defensive in purpose and lead to pathology of character.

It will no doubt be familiar to you that this so-called "deficit" viewpoint has been vigorously criticized by adherents of the "drive/conflict" point of view (Dowling 1991, Gill 1994, Stein 1979). Arlow (1991), for example, poses the problem as follows:

> The question that arises is what makes it difficult or impossible for the ego to effect adequate compromise formations of childhood instinctual conflicts. The issue is crucial insofar as treatment is concerned because every therapeutic approach must at some point interdigitate with a theory of pathogenesis (Arlow 1981). It is at this point that the concepts of trauma and deficit begin to play significant roles in controversy. [p. 6]

Arlow's answer to the first question is that "trauma is a special vicissitude of development, seen in the context of continuing intrapsychic conflict" (1991, p. 7). It is clear that the conflict theory of pathogenesis does not permit the identification of a psychic trauma *except* as it is reflected in conflict, even if the trauma, viewed as an actual external event, appears to be quantitatively large.

In order to avoid an appearance of simply having made an ex-cathedra declaration, Arlow criticizes the concept of deficit on the basis of the *sources* of the data employed in formulating those concepts that lead to modifications of analytic technique. As with many others who adhere to the conflict model, Arlow, too, states that fundamentally the idea of deficit is derived from the field of direct observation of children, and not from the analytic treatment situation itself. The application of these deficit concepts to analytic technique leads, Arlow feels, to unwarranted assumptions about the meaning of material that emerges in analytic treatment. In other words, as the analyst creates observations or facts in the course of his interactions with the patient, too much reliance is placed on complex theories rather than a sparse set of assumptions. As a result, the range of observation is narrowed. Arlow (1991) continues:

> It is an appealing scenario. Where precise genetic material is difficult to obtain, a putative model situation can be involved, which is then foisted upon later manifest symptomatology. This is very appealing to patients, since it takes the origin of their difficulties back to a period of their lives when they had only needs and no responsibilities. Hence there could be no blame and no need to feel guilty. [p. 13]

Perhaps it is possible to find a gentler rejoinder to the deficit viewpoint. In Chapter 2, Jack and Kerry Kelly Novick write on "Omnipotence: Pathology and Resistance." In yet an earlier paper (Novick and Novick 1991), they explore omnipotent fantasies in adults and children from a developmental point of view.

They conclude their theoretical summary with the following.

> [We] have attempted to describe the development of fantasies of destructive omnipotence and how the delusion of destructive omnipotence becomes simultaneously a defense against feelings of helpless rage and humiliation and a pathological source of self-esteem. As such, it contributes to . . . resistance to change through experience or analysis. [p. 322]

Like self psychologists, they suggest that the experience of omnipotence or grandiosity in the infant and young toddler is a normal part of the development of mental structure and object relations, and is promoted by the gratifications obtained from a collaborating "good-enough" mother (Hartmann 1952) who participates in the child's grandiosity by obtaining her own satisfactions, reflected back from the child's responses. At this infantile stage of the child's development, both collaborating partners—mother and child—share a *normal* illusion of the child's omnipotence. Adult pathological omnipotent fantasies, however, have very different qualities of hostility and total control over others. The Novicks show that when there is an *actual* failure of mutual responsiveness between mother and child, it tends to produce pathogenic omnipotent fantasies, and these reappear at later stages of development. Among the pathological outcomes of a failure of normal omnipotence is the reaction of turning aggression against the self, that is, masochism. Implicit in masochistic behavior is a compensatory and pathologically hostile attempt to control others. What has emerged represents, therefore, a defensive and distorted mental structure.

Thus far, the two theories seem fairly compatible, with one very significant exception. This is the presence of the sexual and aggressive drive theory in the Novicks' formulation, while in the self psychological view of early development, it seems to me that a different drive—the impetus for self-actualization—is at work. I think that this issue—drive versus deficit—is an epistemological shibboleth that ideologically divides the two camps, and which may represent an unbridgeable gap between them. It seems likely that adherence to one or another of these schools of psychoanalysis is a function of three factors: the phenomena in question possess great complexity and ambiguity; the data consist of both verbal reports of subjective experience *and* subjective reactions by the observer; and the personality of the adherent is probably the single most compelling factor in his or her advocacy of one or the other viewpoint. Dr. Ornstein has already called to our attention that this last factor, the analyst's *Weltanschauung*, suggests what is apparent to every analyst: an individual's personal metaphysics is an expression of his character. However, it is not necessary to be pessimistic about the prospect that the "schools" will *never* coalesce; there will always be a healthy diversity of personality among analysts. Fred Pine's "four psychologies" (Pine 1990) represents one sophisticated effort to find common ground. His approach, I believe, may be based on an unformulated and unknown substitute metatheory as a replacement for traditional metapsychology.

I would like to turn very briefly to Dr. Ornstein's two clinical examples. In the remarkable story of his escape from the forced labor camp, he seems to have the intention of offering an account of how consciously available omnipotent fantasies promoted his survival. His description seems to refute the distinction between pathological omnipotence and an acceptance of realistic limits. In analytic therapy with adults, Dr. Ornstein maintains, *any* omnipotent fantasy is assumed by traditional analysts who follow the presumed biases of Freud and Ferenczi to be indicative of pathology. If, then, there is a category of "normal" omnipotent fantasies that can enter into adaptational processes of thought, this seems to support a tenet of self psychology, namely that in analytic therapy the analysis of idealizing, mirror, and merging transferences, always containing both omnipotent content and grandiose feelings, is to be conducted with an attitude of acceptance and lack of condemnation—the "morality" he spoke of in his presentation. If, however, *all* theoretical schools of analysis accept the view that normal infantile mental development begins with structures that may be described as containing qualities of omnipotence and grandiosity, the exclusive appropriation of this idea by self psychology is unwarranted as a basis for the introduction of a radically different approach to analytic therapy and technique.

I do not have the space to do justice to Dr. Ornstein's extract of the analysis of Mr. I. The self psychology explanatory theory used as an orienting frame with which Dr. Ornstein was able to carry out this analysis may be questioned on theoretical grounds, but I cannot find very much to criticize on practical grounds. The analysis gives a powerful impression of having been a great success. The essence of the patient's neurosis seems to have been his fear of overstimulation, necessitating his defense against oedipal and preoedipal object needs. A major defensive structure was characterized by conscious and unconscious fantasies of omnipotence and grandiosity combined with phallic-narcissistic exhibitionistic fantasies, in which the stimulation provided by needed objects was magically controlled. The patient's need to obtain (homosexual) gratification from his father for his feats of sexual exhibitionism probably screened deeper needs for oral gratification from the mother. In this atmosphere of defensive, characterological narcissism, it is little wonder that issues of vulnerability to hurt and the sense of being misunderstood would permeate the transference.

I wish only to raise a question. Dr. Ornstein was well aware of the predominance in the patient of needs for omnipotence as a defense-structure for controlling tension and overstimulating objects. Since the analyst was unusually careful in making interventions with tact and acceptance, and even acknowledged his occasional failures of empathy, is it possible that the patient's needs for omnipotent control were gratified too much by giving him the illusion that he was fully in charge of the dosing of interpretations, that is, of the amount of pain he believed he could endure in the analysis? If so, did that not leave a sector of his neurosis relatively untouched in the analysis, despite the very good outcome overall? Finally, if the theory of technique prescribed by self psychology dictates such technical restraints, does this place a limit on what forms of defense can be addressed?

I would like to thank Dr. Ornstein and the Scientific Program Committee for the opportunity to expand my knowledge and understanding of self psychology.

References

Arlow, J. A. (1981). Theories of pathogenesis. *Psychoanalytic Quarterly* 50:488–514.

——— (1991). Conflict, trauma, and deficit. In *Conflict and Compromise: Therapeutic Implications*, ed. S. Dowling, pp. 3–14. Madison, CT: International Universities Press.

Dowling, S., ed. (1991). *Conflict and Compromise: Therapeutic Implications*. Madison, CT: International Universities Press.

Doyle, A. C. (1930). The yellow face. In *The Complete Sherlock Holmes, Vol. 1*, pp. 350–362. Garden City, NY: Doubleday.

Freud, S. (1914). On narcissism: an introduction. *Standard Edition* 14:67–102.

——— (1915). Instincts and their vicissitudes. *Standard Edition* 14:111–140.

Gill, M. M. (1994). Conflict and deficit: Book review of *Conflict and Compromise: Therapeutic Implications*, ed. S. Dowling. *Psychoanalytic Quarterly* 63:756–778.

Hartmann, H. (1939). *Ego Psychology and the Problem of Adaptation*. New York: International Universities Press, 1958.

——— (1950). Comments on the psychoanalytic theory of the ego. In *Essays on Ego Psychology: Selected Problems in Psychoanalytic Theory*, pp. 113–140. New York: International Universities Press, 1964.

——— (1952). The mutual influences in the development of ego and id. In *Essays on Ego Psychology: Selected Problems in Psychoanalytic Theory*, pp. 155–181. New York: International Universities Press, 1964.

Kohut, H. (1977). *The Restoration of the Self*. New York: International Universities Press.

Novick, J., and Novick, K. K. (1991). Some comments on masochism and the delusion of omnipotence from a developmental perspective. *Journal of the American Psychoanalytic Association* 39:307–331.

Pine, F. (1990). *Drive, Ego, Object, and Self: A Synthesis for Clinical Work*. New York: Basic Books.

Stein, M. (1979). Book review of *The Restoration of the Self*, by H. Kohut. *Journal of the American Psychoanalytic Association* 27:665–680.

5

The Trauma of Confronting One's Vulnerability and Death

Henry Krystal, M.D.

Editors' Comments

Dr. Krystal, who has written so eloquently on psychic trauma, considers here the issue of the establishment of a healthy infantile omnipotence, particularly by those people who are exposed to the profound traumas of combat and war atrocity. Those who have an established healthy omnipotence are better able to cope with trauma, and it is frequently those people who have failed to establish healthy omnipotence in childhood who are overwhelmed by trauma. Krystal draws heavily on an eminent professional career in which he worked with post-traumatic patients and he distinguishes differences in traumatic processes as a result of the age and stage of development in which these traumas take place, stressing in particular the difference between adult catastrophic trauma and infantile trauma.

Krystal reviews some of the literature on trauma, pointing out that in recent studies in neuroscience, brain development has been shown to be greatly dependent on psychological factors. He argues that favorable conditions in infancy produce positive core feelings of omnipotence and protection. In working with Holocaust survivors, Krystal found it essential to distinguish between the experience of fear and the emotional reaction to the signal of unavoidable danger, reminding us that confrontation with the kind of danger about which nothing can be done does not evoke fear. Krystal discusses issues of combat exhaustion; the psychiatric casualties of war; abilities to tolerate anxiety; post-traumatic changes in self-confidence and omnipotence; alexithymia, anhedonia, and psychosomatic diseases as a result of trauma; various traumatic confrontations with death; the work of Lifton on death; and the role of emotional support that some individuals were able to give each other in extreme situations such as concentration camps. Important considerations for the psychotherapy of the many disorders resulting from trauma are presented.

Krystal discusses the influence of trauma on the Polish-born writer, Jerzy Kosinski, and how it is reflected in his important autobiographical novel *The Painted Bird*. Krystal then discusses some of the bizarre behavior of Kosinski in real life, such as his fondness for roaming about at night in dangerous places, followed by a general discussion of *The Painted Bird* as an example of stress trauma, narcissistic rage, and sadomasochistic fixation. Krystal demonstrates that in *The Painted Bird* there is a transformation of infantile narcissism and omnipotence by trauma and repeated confrontation with death into the sadomasochistic, moral, and perhaps perverse attitude that filled Kosinski's work and life.

In this chapter, I would like to consider one aspect of the overall topic of omnipotence, namely, the establishment of "healthy" infantile omnipotence. In particular, I will discuss how individuals who are exposed to extreme trauma (for example, combat stress or war atrocities) rely on this healthy infantile omnipotence to cope with the trauma; or, alternatively, are overwhelmed by the trauma because of the initial failure in infancy to establish healthy omnipotence. As an example of such a failure I shall draw on the life and work of the Polish-born author, Jerzy Kosinski.

* * *

In my thirty years of working with post-traumatic patients, and simultaneously with patients who have addictive and psychosomatic disorders, I have discovered that it is useful to distinguish infantile omnipotence from the omnipotence that develops after the toddler years. What I have noticed is that psychosomatic and addictive patients (and also patients who seem to be survivors of infantile psychic trauma) suffer a peculiar inhibition in their capacity for self-caring, self-soothing, and even affective self-regulation. Some of the patients who remained in psychoanalytic psychotherapy while they undertook biofeedback training have revealed in their dreams and associations a profound belief that acquiring control over certain body functions—a control that they assumed to be "autonomic"—would expose them to some terrible danger and punishment (Krystal 1978). In 1988, in considering self-representation in relationship to self-care, and bringing these ideas together with what I had learned in the meantime about the nature of the transferences of such patients, I concluded that they experienced an "idolatrous transference." By this I mean a transference that involves the attribution of control of virtually all vital and affective functions and parts to the Primal Object representation (Krystal 1988a). And this, of course, raises the issue of "infantile omnipotence."

My work on psychic trauma has led me to distinguish traumatic processes and consequences as correlated to the age and stage of development in which they take place. I particularly stress the difference between adult catastrophic trauma and infantile trauma. Infantile trauma takes place when the child is in what most authors describe as a symbiotic state (Mahler et al. 1975), when the mother and infant are still functioning as one physiologically open system of mutual regulation (e.g., Hofer 1981a,b, 1982). I feel that this state must also contain something functionally equivalent to a type of *omnipotence*, in effect, by which the normal infant experiences all the mother's ministrations as if they were his own achievements and functions. My reason for making this claim, which strains the imagination at first, is that if this sentience is interrupted by infantile trauma, thereby confronting the infant prematurely with the near-destructive intensity of his own affect precursors, then the following sequence occurs: the infant is pressured into a premature recognition of the "created" external object representation, and so this object representation is to end up "walled off," and it is more likely to contain within it all the goodness and comforting power, as well as the above-mentioned parts of the self-representation. On first impression, it may seem that this construct attributes to the infant a sense of omnipotence that appears inconceivable; however, the effects of the disruption in infancy of the dyadic affect control are so glaringly evident in post-traumatic states that in my view such an explanation becomes plausible.

Omnipotent Self-view and the Ability to Tolerate Anxiety

In the past, I have described a genetic view of affects as having a developmental history and developmental lines of affect, evolving out of three infantile states: well-being, distress, and a potential cataleptic state (Krystal 1974). The genetic history of affects involves developmental lines of differentiation, desomatization, and verbalization. By this developmental process, emotions become suitable to function as signals in information-processing. Essential to the infant's development of affect balance is the primary object, the mothering parent, who attends empathically to the infant and relieves distress, and fulfills needs with relative promptness. This interaction, as we will learn from Schore, contributes to favorable developments in the orbitofrontal lobes. From a psychological point of view, it represents a process by which a basic trust in the goodness of the world, and a sense of self-worth, are started. If the mothering parent is not able to give adequate empathic responses, then the nature of the infantile affects is such that they can snowball into a frantic, inconsolable state, and infantile psychic trauma sets in—a disaster that may cause various degrees of arrest. As the child develops, both the maturation of the affects and affect tolerance continue to be the major part of upbringing. Parents intervene to encourage the child to utilize his emotions as signals to himself and to use them in information processing. They help the child to learn how to use his emotions as signals as the presumably mature parent does. An emotionally mature adult is able to recognize emotions (as feelings), name them, understand their cognitive components, and use them to select the response to the present situation that is in his best long-term interests. Such use requires being able to distinguish how much (what intensity) of the affect is appropriate to the present situation, and to what degree the intensity of the affect is reinforced by memories. Having made this distinction, the mature person is able to choose the optimal behavior, rather than responding with an ill-considered impulse, perhaps dominated by primitive fantasies. Thus the process of upbringing and the process of maturation proceed along lines where one can use affects as helpful signals to one's self in adaptation. The affects become less somatic and more ideational, and they permit the individual to practice the "art of living" rather than forcing him to merely attend to relieving the distress of the affect itself.

In 1994, Schore published a monumental work, a courageous, groundbreaking opus in which he integrated

> the two rapidly converging streams of developmental research: psychological studies of the critical interactive experiences that influence the development of socioemotional functions and neurobiological studies of the ontogeny of postnatal maturing brain structures that come to regulate the same functions. A triad of fundamental assumptions underlie this work on the neurobiology of emotional development—that the compelling question of human emotion and motivation can only be understood in terms of structure–function relationships, that the primordial conditions in which these evolve occur in the context of caregiver–infant interaction, and that an understanding of human developmental psychobiology is a prerequisite, and powerful impetus to the elucidation of the dynamic mechanisms of all later socioemotional phenomena. [p. xxx]

The explosion in neuroscience demonstrated that there is a precise correlation, harmony, and even locked-step integration between the psychological and interactional developments familiar to us and the neurobiological developments. It turns out that the ontology of the brain renders the neuroanatomical and physiological structure growth greatly dependent on psychological factors, and in turn they set the stage for all future socioemotional functioning.

In the context of this new conception of development, we can postulate an "encoding" of transactional influences into anatomical structures. As Schore states:

> [T]he diadic psychobiological experiences that occur during early reunions serve as imprinting events for the experience-dependent maturation of a structural system that for the rest of the life-span appraises the affective and motivational significance of environmental stimuli. A central component of this system resides in the orbitofrontal cortex, and the critical period for its physiological maturation occurs during the practicing phase. [1994, p. 113]

That kind of development makes it possible for us to assume that favorable conditions in early infancy produce something that operates for life like a hidden (and protected) core feeling of omnipotence. One might say that this concept is comparable to the cognitive idea of omnipotence and even to "basic trust." This omnipotence represents a necessary core of our self, and, moreover, a traumatic derailment of infantile omnipotence is likely to result in significant defects in the psychological maturation of the individual—for life. The most obvious component of infantile omnipotence is its fostering the ability to function in a state of denial of death. It is a paradox of the human psyche that reality testing, and the ability to deal with adversity and disappointment is built on the foundation of infantile omnipotence and the resultant day-to-day emotional denial of death. Only on the basis of infantile and omnipotence can one develop a realistic self-view, and the capacity for self-love (normal narcissism) as well as object love. The impairment and derailment of the development of infantile omnipotence by infantile psychic trauma produces a sadomasochistic fixation, and (as we shall see in the case of Jerzy Kosinski) frantic and heroic attempts at self-repair that are bound to fail. The derailment produces a variety of forms of psychic pain with which we are familiar in post-traumatic states. We have long known of the problems of de-differentiated depression, anxiety, guilt, and envy, and the resulting rage. The above-mentioned work of Schore (1994) further focuses our attention on the happiness-precluding effect of shame. Since we are dealing with early, preverbal, pre-symbolic affects, we have not in the past paid adequate attention to this problem and the resultant tendency to engender a yearning for dominance and to foster sadomasochistic solutions to problems.

The Signal of Danger and the Recognition of Unavoidable Danger

In working with post-traumatic patients, and particularly in working with Holocaust survivors, it became essential to distinguish the experience of fear, which is the signal of impending *avoidable* danger (and consequently involves an activation of the entire organism in both the psychological and physiological aspects) from the emotional reaction to the signal of *unavoidable* danger. Confrontation with the kind of danger about which nothing can be done does not evoke fear, but rather a different affect response referred to by Stern (1951a,b) as *catatanoid reaction.* The catatanoid reaction involves the subjective evaluation of the situation as hopeless, and the self-experience is one of helplessness. With the helpless surrender to the inevitable disaster, the traumatic process is initiated (Krystal 1979a, 1988a). Of course, among other descriptions and definitions of the onset of the traumatic state, Freud (1926) also precisely described this same picture: "[T]he subject's estimation of his own strength . . . and his admission of helplessness in the face of it" was defined as "the essence and meaning" of the traumatic situation (p. 166). The traumatic process is progressive, has an evolutionary determination, and in its basic course is universal in the animal kingdom (Krystal 1979, Seligman 1975). It represents a self-destruct apparatus that guarantees each animal a painless death, that is, death in a state of numbness. The manifestations of the progress, or deepening of the traumatic state, involves an increasingly complete numbing of the ability to experience pain and painful affects. Other developments also take place. There is (1) a blocking of initiative and an obeying of all orders; (2) a progressive deepening of a cataleptic or hypnotic-like submission, which is deepened the more the subject obeys orders; (3) a blocking of conation, such as cognition, perception, recall (including that of "benign introjects"), scanning, judgment, planning, problem solving, and evaluation of self vs. environment; (4) confrontation with death, and ultimately psychogenic death, with the heart stopping in disastole (Krystal 1988a, Meerloo 1959, Richter 1959, Seligman 1975).

As we embark upon consideration of the impact of the confrontation with death, it seems necessary to note the extreme difference in the experience for a person who is possessed of a feeling of safety and basic trust and intact function of the denial of death, and for those who have suffered infantile trauma.

Confrontation with Death and "Combat Exhaustion"

The classical study that distinguishes these two states is one that was written by a Special Commission of Civilian Psychiatrists at the request of the Neuropsychiatry Division, Office of the Surgeon General (Bartemeier et al. 1946). The members of commission traveled to all the psychiatric centers on the European continent and in Britain. They obtained the cooperation of all who were in charge of the psychiatric units. Finally, they described a condition they called "Combat Exhaustion." Statistics indicated that precipitating events were "closely associated with the intensity of combat. Roughly speaking, for every 5 men wounded, one is killed and one becomes psychiatrically disabled" (p. 371). They described the evolution of the clinical picture of "combat exhaustion" in terms of an incipient stage that consists of psychomotor retardation; a tendency to become either morose and withdrawn, or hyperactive, with excessive smoking, drinking, and talking; a discarding of possessions; affective flattening especially related to the love-objects "back home" (letters remain unopened); loss of appetite; apprehension; dependence; reluctance to accept responsibility or exert initiative; and confusion. Physical symptoms also appeared, such as tremor, vomiting, and diarrhea. The most important and characteristic part of the picture was that members of the military would turn their aggression against *their own comrades*, instead of the common enemy. It was stated that "if such patients are not sent back" there may follow complete confusion, with severe (possibly bizarre) or dangerous actions. Any person who had actually become overwhelmed and disorganized (the word *traumatized* was never used) would be sent to an "Exhaustion Center" or a general hospital psychiatric unit, and those who had to be hospitalized for a "month or two" were not expected to be capable of returning to active combat during the war.

From what we have learned since that time about post-traumatic stress disorder, this finding is not surprising. It is impressive only because of the emphasis on the tolerance of exhaustion: of one's capacity to bear combat conditions, that is, regular confrontation with death. In fact, the follow-up studies of World War II showed that significant numbers of these veterans suffered for years, and many could not return to their previous way of maintaining a working state of security. They were unable to restore a workable balance between the narcissistic, omnipotent derivative self-representations that permitted the denial of death, and the realistic self-representations that permitted the tolerance of the perils of everyday life (Beebe and Appel 1958). In fact, long-term follow-ups kept revealing new cases of post-traumatic syndromes, even among those who had not developed an acute panic reaction in the situation of confrontation with death (Archibald et al. 1962, 1965).

Post-traumatic Changes in Self-confidence and Omnipotence

I have observed that a dominant trait in the lives of many Holocaust survivors, as well as Vietnam veterans, is "an all-pervasive and all encompassing distrust and suspicion such that only the destruction of their capacity for basic trust could account for such desolation" (Krystal 1993, p. 842). Actually, this is starting the discussion with the most severely affected cases. We could start at the other side of the spectrum, noting that among Holocaust survivors, especially concentration-camp survivors, it is imperative to note that most managed to restore a state of denial rather quickly. A remarkable number entered into marriages while still in displaced persons camps and had children without delay. The driving force most commonly was not love between the partners, but rather the urgency to bring forth a new generation and "fight Hitler." In my thirty-plus years of follow-ups of these patients, it has been my general impression that those survivors who had a chance to be active in their defense and survival, and, especially, in helping others, had a better prognosis in regard to post-traumatic problems, and especially in regard to restoring their omnipotent, narcissistic unconscious fantasies.

Some interesting reminiscences come to mind in this connection. All those who survived were able to do so by virtue of managing to arrest the progression of the traumatic process at the "automaton" or "robot" stage. In this condition, as in the "pre-combat exhaustion" stage, attention and cognition were narrowed to daily or even moment-to-moment survival. In this state, most of the prisoners (except those who were picked for the "Sondercommando" and actually participated in the killings and cremations) denied witnessing mass murder. Curiously, this applies even to the "Canada Commando," the people who sorted the belongings of the transports and benefited greatly from this activity. However, the helplessness was such a profound narcissistic wound, one that for many has not been possible to heal to this day, that it keeps generating shame. In this connection, Danieli (1981) pointed out that when one or both survivors could identify themselves with the resistance, their orientation became that of "fighters," as opposed to that of "numb" or "victim" families. Danieli identifies the families of "those who made it." These families were especially successful in social and financial adjustments, and many of them have continued to function well to this day. Many of these families had only one member who was a survivor, and many refused to apply for any restitution from Germany for health damages, particularly mental health damages. However, based on my own follow-up of victims (often thirty years later), I have found that many were alexithymic (described below), anhedonic, and suffering from psychosomatic diseases at a rate much higher than average. I have previously reported that while the general survivor population had a 30 percent rate of psychosomatic diseases, the survivors who were adolescents during the Holocaust—among whom many of "those who made it" can be found—had a 70 to 75 percent incidence of psychosomatic illness (Krystal 1971). As these patients got older, they became more severely insomniac and depressive.

My impression is that almost every survivor has preserved a secret spark of omnipotence that whispers to him that he is very special and so he managed to survive the indescribably overwhelming and humiliating near-death experiences. He knows that he just barely made it. Many have one or more terribly painful memories that they have not been able to share with anyone. But these secrets of unspeakable horror, translated into the language of infantile omnipotence and narcissism, may be concealing this message: "Do you want to know how it is that I survived? The secret is, my mother loved me!"

Confrontation with Death in Trauma and Alexithymia

The problem in evaluating any given individual's success in preserving omnipotence is made more difficult by a number of accompanying problems. My conception of alexithymia, which is present to varying degrees in most survivors, is that the definition of the inability to have emotions available in a signal fashion is descriptive, as is the other affective disturbance of not even being able to localize the "expressive" aspect of emotions (Nemiah 1977a,b, 1978, Sifneos 1967, 1973).

We first need to distinguish the emotions that register consciously from those that operate on a subliminal level, where they operate as "switches" in determining the fate, routing, registration, recall, and other choices of information processing. Then we need to reemphasize the genetic point of view of affects: notably, that their developmental lines are of affect differentiation, desomatization, and verbalization. Through this process, emotions evolve from the three infantile states of emotion precursors (the state of well-being, the state of distress, and cataleptic-dissociative state) to adult-type emotions suitable for optimal information processing. In alexithymia we see a regression or arrest in this process, with the result that the emotional responses are mostly somatic and poorly differentiated (Krystal 1974, 1988a). There is also a cognitive disturbance, called "operative thinking" by the French analysts who described it (Marty and de M'Uzan 1963, Marty et al. 1963, 1983), which manifests itself in analysis, when these patients, who at first give the impression of being very well adjusted to reality, produce in analysis a chronologically arranged recitation of all the trivia that happened since the last encounter. These early observers also pointed out that the patients do not develop a "good neurotic transference," but maintain a patient–doctor stance and patiently wait for the analyst to make them feel good. These findings were elaborated by McDougall (1974a,b), who also indicated that in many of these patients one gained the impression that they decathected part of their self- and object-representations, and replaced them with nothing. All these observations allude to yet another alexithymic characteristic: an inhibition in wish-fulfillment fantasy, which I later attributed to the traumatic (especially important in infantile trauma) interruption of the normal development of transitional functions (Krystal 1988b). In sum, all of these problems are part of the post-traumatic inhibition in self-caring and self-soothing (what Horton elaborated as "solacing," 1981), but also self-regulation. In analysis, I found that all these behaviors were part of the development of an *idolatrous transference*—a return, as I mentioned above, to the infantile state in which all the vital and affective parts of one's self are attributed to the Primal Object, and the self-caring is reserved to It too. All self-care must be carried out under a "franchise" from a Primal Object transference surrogate.

To reclaim one's autonomy is experienced as a Promethean transgression punishable by a fate worse than death: Hell, or what it really conceals. This is a doomsday orientation based on the dreaded but expected return of the infantile trauma. Such transferences involve preverbal affects and memories, and possibly results of "Primal Repression" (Cohen 1987, 1993, Cohen and Kinston 1984, Kinston and Cohen 1986). Consequently, we cannot expect the patients to translate these problems for us into the neurotic-type verbal and symbolic productions, but must continue to learn to develop sensitivities, observational strategies, and new techniques to deal with these types of problems. Most of the above-quoted papers by Cohen and Kinston, many of the writings of McDougall (1974a, 1984), and some of my own (e.g., 1979, 1988a, Chapter 15) address themselves to this issue.

Traumatic Confrontations with Death

We come now to the examination of the essence of the kind of confrontation with death that can be presumed to be traumatic, and the consequences that can be expected. Lifton has devoted many years to the study of these questions, and has produced some very significant observations (Lifton 1967, 1968, 1973, 1976, 1979, Lifton and Olson 1978). One of these is the idea of survival priorities. By priorities, we mean dealing with our guilt about surviving (which reinforces feelings of omnipotence) as well as confronting our own mortality in the face of death; whether the omnipotence or the vulnerability predominates is a question of survival priorities. They are part of our concept of life, which we do not need to ponder unless these survival priorities are violated, and as we age there are many evolutionary, social, and psychological processes that enable us to mourn in advance, preparing for our own death with some grace and dignity. I have written about the interference with this process by post-traumatic problems, especially alexithymia, which interferes with the ability to mourn in advance for one's self and also deal with the losses of old age (Krystal 1987). In this connection, I am reminded that in some of Lifton's earlier work (1967), he made the point that we are all survivors; thus, with every loss, we may discover that we also must deal with the idea of the triumph of survivorship. My impression is that the ancient Jewish mourning custom that involves tearing one's clothes and putting sackcloth on one's body and ashes on one's head seems to be an excessive protestation that covers up survivor triumph with behavior protesting the misery of survival.

Interestingly, a number of Holocaust survivors (and even more of their children) were disturbed by the idea of survivor guilt, as if the therapist invented it, or ordered it. And yet, survivor guilt would seem inevitable in those who experience major losses, and certainly in survivors of genocide. Survivor guilt involves the collision between the restoration of one's illusions of omnipotence and the simultaneous confrontation with the failure to rescue loved ones.

When we are considering an individual's death within an intact community, then we can visualize the combined traditions and myths, and the realignment of closeness and caretaking roles among the survivors, that serve to protect the illusion of immortality, by biological, religious, or universal transcendental attitudes. This was even possible (in miniature) in Auschwitz; for example, when transports arrived who had not been totally demoralized by long degradation and starvation in ghettos, small groups of individuals would come together and give each other the emotional support that made possible the maintenance of morale and pre-persecution identity (Ornstein 1985). The context of one's life and death becomes the task of the life-review in which one may respond with despair and anger, feeling that all the untoward things should not have happened because "there was no reason for them." Being able to accept that everything that happened was justified by its causes permits wisdom and integration (Krystal 1981) and even the acceptance of what Weisman and Hackett (1961) elaborated in the idea of an "appropriate death." All one's spiritual resources and emotional reserves can be overwhelmed by catastrophes and major disasters, and thus a traumatic confrontation with death results. If the use of "primary repression" does not occur, then at the very least one is condemned to living with survivor guilt (which may not be verbalized as such) and one is condemned to a life of increasing pain. While most of the chronic pain reactions are generated by painful affects such as guilt, rage, shame, and depression (Lifton describes it as "stasis and negation" 1979, p. 182), there also occur processes which we might think of as the obverse of healthy narcissism and omnipotence. For example, one can react to massive death by identification with death, the dead, or a life of death and/or mortification.

The overt identification with death is illustrated in the following case of schizophrenia.

Nemeth (1971) described a patient who was a concentration camp survivor, and among whose delusions were that "every other day he ascends to the seventh heaven, where accompanied by three officers and four women (the fourth one is for him), he conducts a 'selection.' Unlike the Nazis, he sends the selected subjects to America" (p. 142). At the time, he was a chronic State Hospital patient, who had worked for several years as a barber in the patients' barber shop. He then made some symbolic gestures of escaping from the hospital, and finally settled down to a life of solitary immersion in his delusions and hallucinations. This case illustrates what we have touched on before, namely, that although the development of alexithymia produces the misfortune of regression in affects, affect deverbalization, and desomatization and the problems of physical pain and psychosomatic disease, there are also some benefits from it. One benefit is that this development protects some of the narcissistic views of one's self. The patients isolate their "disease" or "survivor syndrome" (where that now ancient term [Niederland 1961] applies), and proceed to use a variety of defenses to rebuild their self-worth and greatly subdued, or "borrowed," omnipotent beliefs. Holocaust victims, for example, may return to their religion, covering up their gnawing (unconscious) doubts with rituals. They may develop an identification with the revived Jewish State, the new generation, and a multiplicity of other substitutes for the object of the idolatrous transference. However, as already mentioned, to an important extent these defenses crumble with aging. As part of Germany's efforts to compensate Holocaust survivors, a couple of years ago they permitted those survivors who could demonstrate that a "persecution connected condition, which was recognized 30 or so years ago, got much worse (over 70 % occupationally disabling)," to apply to be reexamined. I have done psychiatric re-evaluations of 45 such individuals since September 1992, as the psychiatric examiner for the Consul General of Germany in Detroit. The findings were quite surprising for their consistency, even though the group was small. The patients, many now retired, complained of insomnia; pains in their muscles, joints, and body in general; and a multitude of psychosomatic diseases, besides the illnesses that they developed that were not persecution related. They frequently mentioned that when they do fall asleep they often wake up—a couple of hours early and then usually way before dawn—terrified, and sometimes remain depressed all day. Depression and anhedonia were virtually the rule. However, they showed a most extraordinary inability to verbalize the ideas or memories that went with the present-day dysphoric states. In some cases the reaction was so severe that it seemed that the patients had developed a pseudo-dementia. Some would become extremely angry, defiant or even paranoid when I questioned them about their present feelings, relations with their family, and particularly their thoughts and fantasies. This behavior seems to be part of a problem I reported in 1988 (1988a, p. 236) and more recently in connection with therapeutic problems (Krystal 1994); namely that the most profoundly repressed contents of the "post-traumatic black hole" involve the *unconscious identification with the "other side"* of a genocidal sado-masochistic relationship.

The transference to the examiner displayed in the claimants' behavior was only the surface of a problem related to what Cohen

(1987, 1993) and Cohen and Kinston (1984) referred to as "primal repression." Individuals, particularly victim-survivors forced to discover this seemingly eradicated secret, may become psychotic and reveal a primitive type of submission based on primitive love—the very opposite end of the spectrum from narcissistic omnipotence. Although Kinston and Cohen (1986) described the dangers of psychoanalytic treatment after post-traumatic primary repression, the most beautiful description of this issue is an artistically intuitive one, by the late British actor R. Shaw (1967) in his play, *Man in the Glass Booth*.

Considerations of Therapy

The major point of the above discussion is that in the treatment of post-traumatic states, the emphasis will be on the reconstruction of structures, initially and for a long time. The reconstruction of the traumatic state and its aftereffects takes a distant second place and is a slow and drawn-out assignment; and the reconstruction of the traumatic *situation* may be just an occasional event, in exceptional patients, under exceptional circumstances. Actually, if we are going to attempt psychoanalytic psychotherapy, then we must first demonstrate and explain to the patient the nature of their affective and cognitive disorders related to alexithymia. This discovery may arouse an ambivalent reaction. At first the patient may be relieved to gain some understanding of his or her affective disturbance, which for so long was mistaken even by experts as "emotional anaesthesia" (Minkowski 1946). Subsequently, however, the uncovering work becomes more painful, even unbearable. This is so when we delve into the somatic equivalents of depression and shame, and thus reveal that the affective regression was part of the traumatic surrender, and later, helped the individual to survive in the dehumanized "robot" manner, and still later, was put to use to protect what narcissistic omnipotence could be salvaged by substituting for the never-achieved mourning, psychosomatic diseases, as well as chronic depression, shame, survivor guilt, and other painful or threatening affects. When we demonstrate to the alexithymic post-traumatic patient his serious impairment in taking care of himself, we may encounter resistance to interfering with extreme overwork, or a driveness to maintain activities that serve to avoid the return of the horror and shame of helplessness. The confrontation with the Idolatrous Transference has to wait for evidence that affect tolerance has been increased to the point that it is possible to avoid the kind of crises which Cohen (1987, 1993) anticipated—crises that follow if we prematurely uncover the traumatic information that has never been made part of one's self-representation. In short, death, murder, or suicide are very real possibilities.

I cannot, without some cautions and reservations, share the optimistic report of Ornstein (1986) who, applying a self psychological view, felt that some survivors of severe trauma, treated with emphatic attunement, can restore their self-cohesion. She went on to say that some Holocaust survivors may be able to reintegrate their memories and restore their psychic continuity because "fellow survivors, emphatically responsive, tolerant friends as well as their own spouses and children had frequently performed these necessary selfobject functions" (p. 191). I do believe that in exceptionally good and prolonged psychoanalytic treatment it is possible to repair some narcissistic injuries and restore some feelings of omnipotence. However, the lengthy discussion of the infantile sources of narcissism was presented in preparation for the present considerations. As I have observed in my work (1988a) and McDougall stressed (1978a,b, 1984), entering the arena of infantile conflict requires the use of empathy with preverbal communications, sometimes just affect-precursors. Dealing with failure in self-solacing involves the study of the utilization of transitional functions (Horton and Sharp 1984). The approaches to infantile states do not take place in the cool and "neutral" position of the neurotic transference. The situation bears a closer resemblance to the kind of state in which we deal with childhood incestuous abuse. In those situations, since the patients were frequently in trances during the abuse, they tend to reexperience trances and/or dissociations in the treatment. It is necessary to recognize the regressed and dissociated state, and have an experience-proximate attitude to it. In other words, we are not going to play the hypnotist game but, as much as possible, empathically enter the infantile state, as a good mother does. The reason that most post-traumatic patients are "best left to the internist," as Sifneos once candidly observed about psychosomatic patients (1975), is that these states are difficult and painful to treat, and respond slowly if at all to our best efforts.

Some Comments on the Relationship between the Life and Work of Kosinski

In light of the above analysis, I now would like to discuss some aspects of the life and work of the Polish-born author Jerzy Kosinski, who is generally regarded as a Holocaust survivor-victim, and whose works are widely considered to reflect this personal history. I hasten to add that I shall not attempt anything like an analytic study of his character, or of the available literature by and about Kosinski. I wish to restrict myself to the question of his reactions to what was generally assumed to have been his traumatic confrontation with death. That this confrontation significantly influenced his behavior and writing, and that his suicide represented his final "victory" over the incurable wounds he suffered from all his life are compelling ideas.

After the publication of *The Painted Bird* in 1965, Kosinski told many people in public and private that it was an autobiographical novel. Elie Wiesel wrote the following in the *New York Times Book Review*: "Written with deep sincerity and sensitivity, this poignant account transcends confession." At the time of Kosinski's suicide, Wiesel added, "I thought it was fiction, and when he told me it was autobiography I tore up my review and wrote one a thousand times better" (cited in Sloan 1994, p. 46). Kosinski encouraged *The Painted Bird*'s acceptance as autobiographical recollections, and it was compared to the diary of Anne Frank. Its success and critical and international acclaim surprised even Kosinski. As Sloan (1994) put it:

> "Account," "confession," "testament," "document," "testimony": these were the key words in the book's critical reception. What made *The Painted Bird* such an important book was its overpowering authenticity. Perhaps it wasn't exactly a diary—six-year-olds don't keep diaries—but it was the next best thing. And in one respect it was better; Kosinski was Anne Frank as a survivor, walking among us. [p. 47]

As time went on and Kosinski produced more books and emerged as a most impressive person both in his gifts and achievements, and revelations appeared about his bizarre lifestyle (most of all his *symptomatic* life), the book took on increasing poignancy as a challenge and an opportunity to learn something very important about the psychological impact of prolonged exposure to near-death experiences.

The format of *The Painted Bird* is quite striking. The protagonist, a 6-year-old boy when we first meet him, is sent to the Polish countryside by his parents to avoid being caught and arrested by the Nazis. Over a period of about six years he goes from one situation of danger and horror to another. Each time he barely escapes with his life. What is striking in all this is that there is hardly any description or recollection of the subjective nature of the experiences. Each episode stops abruptly with an escape and we then enter a new horror story. I found the style of *The Painted Bird* illustrative of the cognitive constriction that takes place in trauma, and consistent with the dearth of survivor accounts about trauma (1988a). I also found in surveying the autobiographical writing of post-traumatic individuals, that the "fact" orientation—the inability to observe, describe, and utilize one's own feelings—is common, conspicuous, and pathognomonic. As I have said, "*The Painted Bird* is probably the best illustration of this phenomenon" (Krystal 1978, p. 102).

Thus, in *The Painted Bird* a rescuer, Martha, accepts the abandoned child, saves him and reinforces his magical thinking by practicing a mixture of folk medicine and magic; she soon dies in a mysterious fire. The protagonist then moves on to a jealous miller, who enucleated the eyes of his plowboy, whom he suspects of "eyeing" his wife. This is followed by the adventures of Lech, a birdcatcher, who amuses himself by painting crows with lime and watching them get killed by other crows. Then comes the story of "stupid Ludmila," which culminates in a sex orgy, after which the women of the village beat her to death. Next is the blacksmith incident, ending in bloody carnage and total destruction. Then there is the episode that starts with a wedding, during which a farmer gets stabbed to death. The episode ends with the protagonist's being chased by a band of village boys who try to kill him. Although wounded, he manages to escape and leaves the village. In the next episode a "Jewess" is raped by a peasant, Rainbow, the whole incident being watched by the little boy through a knothole. Next, a group of SS men resplendent (to the boy) in their uniforms pay a visit to the village and kill some hiding Jews.

What follows is the sadistic, and almost unimaginable, story of Gardos and his vicious dog. Gardos hangs the boy by his arms from the ceiling just out of reach of the deadly dog. Gardos also beats the boy with whips and willow canes, and finally, after a visit by a priest, the boy escapes and runs to the church. There he learns about prayer, and thus becomes able to replace the terrible feeling of helplessness with the power of prayer. This religiosity leads to his running one day to the church, where Mass is about to be celebrated. An altar boy is missing so the priest picks our "Gypsy" boy as a replacement. Weak from the previous night's beating, he drops a Missal. For this he is punished by being thrown into the cesspool behind the village outhouse to drown. This episode is the only one in which Kosinski (1991) actually makes some attempt to describe the boy's experience (though not his feelings):

> I retched. The peasants swung me by the hands and feet. The pale clouds in the sky swam before my eyes. I was hurled into the very

> center of the brown filth which parted under my body to engulf me. Daylight disappeared above me and I began to suffocate. I tossed instinctively in the dense element, lashing out with my arms and legs. I touched bottom and rebounded as fast as I could. A spongy upswell raised me upward toward the surface. I opened my mouth and caught a dash of air. I was sucked below the surface, and again pushed myself up from the bottom. The pit was only twelve feet square. Once more I sprang up from the bottom, this time toward the edge . . . I caught hold of a creeper. . . . [p. 124]

In the one conversation I had with Kosinski, some ten years ago, I tried to probe his alexithymia by inquiring about *his feelings* during the above-described episode. When I asked him how *he* felt being thrown into the cesspool, he responded, "It felt warm."

There is one more episode from *The Painted Bird* that is relevant to our investigation. Kosinski describes how some Polish boys, whom he tried to join in skating, attempt to drown him by pushing him under the ice in a hole. Years later, he repeated that story in an essay written on the tenth anniversary of the publication of *The Painted Bird*, which was reprinted in the collection of his nonfiction published posthumously by his widow, Kiki: "At the age of ten, while ice skating on a lake in Poland I was pushed under the ice as a prank by village kids and, choking, barely made it to the surface" (1991, p. 69). Recently, a very different account of this episode has been obtained by Sloan, who has interviewed Kosinski's rescuer on that occasion. According to Sloan, Jerzy had not been allowed to leave his backyard (where he spent his free time hanging on a fence). However, he did get away on two occasions, trying to skate with his friend, Andrzej Migdalek, while the other boys were not skating on the lake. "But they were back very quickly. Older boys, excellent skaters from the neighborhood, started chasing them, skated right in front of them, and shouted at Jurek [Polish diminutive of *Jerzy*]: 'A Jew, a Jew'" (Kosinski 1991, p. 69). He was so frightened that he wanted to get home right away. But Jerzy soon forgot about it, and he begged to go out again to skate with little Andrzej Migdalek. Once again they met their tormentors, older boys from Dabrowa, together with their ringleader, Swietlik. These tormentors shouted to Jurek to take his pants off and show his penis to prove he was not circumcised. Andrzej Migdalek told Swietlik to show his own penis. Everybody knew that Swietlik was a converted Jew, so this enraged him. Together with the gang, he got hold of Jurek, threw him on the ice, and started taking his pants off. Jurek fought, struggled, shielded himself with his hands, shrieked, and wailed: "*Mameh! Mameh!*" Never before had Migdalek heard Jurek utter a Jewish word. He tried to help, to pull Jurek from underneath the assailants, but nobody knows how it might have ended if it had not been for Edek Warchol, the landlord's son, who was strong and almost an adult. Alarmed by Jurek's cries, he skated toward him. Swietlik and his friends, much younger, scattered in different directions, frightened. In the meantime, Jurek got up and ran home. (This episode is from Siedlecka [1994], an English translation manuscript.)

I have focused at some length on *The Painted Bird*, which, unlike Kosinski's other novels, deals directly with his early life in Poland and his (supposed) experiences during the Holocaust. I have also pointed out the unusual style and format of this novel. Significantly, from a psychological point of view, this same style is apparent in most of his other works. Almost every novel shows the same two stylistic characteristics: Each novel consists of a series of episodes, most of which do not continue in the next story; there is always some major discontinuity. Even if the protagonist is the same, he appears in a different guise, or reflects a different milieu or motivation. Each story is abruptly dropped; consequences, aftereffects, and the need to return to "home base" are not explored (Kosinski 1968, 1971, 1988).

Kosinski's quick-change artistry, if I may call it that, was reflected in his life as well as in his literary technique. As is well known, in his (symptomatic) life, Kosinski used to delight in donning different disguises/personas, and he had a fondness for roaming about at night in dangerous, or at least unsavory, places. He also used to enjoy hiding and impressing his friends with his ability to do so. His friends learned that he could hide any time when he had company or was visiting in their homes. Once, for example, he hid out in the chimney, and another time in the drawer of his photography lab. In a discussion with Stokes (one of the two men who tarnished his reputation in an article in the *Village Voice*), Kosinski said, "All my life I have been hiding." He also bragged, "Give me half an hour and I will find a hiding place anywhere" (Taylor 1991, p. 34).

Tanay (1968) commented in a work on psychotherapy with Holocaust survivors that the thought of finding a good hiding place crossed the mind of his patients in every new surrounding. Frankiel (1993) demonstrated that "children who introduce hide-and-seek games into their therapies have good reasons to be preoccupied with loss" (p. 345). Although this game served to reassure the children that they would not be abandoned, Frankiel concluded: "the child who has lost a love object feels incomplete—physically and psychically—and narcissistically damaged." She adds a point relevant to our discussions, namely, that "the finding of a new object rekindles the hope of setting everything right," but, "This includes not only the recapture of the lost love object, but the restoration of the lost intact self; it also includes some compensation and revenge for the suffering endured in the long days of waiting" (p. 358).

The Nature of Confrontation with Death and Trauma to Jurek

The Painted Bird was translated into virtually every language except Polish. In Poland it was not published until 1985. The Polish official attitude was that the book was slanderous, and thus even the importation of the book was prohibited. Kosinski felt that "these diverse criticisms were part of a large scale attempt by an extreme nationalist group to create a feeling of danger and disruption in my homeland, a plot intended to force the remaining Jewish population to leave the state" (Kosinski 1991, p. 189).

Among those who attacked Kosinski was a journalist, Joanna Siedlecka. She devoted a great deal of time and energy to attempting to establish the inaccuracy of Kosinski's "autobiographical" account in *The Painted Bird*. Siedlecka published her findings in a book entitled *Czarny Ptasior* ("disgusting black bird"). In it she revealed that Jurek was never separated from his parents. With his parents, Moses and Elizabeth (original surname, Lewinkopf), he apparently moved in October or November 1939 from his home town of Lodz to the eastern city of Sandomierz. The fate of the Kosinskis has been studied and reported by other authors, for example Taylor, who confirms that Siedlecka's account is correct. They lived in an apartment house occupied by Jews but owned by a Pole. There they obtained false papers, changing their name to Kosinski and their religion to Catholic. Moses Kosinski was a philologist and student of ancient languages and had worked in Lodz translating technical manuals and instructions for textile factories (Taylor 1991). Although he was short, pot-bellied, and balding, he was able to impress people with his knowledge, cunning, and willingness to teach and help. According to Siedlecka, soon all the people called him "Professor," and his wife "Pani Profesorowa" (Madame Professor). Moses Kosinski seemed to have had a keen sense of the political situation, and consequently he managed to get his family away from Sandomierz to an isolated village called Dabrowa Rzeczycka before a ghetto was established in Sandomierz. (The ghetto eventually liquidated and all Jews were sent to their death in Treblinka.) In addition, he seemed to have enough money, dollars, gold, jewelry to keep the family in relative luxury, beyond anything imaginable to the local population.

Professor Sloan of the University of Illinois went to Poland and interviewed the people mentioned by Siedlecka, and wrote an article in *The New Yorker* (1994) that confirmed most of the basic facts of the Kosinskis' survival. He continues to search for all contacts of the family and is writing a book about the findings. I am most obliged to him for sharing with me information, as well as the translated manuscript of Siedlecka's book. Sloan was not only able to identify the son of "Martha" of *The Painted Bird*, but the man turned out to be a docent of war-time memorabilia, having access to public documents and the historical museum housed in the former Jewish Synagogue. The "acting curator" then took Sloan to Dabrowa Rzeczycka, where he met Lech, the man who used to trap crows, paint them with limewash, and release them in order to watch the rest of the flock attack them. Professor Sloan recently related to me (June 9, 1995) that he had been back to Poland a couple of times since then and attended an academic meeting of literary students of Kosinski. At this meeting Sloan was able to confirm that *The Painted Bird* was *not* an autobiographical book, but more in the nature of a historical novel. Moreover, and most important for our considerations, he found *no* evidence that Jurek was ever exposed to a confrontation with death. There was no history of catastrophic trauma during the Holocaust period.

Since we have no such history in the case of Jurek, how then can we explain the curious phenomena already described, that is, Kosinski's pathological or symptomatic behavior? I propose that to do so we should return to the idea of "combat exhaustion" and consider if it can explain the life and death of Kosinski, which *seemed* to be so well explained by the traumatic events of *The Painted Bird*. I identify the condition as an exhaustion of all the emotional resources of an individual, such that there is a reactive rage against the whole world, one's self, and even one's benign introjects.

Narcissistic and omnipotent feelings, including infantile omnipotence, turn into a form of pain: love outraged becomes the motive for a mixture of sadomasochistic attempts to regain the primary object, but under the rules of power and submission, since the search for love is experienced as hopeless. As with the "combat exhaustion" paradigm of World War II, we see a turning against one's previous sources of security and comfort; there is always a suicidal potential. Only in extraordinarily fortunate circumstances can psychogenic death or severely disabling character deformation be avoided; instead what develops is pathological narcissism, in which significant areas of function are preserved, despite severe and deforming post-traumatic psychopathology. I think we can understand the fate of Kosinski as a reaction and restitutive self-aggrandizement to try and restore an impoverished self.

Stress Trauma, Narcissistic Rage, and Sadomasochistic Fixation

The Kosinskis did not fit in with the Jewish population of the apartment house in Sandomierz. Mrs. Kosinski, younger than her husband, was slim and elegant and—along with her husband and son—had a contempt for the local Jews, who tended to wear the gabardine black clothes, skull-caps, and earlocks, and to speak with a Jewish accent. The Kosinskis prided themselves on their impeccable Polish diction and enunciation. They lived a life of leisure, and Jurek, whom they adored, never attended Jewish or public school, and was not allowed to play with the Jewish children, whom he learned (and was encouraged) to despise. On one occasion, when he considered playing with one, his mother whispered, "Remember your accent!"

Jurek considered himself a Polish Catholic boy and practiced the appropriate prayers. The Jewish boys would tease him and call him "Josek" (the Polish-Jewish diminutive of Joseph to which he always responded with rage, and sometimes with fist-fights). When he was asked by a Jewish girl, Rebeka Blusztajn, to go out to play, he kicked her, spat on her, and called her a "dirty Jew" (Siedlecka 1994, p. 9). Sloan writes: "It was the father that could have made Jurek aware that to be a Jew was to be in mortal danger. What he could have told him must be interesting, since the seven-year-old took it so much to heart. He got so scared that he shunned his little compatriots. He beat them up and kicked them. And wanted to be only Jurek Kosinski and not Josek Lewinkopf" (p. 11).

Eventually, the Kosinskis went to the village of Dabrova, where Jurek continued to spend all of his time with his parents. He was confined to the yard of his cottage. Whenever he ventured out, the Polish boys called him "Jew," attacked him, and threatened him. Thus, he was alienated from everyone. At this time his "adopted stepbrother" appeared on the scene, complete with a Polish nanny who loved him and, apparently, a lot of money. Although Mrs. Kosinski agreed to have Henio, a young Jewish boy, and his nanny join their household (apparently for the financial gain), she refused to handle him in any way. This behavior was apparently so extreme that it shocked all observers. Jurek hated Henio, had nothing to do with him, and eventually broke his arm.

Mrs. Kosinski was allegedly preoccupied with her clothes and appearance. She also used to enjoy very costly food (though when her neighbors and their children were starving no help came from the Kosinskis). While in Sandomierz Mrs. Kosinski had one friend whom she considered worthy of her company as a fellow rich "inteligencia" person. This woman had a son, Stefan, who was about Jurek's age, and so the children played with Jurek for the sake of Stefan.

> The children did not like Jurek: he was different from other children. More mature, thoughtful. A little removed, more a viewer than a participant, he avoided active games: chasing, fighting, digging in the sand, and on the whole everything that would soil his clothes. He immediately brushed the dirt off. They recall the gesture that made them laugh to this day. He was very clean and beautifully dressed, in knitted sweaters, smart shoes, though more and more Jewish children were running around in rags and barefoot. Yet most relevant was the fact that he was very intelligent, but malicious, domineering, demonstrating his superiority, always having everything his way. One day while playing . . . the boys put little Marysia in a baby-carriage, and with all their might pushed it down a slope. It went down fast like an arrow, and was luckily stopped by a tree, so nothing happened to the girl. But it could have ended not quite so well. As it was, the girl cried a lot, frightened. So did Stefan, who obviously regretted what he had done. Not Jurek though. He laughed. He could do anything. His doting parents, and especially the mother, never rebuked him. [Siedlecka 1994, p. 15]

When the Kosinski family was living in Dabrowa—according to Siedlecka—the local boys conspired to see Jurek's circumcised penis, which he was very careful to protect. Unlike other boys, he always went to the latrine. When he went there, the boys would throw burning cans filled with carbide at the door. They counted on him to be so terrified by the explosion and fire that he would run out with his pants down. But though they smoked him out like that several times, he always managed to pull his pants up, and they never saw anything! So finally, one time when Jurek sneaked out of his yard and ran to the pasture, the boys attacked him. They snatched him, stretched him out on the grass, and started taking his pants off. He fought and screamed, and fortunately just then a neighbor, Stanislaw Rybak, arrived on the scene. If it had been just local boys fighting, he would not have paid attention, but he saw the "Professor's little son," so he got a stick and chased off the boys. But that's not all. He went running to the Kosinskis to tell them about the boys. Jurek did not know who they were or where they lived. Thanks to Rybak, Jurek went around the neighborhood with his father, "pointing out" the ones who had grabbed him. Jan Szkutnik remembers the visit well.

> "Szkutnik," the Professor shouted from the door (he called the peasants by their last name, and they called him "Professor"!), "Your son hurt mine!"
>
> So Szkutnik's father gave him such a spanking that he avoided "Professor's little son." Like his friends, who also had to pay the price.
>
> But in spite of this, they felt sorry for him.
>
> True, he had an educated father, [a] mother with polished nails, a servant. A part for the first communion. English lessons. A ball, books, it was said even a globe! He sat on the porch eating sausages and veal, drinking cocoa. On the one hand he was the Professor's little son but on the whole a poor meager fellow.
>
> For he could not leave the yard, swim in the river, look after cows in the pastures, go to the forest, throw burning cans filled with carbide, bake potatoes in the ashes of bonfires.
>
> He was only hanging on the fence, guarding his "bird" that no one could see.
>
> So maybe when it came like a bomb-shell after the years that he wrote, apparently, *The Painted Bird* at first they thought that maybe it was about "it." After all, there had been so many fights, actions, and

battles over the matter. But no, it was about Lech Tracz's crows. [Siedlecka 1994, pp. 50–51]

Discussion, and a Few Comments by Kosinski

In my earlier work on trauma (1988a), I came to the conclusion that it was not advantageous to keep anxiety as the model affect. I felt that love was much more central to all affective reactions. Thus, it is helpful for me to be able to consider rage as love outraged; and, further, all painful affects as transformations or reactions to injured love. Moreover, it is essential to distinguish pleasure from gratification, and suffering from pain. What is more, it is possible to develop an addiction to pain, and to painful affects, on the basis that the conscious painful experience is accompanied by unconscious gratification. Rado (1964) had an early insight about the problem of "traumatophilia" as a major post-traumatic sequel.

In my experience, when everything about the patient indicates the prevalence of post-traumatic problems, yet I cannot discover a history of adult or childhood catastrophic trauma, I then become convinced that there is also a history of infantile psychic trauma. This assumption is difficult to prove because of the preverbal level of problems, which, contrary to our earlier expectations, is not translated into words when language is acquired (Stern 1985). In the example of Jerzy Kosinski, we do have a plethora of traumatic factors and episodes: his uprooting, isolation, and raw castration anxiety are quite adequate to explain many of the post-traumatic problems. However, I have been searching in vain for the precise moment of confrontation with death, and development of trauma. We have a number of clues to consider: his mother's narcissism and her behavior with Jurek suggest that from the beginning he was treated as an extension of herself, and that she insisted on being his sole source of love and comfort. By sticking to her side, the boy was perceived by many people either as a "black spider" or as a "princeling." Professor Sloan (personal communication December 15, 1994) ventured that there was a "folie à Deux" relation between the mother and son, because after the fictional nature of *The Painted Bird* became known, she kept writing letters to Jerzy confirming the original version of the tale as factual.

However, there is another major issue involved here: notably, the transformation of infantile narcissism and omnipotence by trauma and repeated confrontations with death into the sadomasochistic moral and perhaps perverse attitude that fills Kosinski's work and life. Kosinski liked to talk about it in terms of "dominance":

> If there is anything in an individual that enables that person to remain independent, the protagonist of *Steps* [one of Kosinski's novels, 1968] attempts to conquer that independence; if he succeeds he feels only indifference. But in a seemingly prolonged moment when the dominance becomes his, he feels a kind of passion, a gratefulness so total, a joy at winning so deep as to be love. There grows within him also a great relief at having finally freed himself of a struggle, of finally being able to acknowledge himself the stranger. In that instant one partner loves the other's susceptibility, he loves passionately.
>
> But when that instant passes, he feels only emptiness and he moves again from threat to conquest, from love to indifference. . . . [F]rom the point of view of the protagonist of *Steps* the only truly satisfying relationship is one growing out of domination; one in which his experience of a certain form of the past can be projected onto the other person. [1991, p. 229]

The joy of dominance may be ephemeral, but it is much preferable to what it serves to avoid: submission to a sadomasochistic relationship, and even the return of an infantile trauma state. That is Hell. It is the kind of suffering that gets worse and worse and continues forever (because of the absence of any sense of time). His mother's insistence that he must cling to her and that any contact with Jewish or Polish children would contaminate him with the taint of death, combined with his father's man-to-man explanations of the danger and the probability of death if Jurek did not follow his instructions to the letter, provide an example of what Shengold (1989) called "soul murder."

In addition, in the hours of hanging on the fence Jurek observed many cattle cars filled with Jews on the way to their death, with only a few victims able to reach the opening covered with barbed wire and plead for a drop of water. The most conspicuous aspect common to Jurek's reaction and that of soldiers who developed "combat exhaustion" is that aggression was turned from the enemy to one's comrades. Once started, this rage turned also against oneself and one's loved ones. Jerzy hated Jews and Poles, and admired and identified with the SS men. This aberration continued throughout his life. One of his favorite games was to design esoteric uniforms, and go to countries where people would defer to him and obey him because of the uniform (mentioned in an interview with Gene Shalit in 1980; also published in *Vanity Fair* in October 1991). He was cruel to dogs, and until his last few years, also to children (Sloan, personal communication December 15, 1994). He was so afraid of being "engulfed" by a woman that during his marriage to Mary Hayward Weir, the widow of a steel magnate, whenever they moved from one of her mansions to another, he insisted on putting all of his things in one room—his bedroom, which the maids and other workers complained that they could not keep in order.

He reflected on the irony of his life: "Whoever sheltered me in Poland faced the death penalty. What kind of childhood did that produce? Traumatic, no question about it. I, the child, was responsible for the endangerment of adults" (Kosinski 1991, p. 34). In the wake of trauma, especially childhood and infantile trauma, people develop what I call "a doomsday orientation," an expectation and even conviction that sooner or later the "fate worse than death" will occur. Kosinski not only had this fear, and a psychosomatic expression of his anxiety (heart irregularity), but it was very clear that he would rather die than return to his traumatic state. He said: "Mercy killing interests me; mercy living does not" (1991, p. 23). He discussed in detail his plans for suicide (which were also reflected in *Steps* and

The Hermit of 69th Street). The following quotation is from *Passing By* (1968, p. 231):

> [F]or the protagonist of *Steps* suicide is an act stemming out of the present. In performing suicide a man chooses to escape from his future and from his past, thus overcoming the knowledge that he will die. . . . But even in self-destruction, his shadow outlives him. He imposes on other people the necessity for remembering and for judging him, for summarizing his character. He creates the means to outlive himself.

And we may add, in summary, that he exits fighting, dominant against the forces of death, and does not return to submission.

References

Archibald, H. C., Long, D. M., Miller, C., and Tuddenham, K. D. (1962). Gross stress reaction in combat: a 15 year follow-up. *American Journal of Psychiatry* 119:317–322.

——— (1965). Persistent stress reaction after combat. *Archives of General Psychiatry* 12:425–481.

Bartemeier, L. H., Kubie, L. S., Menninger, K. A., et al. (1946). Combat exhaustion. *Journal of Nervous and Mental Disease* 104:358–389.

Beebe, G. W., and Appel, J. W. (1958). *Variations in Psychological Tolerance to Ground Combat in World War II*. Washington, DC: National Academy of Sciences, National Research Council.

Cohen, J. (1987). Trauma and repression. *Psychoanalytic Inquiry* 5:163–189.

——— (1993). Primal repression. Paper presented at the meeting of the American Psychoanalytic Association, May.

Cohen, J., and Kinston, W. (1984). Repression theory: a new look at the cornerstone. *International Journal of Psycho-Analysis* 65:411–422.

Danieli, Y. (1981). Differing adaptational styles in families of survivors of the Nazi Holocaust: some implications for treatment. *Children Today* 10:34–35.

Frankiel, R. V. (1993). A symposium. The game of hide and seek: origins, meaning, enactments. *Psychoanalytic Review* 80:327–329.

Freud, S. (1926). Inhibitions, symptoms, and anxiety. *Standard Edition* 20:74.

Hofer, M. A. (1981a). Towards a developmental basis for disease predisposition: the effect of early maternal separation on the brain, behavior, and cardiovascular system. In *Brain Behavior and Bodily Diseases*, ed. H. Werner, M. A. Holdes, and A. J. Stunkard, pp. 135–166. New York: Raven.

——— (1981b). *The Roots of Human Behavior*. San Francisco: Freeman.

——— (1982). Some thoughts on "the transduction of experience" from a developmental perspective. *Psychosomatic Medicine* 44:19–28.

Horton, P. L. (1981). *Solace: The Missing Dimension in Psychiatry*. Chicago: University of Chicago Press.

Horton, P. L., and Sharp, S. L. (1984). Language, solace and transitional relatedness. *Psychoanalytic Study of the Child* 39:167–194. New Haven, CT: Yale University Press.

Kinston, W., and Cohen, J. (1986). Primal repression: clinical and theoretical aspects of the mind. The realm of psychic states. *International Journal of Psycho-Analysis* 67:337–356.

Kosinski, J. (1965). *The Painted Bird*. Boston: Houghton Mifflin.

——— (1968). *Steps*. New York: Random House.

——— (1988). *The Hermit of 69th Street*. New York: Seaver.

——— (1991). *Passing By: Selected Essays, 1962–1991*. New York: Random House.

Krystal, H. (1971). Trauma: consideration of its intensity and chronicity. In *Psychic Traumatization. International Psychiatric Clinics*, ed. H. Krystal and W. G. Niederland, vol. 8, pp. 11–28. Boston: Little Brown.

——— (1974). The genetic development of affects and affect regression. *Annual of Psychoanalysis* 2:98–126.

——— (1978). Trauma and affect. *Psychoanalytic Study of the Child* 33:81–118. New Haven, CT: Yale University Press.

——— (1979). Alexithymia and psychotherapy. *American Journal of Psychotherapy* 33:17–31.

——— (1981). Integration and self-healing in posttraumatic states. *Journal of Geriatric Psychiatry* 14:165–189.

——— (1985). Trauma and the stimulus barrier. *Psychoanalytic Inquiry* 5:131–161.

——— (1987). The impact of massive trauma and the capacity to grieve effectively: Later life sequelae. In *Treating the Elderly with Psycho-*

therapy, ed. J. Sadavoy and M. Leszcz, pp. 67–94. New York: International Universities Press.

——— (1988a). *Integration and Self-Healing*. Hillsdale, NJ: Analytic Press.

——— (1988b). On some roots of creativity. In *The Hemispheric Specialization*, ed. K. D. Hoppe, pp. 475–491. New York: Saunders.

——— (1993). Beyond DSM-III-R: Therapeutic considerations in posttraumatic stress disorders. In *International Handbook of Traumatic Stress Syndromes*, ed. J. P. Wilson and B. Rafael, pp. 841–853. New York: Plenum.

——— (1994). Psychic trauma and psychoanalytic approaches to somatization and addiction. Presented at the 5th Annual Day in Psychoanalysis, Toronto Psychoanalytic Society, April.

Lifton, R. J. (1967). *Death in Life: Survivors of Hiroshima*. New York: Simon & Schuster.

——— (1968). Observations on Hiroshima survivors. In *Massive Psychic Trauma*, ed. H. Krystal, pp. 169–189. New York: International Universities Press.

——— (1973). *Home from the War*. New York: Simon & Schuster.

——— (1976). *The Life of the Self*. New York: Touchstone.

——— (1979). *The Broken Connection: On Death and the Continuity of Life*. New York: Simon & Schuster.

Lifton, R. J., and Olson, E. (1976). The human meaning of total disaster: The Buffalo Creek experience. *Psychiatry* 39:1–18.

Mahler, M. S., Pine, F., and Bergman, A. (1975). *The Psychological Birth of the Human Infant: Symbiosis and Individuation*. New York: Basic Books.

Marty, P., and de M'uzan, M. (1963). La "penseé opèratoire." *Revue Francais Psychanalitique* 27 (Suppl.):345–356.

Marty, P., de M'uzan, M., and David, C. (1963). *L'investigation Psychosomatique*. Paris: Presses Universitaires Paris.

——— (1983). Process of somatization. In *Psychosomatic medicine*, ed. A. J. Kudkowski and C. P. Kimball, pp. 455–461. New York: Plenum.

McDougall, J. (1974a). *Plea for a Measure of Abnormality*. New York: International Universities Press.

——— (1974b). The psychosoma and psychoanalytic press. *International Review of Psycho-Analysis* 1:437–454.

——— (1984). The "dis-affected" patient: reflections on affect pathology. *Psychoanalytic Quarterly* 53:386–409.

Meerloo, J. A. M. (1959). Shock, catalepsy and psychogenic death. *International Record of Medicine* 172:384–393.

Minkowski, E. (1946). L'anestheste affective. *Annual of Medico-Psychology* 104:8–13.

Nemeth, M. C. (1971). Psychosis in a concentration camp survivor. In *Psychic Traumatization: Aftereffects in Individuals and Communities*, ed. H. Krystal and H. G. Niederland, pp. 135–146. Boston: Little Brown.

Nemiah, J. C. (1977a). Alexithymia: theoretical considerations. *Psychotherapy and Psychosomatics* 28:199–296.

——— (1977b). Alexithymia: theories and models. *Proceedings of the 11th European Conference on Psychosomatic Research*. Basel, Switzerland: Karger.

——— (1978). Alexithymia and psychosomatic illness. *Journal of Continuing Medical Education in Psychiatry*, pp. 25–37.

Niederland, W. G. (1961). The problem of the survivor. *Journal of the Hillside Hospital* 10:233–247.

Ornstein, A. (1985). Survival and recovery. *Psychoanalytic Inquiry* 5:99–123.

——— (1986). The Holocaust reconstruction and establishment of psychic continuity. In *The Reconstruction of Trauma: Its Significance in Clinical Work*, ed. A. Rothstein, pp. 191–205. Madison, CT: International Universities Press.

Rado, S. (1964). Hedonic self-regulation of the organism. In *The Role of Pleasure in Behavior*, ed. R. Heck, pp. 257–264. New York: Harper & Row.

Richter, C. P. (1959). The phenomenon of unexplained sudden death in animal and man. In *The Meaning of Death*, ed. H. Feifel, pp. 302–313. New York: McGraw Hill.

Schore, A. N. (1994). *Affect Regulation and the Origin of the Self: The Neurobiology of Emotional Development*. Hillsdale, NJ: Erlbaum.

Seligman, M. E. P. (1975). *Helplessness: On Depression, Development, and Death*. San Francisco: W. H. Freeman.

Shaw, R. (1967). *The Man in the Glass Booth*. London: Chatto & Winders.

Shengold, L. (1989). *Soul Murder*. New Haven, CT: Yale University Press.

Siedlecka, J. (1994). *Czarny Ptasior*. Gdansk, Wydawnitstwo Marabut Warszawa, Wydawnitstwo D. F. S. English translation manuscript, trans. Agnieszka Kmin.

Sifneos, P. E. (1967). Clinical observation on some patients suffering from a variety of psychosomatic diseases. *Acta Medica Psychosomatica*. Proceedings of the 7th European Conference on Psychosomatic Research. Rome, Sept. 11–16, pp. 452–458.

——— (1973). The prevalence of "alexithymic" characteristics in psychosomatic patients. *Psychotherapy and Psychosomatics* 22:255–262.

——— (1975). Problems of psychotherapy of patients with alexithymic characteristics and physical disease. *Psychotherapy and Psychosomatics* 26:65–70.

Sloan, J. P. (1994). Kosinski's war. Life and letters. *The New Yorker*, October 10, pp. 46–53.

Stern, D. N. (1985). *The Interpersonal World of the Infant*. New York: Basic Books.

Stern, M. M. (1951a). Pavor nocturnus. *International Journal of Psycho-Analysis* 32:302–309.

——— (1951b). Anxiety, trauma, and shock. *Psychoanalytic Quarterly* 20:179–203.

Tanay, E. (1968). Initiation of psychotherapy with survivors of Nazi persecution. In *Massive Psychic Trauma*, ed. H. Krystal, pp. 219–233. New York: International Universities Press.

Taylor, J. (1991). The haunted bird: the death and life of Jerzy Kosinski. *New York Magazine*, July 15, pp. 25–37.

Weisman, A. D., and Hackett, T. P. (1961). Predilection to death. *Psychosomatic Medicine* 23:232–256.

Wilson, J. P., and Rafael, B., eds. (1993). *International Handbook of Traumatic Stress Syndromes*. New York: Plenum.

Discussion

Rita V. Frankiel, Ph.D.

Editors' Comments

Dr. Frankiel, in her appreciative discussion of Dr. Krystal's paper, attempts to bridge his contribution to everyday psychoanalytic work, not only with Holocaust survivors but with those reared in families with profoundly damaging effects on personhood. She provides a long quote from Primo Levi's haunting autobiography, *Survival in Auschwitz*, that illustrates the total dehumanization of the concentration camp experience. Both Levi and Kosinski eventually ended their own lives. She states that Krystal's work helps us as analysts to tolerate many of the frustrating resistances of victims of abuse and to understand our countertransferences.

It is a pleasure to respond to Henry Krystal's rich and far-ranging presentation. I have had the opportunity to read a longer version of this chapter and his book *Integration and Self-Healing* (1988), and so have had the chance to try to encompass the range and variety of the interests and commitments that have informed his productive career. Dr. Krystal starts by telling us of new findings in developmental neurobiology that demonstrate changes in brain structure that encode early experiences with primary caretakers. This research may ultimately show us why and how early disasters and omissions have such long-lasting consequences.

At the risk of some simplification, I would say that his central areas of research interest have been trauma and its consequences, survivorship and its costs, and alexythymia and its hazards and benefits for survival. I hope in my remarks to offer some bridges that will clarify the usefulness of these contributions to everyday psychoanalytic work not only with Holocaust survivors, but also with those patients who are struggling to survive early years in families whose dominant modes of relatedness have had damaging effects similar to the efforts to eliminate personhood in the concentration camps. I will review those of his research findings that I think most significant for us as psychoanalysts working with such patients.

Primo Levi's *Survival in Auschwitz* (1960), originally published as *If This Is a Man*, describes the process of stripping away all outer reminders and remnants of identity and attachment and their replacement with the identity of the prisoner, with a shaved head, rags for clothes, and a number tattooed on his arm. The senseless, useless, and crushing work required of the starving and brutalized prisoners also played its part in the program of exterminating first personhood, then persons. All in the camp were either "slaves or masters, the masters slaves themselves. Fear motivates the former, hatred the latter, all other forces are silent. All are enemies or rivals."

I have chosen a passage I think will illuminate some of Dr. Krystal's work about the special hazards that befell the adolescents in the camps. In his research on psychosomatic symptoms among survivors as they age, Dr. Krystal has noted that among survivors who were adults in the camps, 30 percent have such symptoms, with severity increasing with age; among those who were adolescents, the percentage climbs to 70 percent.

> He is Null Achtzehn. He is not called anything except that, Zero Eighteen, the last three figures of his entry number; as if everyone was aware that only a man is worthy of a name, and that Null Actzehn is no longer a man. I think that even he has forgotten his name, certainly he acts as if this was so. When he speaks, when he looks around, he gives the impression of being empty inside . . .
>
> Null Achtzehn is very young, which is a grave danger. Not only because boys support exhaustion and fasting worse than adults, but even more because a long training is needed to survive here in the struggle of each one against all, a training which young people rarely have. Null Achtzehn is not even particularly weak, but all avoid working with him. He is indifferent to the point of not even troubling to avoid tiredness and blows or to search for food. He carries out all the orders that he is given and it is foreseeable that when they send him to his death he will go with the same total indifference . . .
>
> But as all the rest of us try by every possible means to avoid work, Null Actzehn is the only one who works more than all. It is because of this, and because he is a dangerous companion that no one wants to work with him; and as, on the other hand, no one wants to work with me, because I am weak and clumsy, it often happens that we find ourselves paired together. [pp. 42–43]

Levi is injured as they work together. They are carrying a crushingly heavy support. Levi is in front. "At every step, I feel behind me his feet which tread on mine, as he is unable or cannot be bothered to keep in step." There is an "accident"; the load is dropped, and Levi cannot get out of the way so his foot is badly injured. He is in danger of being considered unfit for work—a sure death sentence.

In this incident, Levi pictures the state that Dr. Krystal had so vividly characterized in his work. Null Achtzehn's awareness of himself as human and connected with others is gone. Even his life is unimportant to him. Adolescent rebelliousness—thinking for oneself and making the others know it—is gone. The murderous feeling that would be so expected and so significant an aspect of health in these circumstances is gone and in its place is the automated, robotized death-in-life. Was this murderous feeling turned on Levi? We can't really tell. Levi does not judge. But we must allow ourselves to speculate: Was this accident one way that this boy could discharge some of the crushing burden of rage against one who was smaller, weaker, and a forgiving target? When we think about this boy, who becomes depersonalized and turns all of the hatred he would ordinarily have to work through in adolescence on himself and those around him, we can appreciate the survival mechanisms of the workers in wanting to stay as far away as possible.

In thinking about this incident and description by Levi, we can appreciate the contribution Dr. Krystal has made to our understanding of the consequences of these horrific experiences, culminating in a kind of auto-hypnotic state that takes over and surrenders them to inevitable death. Death for some, perhaps many, came in response to the extremes of hopelessness and helplessness.

Many who have survived have done so with remnants of the living death that precedes physical death. Some are plagued by the continuity of that state in the form of emotional blunting, regression of affects, the loss of the capacity to name intense emotional states, and the return to the body as the vehicle for recording and experiencing intense states in the form of psychosomatic diseases and intense pain. Where it was possible to have been active (as Levi was as a partisan who was caught and sent to Auschwitz only in 1943), the outcome of survivorhood was less dangerous and damaging than it was for others.

For Dr. Krystal, early empathic attunement and devoted caretaking leaves the person with a profound identification with the primary caretaker and his or her fantasied omnipotence. That identification provides the person with the conviction that he or she has the wherewithal to "make it." In Paul Ornstein's chapter in this book he invoked a similar phenomenon to explain his ability to plan and execute his escape from imprisonment in a work detail under the control of the Hungarian Army. In Dr. Krystal's view, this conviction of a benign omnipotence (mother's love) made it possible for many of those who survived to do so. This conviction also mitigated to some extent their survivor guilt, and allowed them to establish new marriages and new families in the camps long before they could have dealt with their grief over what had been lost—their loved ones and their entire world. I wonder to what extent incomplete mourning is actually at work in the impacted guilt, the psychosomatic symptom-formation, and the ongoing depression and insomnia of so many.

All of this also has implications for our work with other abused and damaged patients. In addition to his work with survivors, Dr. Krystal has illuminated the acute and chronic suffering of those who, as children, were raised in environments where there was limited capacity to meet physical and/or emotional needs even in earliest infancy, and so emerged traumatized. It is an accomplishment to tolerate awareness of these panic states and/or the numbness that defends against remembering or experiencing in a decodable fashion the painful messages that their bodies carry. One wants to block these messages or turn them into something else. Dr. Krystal's work has helped us reach the better level of awareness we need in order to tolerate frustrating resistances and resonate with the inner states of these victims of abuse, for that is the single best therapeutic method—exhaustingly painstaking and deadening as it may be—to see the patterns in the transference and countertransference that will slowly lead to decoding.

Derealization and depersonalization and other states of modified consciousness also derive from infantile traumatic states. They can be glimpsed only if we join with the victim by becoming aware of ourselves as captive, persecutor, or persecuted in his or her transference fantasies and/or enactments. In this regard, the work of Betty Joseph (1983) clarifies that we may be working with patients who want us to fail and not understand them while sometimes also hoping that we can nevertheless succeed in liberating them from their addiction to psychic states that cause self-neglect and failures of self-protection that brings them close to death. Ferenczi (1933) and Shengold (1989) have also made significant contributions to our understanding of how, in the analytic situation, we can find these phenomena repeated again and again. Shengold especially has offered ways of thinking about the role of analytic treatment in the recovery of early destructive affects, perpetuated in repetitively self-destructive ways as a defense against murderous feelings toward abusive and destructive caretakers.

Dr. Krystal points out that some Holocaust survivors and the grown-up survivors of infantile trauma and abuse have lost the capacity and perhaps even the interest in soothing and comforting themselves and in controlling and managing themselves. In his book *Integration and Self-Healing*, Krystal (1988) reminds us that denial of our mortality is an indispensable ingredient in our feeling of confidence in "going on being." He points out that the gift of Prometheus—blind hopes—conveys permission for self-protection, self-caring, and solace. In the myth, this self-caring and protecting function is violently opposed by Zeus, who seems to symbolize in this myth a thrust toward, and love of, death. Patients fear committing a "Promethean transgression" by facing their mortality; instead, they manifest a transference need that we as omnipotent analysts provide them the means for escaping; we must spare them the death-dealing hubris of taking care of themselves. In treatment, they develop what Dr. Krystal has called an "idolatrous transference," that is, a return to the infantile state in which all the vital and affective parts of one's self are attributed to the Primal Object and the self-caring is reserved to it too. All self-caring must be carried out under a 'franchise' from a Primal Object transference surrogate.

In their transferences some of these patients are willing to believe anything in order to feel that they have an alliance with the powerful one. The patient says, "Tell me what you want and I will deliver it to you." But it is more than an offer, it is an effort at coercion in the transference. Although such patients are superficially compliant, they are deeply cynical, disappointed, and prepared for further traumatization; one might say that they seem to seek and insist on it. In my experience, these patients often offer idealizing transferences behind which lies the wish to force the abuse they expect into the open. If idealization comes, can persecution be far behind?

At the end of his paper, Dr. Krystal turns to the life of Jerzy Kosinsky and with his customary thoroughness he reveals the story behind the story of Kosinsky's life for our inspection and compassion: the voyeuristic sadomasochism that was the legacy of his pathological relationship with his mother, intertwined with the personality-deforming fantasy distortions of the ominous fear- and hate-filled world within and without.

Dr. Krystal is to be thanked for the riches he has brought us in this article and in the years of work that have led up to it.

References

Ferenczi, S. (1933). On the confusion of tongues between adults and the child. In *Final Contributions to the Problems and Methods of Psycho-Analysis*, pp. 155–167. New York: Basic Books, 1955.

Joseph, B. (1983). On understanding and not understanding: some technical issues. *International Journal of Psycho-Analysis* 64:291–298.

Krystal, H. (1988). *Integration and Self-Healing*. Hillsdale, NJ: Analytic Press.

Levi, P. (1960). *Survival in Auschwitz: The Nazi Assault on Humanity*. New York: Collier, 1993.

——— (1960). *If This is a Man*. New York: Orion.

Shengold, L. (1989). *Soul Murder: The Effects of Childhood Abuse and Deprivation*. New Haven, CT: Yale University Press.

6

Narcissism and the Quest for Political Power

Jerrold M. Post, M.D.

Editors' Comments

Jerrold Post is a psychiatrist who has devoted his career to the field of political psychology. He has systematically examined influences of personality upon political behavior and has written broadly on the effects of illness and age upon leadership. He reminds us that there have been leaders who have been motivated by dreams of glory, some of whom have evidenced a drive for destructive power. In his carefully reasoned paper, he explores the relationship between narcissism and power, and illustrates this with material from leaders of the twentieth century. Post reminds us that if leaders with narcissistic characteristics were taken from the ranks of the public we would have very few leaders left, further suggesting that the differences between individuals with severe narcissistic personality and full-blown character disorders are only differences of degree.

Post defines narcissistic personality disorder, emphasizing the traits that have particular relevance for political behavior. He summarizes both Kohut's and Kernberg's psychoanalytic inquiries into narcissism. The phenomenology for the narcissistic personality is spelled out, drawing again on the work of Kernberg and Kohut, as well as that of Vamık Volkan. The psychogenesis of narcissism is also explicated.

As to the severely pathological leaders, Post tells us of Idi Amin Dada of Uganda, Nicolai Ceausescu of Rumania, Anwar Sadat, Hitler, Mussolini, Stalin, and Saddam Hussein. Drawing on psychobiographic and descriptive material concerning Saddam Hussein, he explores malignant narcissism and narcissistic rage. He also draws attention to the self object relationship narcissistic leaders have with their close advisors, emphasizing the potential for sycophantic advisers and resultant distortion of political decision making.

He also explores the charismatic leader–follower relationship, emphasizing the lock and key fit between the "mirror-hungry" leader and the "ideal-hungry" follower. He distinguishes between reparative charismatics, exemplified by Ataturk, the founder of the modern state of Turkey, and destructive charismatics, exemplified by Hitler. As Post reminds us, the range of themes relevant to political leaders illuminated by psychoanalytic understandings of narcissism and self psychology is very broad.

For the individual with dreams of glory and power, the political stage may be an irrestible platform on which to play out these dreams. Leaders impelled by dreams of glory have been responsible for some of the most glorious moments in human history, but leaders driven by an insatiable drive for power have been responsible for some of the most violent moments as well. This essay explores the relationship between narcissism and the quest for political power, using illustrative material from twentieth-century leaders.

It is probably not an exaggeration to state that if individuals with significant narcissistic characteristics were stripped from the ranks of public figures, the ranks would be perilously thinned, for the upper levels of government and industry are filled with "successful narcissists." After all, at one level narcissism is nothing more than extreme self-confidence, and the wedding of self-confidence and abilities is what makes for success. The differences between individuals with significant narcissistic personality features and those with the full-blown character disorder are differences of degree, not of kind, and under stress, mild narcissistic characteristics can become extreme and temporarily resemble the full-blown picture.

The Narcissistic Personality Disorder

The essential features of Narcissistic Personality Disorder as described in *DSM-IV* (1994) are a pervasive pattern of grandiosity, need for admiration, and lack of empathy. Narcissists are preoccupied with fantasies of unlimited success, power, brilliance, beauty, or ideal love. Individuals with this disorder have a grandiose sense of self-importance, believe that they are "special," and expect to be recognized as superior. They routinely overestimate their abilities and inflate their accomplishments, often appearing arrogant, haughty, boastful, and pretentious. Implicit in their inflated judgments of their own accomplishments is an underestimation of the contribution of others. They require excessive admiration and are hypersensitive to criticism. They have a sense of entitlement, that is, unreasonable expectations of especially favorable treatment or automatic compliance with their expectations. Often envious of others, they believe that others are envious of them and begrudge them their success. They lack empathy and are unwilling or unable to recognize or identify with the feelings and needs of others. This sense of entitlement combined with a lack of sensitivity to the wants and needs of others results in their being interpersonally exploitative, that is, in their taking advantage of others to fulfill their own needs. Close relationships invariably suffer because of the lack of empathy, the sense of entitlement, and the interpersonal exploitativeness.

The full-blown clinical narcissistic personality disorder is inconsistent with the ability to sustain effective leadership, but a number of the features described have obvious relevance to the decision-making and behavior of political leaders.

This article will first review in summary form current understandings of narcissism, considering its phenomenology, psychodynamics, and psychogenesis. In so doing, those features of the narcissistic personality that may influence the conduct of leadership and followership will be highlighted. Implications for political psychology will then be reviewed.

While not attempting an historical review of the development of the concept of narcissism, I would be remiss not to acknowledge the seminal role of the contributions of Sigmund Freud. In a 1914 article, "On Narcissism," Freud introduced the concepts of primary and secondary narcissism, the former being a natural phase of early pyschosexual development, the latter reflecting a withdrawal of libido from objects as it is redirected to the self. Thus narcissism reflects a return of the libido into the ego, with an excess of libidinal investment in the self and insufficient attachment or psychological investment (cathexis) in other (objects) (Freud 1915–1917). This imbalance of self versus other is at the heart of many of the narcissistic phenomena of particular relevance to political psychology.

In these early considerations of narcissism and its associated problems with object relations, Freud was laying the foundation for object relations theory. Later theorists who focused on object relations made major contributions to furthering understandings of narcissism. The contributions of these theorists and the role they played as foundations of the self psychology of Heinz Kohut are admirably summarized by Bacal and Newman (1990).

During the past two decades, psychoanalytic theorists have been concerned with illuminating the psychology of narcissism and borderline conditions. Heinz Kohut and Otto Kernberg have played leading roles in elucidating the developmental psychology, phenomenology, and psychoanalytic treatment of these conditions. Because of the importance of their contributions to the understanding of narcissism and the psychology of the self, the concepts of Kohut and

Kernberg will be given particular emphasis (See Kohut 1971, 1977, 1978, 1984 and Kernberg 1975, 1984).

In entering the Kernberg-Kohut thicket, the reviewer is fully award of the fierce partisanship of their loyalists. There is no intent to serve as arbiter, but rather to acquaint the reader with the breadth of their contributions. While there are some fundamental theoretical differences, and they often employ different technical language, each has addressed similar theoretical issues and clinical phenomena, and their work is often mutually reinforcing. Rather than systematically translate equivalent terms, the concepts of one of them will be presented when it is felt to be especially relevant to political psychology. Both Kernberg and Kohut have addressed the idealizing transference, for example, but the transferential postures identified by Kohut are notable for their presentational clarity and are presented because of their power in understanding leader–follower relationships. Similarly, both Kernberg and Kohut have addressed primitive narcissism, with Kohut referring to the archaic form of narcissism and Kernberg to malignant narcissism. Because of the clarity of Kernberg's conceptualization, and its utility for understanding certain leadership phenomena, such as the psychology of the destructive charismatic, his delineation of malignant narcissism has been presented.

Vamık Volkan, whose work is in the Kernbergian tradition, has made important clinical and theoretical contributions to the phenomenon of narcissism (1976, 1981, 1982). His scholarship is particularly notable for his applications of psychoanalytic understandings of narcissism to political leaders, as exemplified by his psychobiographic study of Ataturk (Volkan and Itzkowitz 1984) and his analysis of the manner in which the need for enemies contributes to international conflict (1988).

Charles Strozier and Marvin Zonis, both of whom work in the Kohutian tradition, have made valuable contributions to the relationship between narcissism and political phenomena. An especially valuable contribution of Strozier (1983) is his application of Kohut's concept of the "group self" to leader–follower phenomena. Zonis's

(1991) analysis of the relationship between the Shah of Iran's narcissistic personality and the political history of his nation is a notable example of psychoanalytically informed psychobiography.

Phenomenology

The narcissist's exaggerated sense of self-importance tends to be manifested as extreme self-centeredness, egocentricity, and self-absorption. Abilities and achievements tend to be unrealistically overestimated, but even minor setbacks can lead to a sense of particular unworthiness.

There is a preoccupation with fantasies involving unrealistic goals. These goals may include achieving unlimited power or fame. The fantasies frequently substitute for realistic activity in pursuit of success. But even when the goals are satisfied, it is usually not enough; there is a driven "pleasureless" quality to the ambitions that cannot be satisfied.

Kernberg (1975) has stressed an apparent paradox in the work life of narcissistic individuals. They may be quite successful professionally, apparently devoting their energies to socially productive endeavors, but this is, to use Kernberg's phrase, "pseudo-sublimatory," for the goal of their efforts is actually exhibitionistic, to gain recognition, fame, and glory. This search for recognition and adulation that drives these individuals springs from their excessive self-absorption, their intense ambition, and their grandiose fantasies. Underlying and impelling this quest is an inner emptiness and uncertainty about identity. Tartakoff (1966) has written of "the Nobel Prize complex," the search for acclaim by intellectually gifted narcissists.

The certainty of ultimate success to which narcissists feel entitled leads to both a sense of omnipotence and a feeling of invulnerability, a feeling that they cannot go wrong. This underlies the narcissist's capacity for risk taking; he behaves as if someone is watching over him, as if divine protection or charmed fate will ensure his success and well-being (Meissner 1979).

There is a constant search for admiration and attention, and more concern with appearance than substance. This quality, too, is insatiable, so there is a constant need for reassurance, a constant concern for how well the narcissist is doing, how well others think of him, and an exaggerated response to criticism or defeat that can lead to feelings of rage, inferiority, shame, humiliation, or emptiness.

The interpersonal relationships of narcissists are regularly and characteristically disturbed. Close relationships tend to vacillate between extremes of over-idealization and devaluation. Because these individuals are so self-absorbed, there is a failure of ability to empathize with others. Indeed others are seen as extensions of the self who are there only to supply admiration and gratification. The narcissist surrounds himself with admirers and requires a constant stream of adulation from them. Yet it is a one-way street, and when the follower is no longer useful to the psychological economy of the narcissist, he can be dropped suddenly without a backward glance. This precipitous fall from grace will frequently be bewildering to the individual dropped, who mistakenly believed he was highly valued by his hero. Indeed, his provision of psychological supplies, of adulation, *was* valued, but he was not seen as a separate individual with needs of his own. The narcissist is often extremely charming and delightful to be with, contributing to the false spell cast over his intimates.

An aspect of the "special" quality of these individuals is the feeling of entitlement they convey. They expect special treatment from others, expect others to do what they want, and will be angered when others fail to live up to their unreasonable demands. They regularly ignore the rights and needs of others in the service of their own self-aggrandizement. Thus arrogance is a characteristic feature of the narcissist, who is wrapped up in himself and contemptuous of others (Meissner 1979). There is accordingly a major inability to sustain loyal relationships over time. This quality of personal exploitiveness, with disregard for the feelings and needs of others, often leads narcissists to be described as "sharks."

The mirror image of the quest for adulation is sensitivity to slight and criticism. The narcissist is vulnerable and easily hurt, and goes through complicated maneuvers to avoid being hurt. He can put on a mask of cold indifference and can envelop himself in what Volkan (1982) has called "the glass bubble." Like the Little Prince, the narcissist feels he lives by himself in splendid isolation, a glorious but lonely existence enclosed by an impervious but transparent protection.

Because the narcissist is so vulnerable to injury psychologically, he can not afford to acknowledge ignorance. This in turn leads to major difficulties with learning, for the learning process carries with it an implicit assumption of lack of knowledge. Dogmatic certainty that has no foundation of knowledge is a posture frequently struck by the narcissist. This discomfort with learning is related to the sensitivity to constructive criticism noted above. If the narcissist's self-concept of perfection and brilliance is to be sustained, no one can give him new knowledge, and no aspect of his understanding is to be faulted.

Kernberg (1975) describes patients with narcissistic personalities as

> presenting excessive self-absorption usually coinciding with a superficially smooth and effective social adaptation, but with serious distortions in internal relationships with other people. They present various combinations of intense ambitiousness, grandiose fantasies, feelings of inferiority and over-dependence on external admiration and acclaim. Along with feelings of boredom and emptiness, and continuous searching for gratification of strivings for brilliance, wealth, power and beauty, there are serious deficiencies in their capacity to love and to be concerned about others. This lack of capacity for empathic understanding of others often comes as a surprise considering their superficially appropriate social adjustment. Chronic uncertainty and dissatisfaction about themselves, conscious or unconscious exploitiveness and ruthlessness toward others are also characteristic of these patients. [p. 264]

Volkan (1982) describes the narcissistic individual as

> regarding himself as endowed with great power, physical appeal and the right to assert his will. He gives the impression of ambitiously striving for brilliance in all he does. He seems to regard others—especially those not among his worshippers—as beneath notice. Although he views his supporters as adjuncts to himself, he is quick to deny their existence if they withdraw their awestruck allegiance. Behaving as though self-sufficient in a superior way, he feels he exists for others to admire. Nevertheless, close scrutiny of the behavior of such a person will reveal that, although he lives a glorious albeit lonely life in such isolation that he could be said to dwell within a "plastic or glass bubble," he is, paradoxically, constantly engaged with others on another level because he is object hungry. He actually has feelings of inferiority and thus is overdependent on the approving attention of other people. [p. 270]

Akhtar (1989) has usefully identified six characteristic dimensions of the Narcissistic Personality Disorder: self-concept; interpersonal relations; social adaptation; ethics, standards, and ideals; love and sexuality; and cognitive style. For each of these dimensions, there is both an overt and covert aspect. In effect, the covert aspect is the underlying feeling that is psychodynamically driving the surface manifestation. This helps explain some of the apparent contradictions in the narcissistic personality. Thus the overt picture of haughty grandiosity overlies feelings of inferiority; the overt picture of zealous morality overlies a corruptible conscience. The following chart summarizes the overt and covert aspects of these six dimensions.

Clinical Features of the Narcissistic Personality Disorder

I. Self-concept

Overt: inflated self-regard; haughty grandiosity; fantasies of wealth, power, beauty, brilliance; sense of entitlement; illusory invulnerability

Covert: inordinate hypersensitivity; feelings of inferiority, worthlessness, fragility; continuous search for strength and glory

II. Interpersonal Relations

Overt: lacks depth and involves much contempt for and devaluation of others; occasional withdrawal into "splendid isolation"

Covert: chronic idealization and intense envy of others; enormous hunger for acclaim

III. Social Adaptation

Overt: social success; sublimation in the service of exhibitionism (pseudo-sublimation); intense ambition

Covert: chronic boredom, uncertainty, dissatisfaction with professional and social identity

IV. Ethics, Standards, and Ideals

Overt: apparent zeal and enthusiasm about moral, sociopolitical, and aesthetic matters

Covert: lack of any genuine commitment; corruptible conscience

V. Love and Sexuality

Overt: seductiveness; promiscuity; lack of sexual inhibitions; frequent infatuations

Covert: inability to remain in love; treating the love object as extension of self rather than as separate, unique individual; perverse fantasies; occasionally, sexual deviations

VI. Cognitive style

Overt: egocentric perception of reality; articulate and rhetorical; circumstantial and occasionally vague, as if talking to self; evasive but logically consistent in arguments; easily becomes devil's advocate

Covert: inattention toward objective aspects of events, resulting at times in subtle gaps in memory; "soft" learning difficulties; autocentric use of language; fluctuations between being over-abstract and over-concrete; tendency to change meanings of reality when self-esteem is threatened*

*From Akhtar 1989, p. 520; reprinted by permission of the author.

Psychogenesis[1]

In the earliest stage of development—the stage of primary narcissism—the infant does not distinguish between himself and others. He experiences the external world—his mother—as part of himself. He is not just the center of the universe, he is the universe. As the young child experiences the frustrating reality of the external world's less-than-perfect response to his needs, he begins to differentiate himself from it. He is demoted from being the universe to becoming merely its center. Two psychological constellations develop as ways of restoring a sense of completeness.

The first is the ideal or grandiose self.[2] The "mirroring" response of the mother—her admiration and loving attention—leads the child to feel special and highly valued. This treasured position is maintained by an important psychological mechanism: *splitting*. The

1. This summary of the normal and abnormal developmental psychology of narcissism is drawn from Post (1986a).

2. A major distinction between the theoretical formulations of Kohut and Kernberg is in relationship to the grandiose self. Kohut believes it reflects the fixation of an archaic "normal" primitive self, the basis for his positing a healthy line of narcissistic development. In contrast, Kernberg believes the grandiose self is always pathological, differing from normal infantile narcissism in that the internalized object images are pathological. The resulting pathological grandiose self is associated with primitive and defective superego formation (Kernberg 1985).

very young child is unable to tolerate the bad aspects of himself and his environment and to integrate them with the good ones into a realistic whole. He splits the good and the bad into the "me" and the "not me." By rejecting all aspects of himself that do not fit his ideal or grandiose self, the child attempts to maintain it.

The child's second mechanism for remedying frustration and incompleteness is to attach himself to an ideal object (Kernberg), or idealized parent imago (Kohut), which derives particularly from the father. This is the fantasized image of the all-powerful, all-knowing, all-giving, all-loving parent. The child gains his own sense of being complete and worthwhile by experiencing himself as connected to, or united with, his idealized object. In Crayton's (1983) formulation, "If I am not perfect, I will at least be in a relationship with something perfect."

If the child is traumatized during this critical period of development, his emerging self-concept is damaged, leading to the formation of what Kohut (1971) calls "the injured self." Such damage can occur in several ways. Children rejected by cold and ungiving mothers may be left emotionally hungry, with an exaggerated need for love and admiration. A different form of rejection is overprotection by the intrusive narcissistic mother. She cannot let her child individuate because she sees him as an extension of herself. Her own sense of perfection seems to depend on her child's perfection.

Kohut (1971) describes two principle vicissitudes of the "injured self," two personality patterns, two transferential postures. The first is the *mirror-hungry personality*. These individuals, whose basic psychological constellation is the grandiose self, hunger for confirming and admiring responses to counteract their inner sense of worthlessness and lack of self-esteem. To nourish their famished selves, they are compelled to display themselves in order to evoke the attention of others. No matter how positive the response, they cannot be satisfied, but continue seeking new audiences from whom to elicit the attention and recognition they crave. The relationship sought from others is the *mirroring selfobject* relationship, in which "recognition is felt to be provided by a significant other for what one has to offer, such as one's unique capacities, talents, abilities, and personal attractiveness" (Bacal and Newman 1990, p. 232).

The second consequence of the injured self is the *ideal-hungry personality*. These individuals can experience themselves as worthwhile only so long as they can relate to individuals whom they can admire for their power, prestige, beauty, intelligence, or moral stature. They forever search for such idealized figures. Again, the inner void cannot be filled. Inevitably, the ideal-hungry finds that his God is merely human, that his hero has feet of clay. Disappointed by discovery of defects in his previously idealized object, he casts him aside and searches for a new hero, to whom he attaches himself in the hope that he will not be disappointed again. Such individuals develop an *idealizing selfobject* relationship. An idealizing selfobject relationship "denotes the experience of feeling linked to the admired other: the self, in effect, walking proudly in the shadow of his admired object" (Bacal and Newman 1990, p. 232).

The descriptions of the narcissistic personality that introduce this article are those of the *mirror-hungry personality*, which Bach (1985, 1990) has termed Type I narcissism. It is this Type I narcissism that has important implications for leader psychology. The *ideal-hungry personality*, which Bach has termed Type II narcissism, has important implications for the psychology of followers. For political psychology, these well-delineated transferential postures described by Kohut represent a significant contribution to understanding leader-follower relationships.

The Narcissistic Personality: Implications for Political Decision-Making and Behavior

The Relationship of the Narcissistic Leader with His Advisors

Am I the lover
Or beloved? Then why make love? Since I

Am what I long for, then my riches are
So great they make me poor.

Ovid, *Metamorphoses* (on the myth of Narcissus)

Narcissism can be considered infatuation with the self so extreme that the interests of others are ignored and others serve merely as mirrors of ones own grandiosity (Alford 1988, p. 2). Because the primary loyalty of narcissists is to themselves, they accordingly have a difficult time sustaining loyal relationships over time. The narcissist tends to relate to individuals in his interpersonal environment as psychological extensions of himself, so that psychologically they are not experienced as individuals in their own right, with needs and wants of their own. Their major psychological function is to maintain the narcissist's self-esteem. Because the primary function of relationships is the maintenance of the fragile self-esteem of the narcissist, they are called *selfobject relationships* (Kohut 1971). An object is a selfobject when it is experienced intrapsychically as providing functions in a relationship that evoke, maintain, or positively affect the sense of self (Bacal and Newman 1990, p. 229). Strictly speaking, selfobjects are neither self nor object; they are the subjective aspect of a function performed by a relationship (Wolf 1985, p. 271).

The Narcissist in Power

Volkan (1980) has emphasized that the narcissist in power has special psychological advantages in terms of sustaining his grandiose self-image. He can actually restructure his reality by devaluing or even eliminating those who threaten his fragile self-esteem. A striking example follows.

Idi Amin Dada of Uganda: Executing Threats to His Self-Esteem

His Excellency President for Life Field Marshall Al Hadj Dr. Idi Amin Dada, V.C., D.S.O., M.C., Lord of All the Beasts of the Earth

> and Fishes of the Sea and Conquerer of the British Empire in Africa in General and Uganda in Particular. [Self-assigned full title of Idi Amin]

Idi Amin Dada took over the reins of the country in a military coup in 1971. The most striking features of his regime were the extent of his narcissistic grandiosity and his defensive violence against those who threatened his fragile self-esteem. During his eight-year rule from 1971 to 1979, Amin killed approximately 375,000 Ugandans out of a population of eleven-and-a-half million.

Amin's largely self-awarded official titles betray not only the massive underlying insecurity that required such exaggerated grandeur, but also the lack of sense of impact upon his audience. The finishing flourish to the composite title, "Lord of All the Beasts of the Earth and Fishes of the Sea, and Conqueror of the British Empire in Africa in General and Uganda in Particular," while comic, reflects a deep pathology.

These grandiose titles were consistent with his modest self-evaluation: "I myself consider myself the most powerful figure in the world" (Melady 1977, p. 17). On several occasions Amin claimed that God had come to him in a dream and chosen him for this paramount role. God had also told him in a dream to expel Uganda's Asians. Out of a desire to show his importance (and please his supporters) he demanded that "any British citizen who wants to see me must kneel before me" (Melady 1977, p. 18–19). He may not have carried out that demand but he did have squads of mostly elderly Britishers carry him for twenty-five miles on a sedan chair in public procession. That was later in his rule, and by then he weighed over three hundred pounds. In a speech on that day he said he would go to London, with or without the British government's permission, and be carried through that city's streets.

Amin would write long and ill-informed advisory cables to world leaders and publish them. He criticized President Nixon for his conduct of the Vietnam War, and when the Watergate scandal broke, wrote letters of advice to Nixon. The context of the grandiose self-evaluation quoted above suggests how threatened and powerless Amin felt under his boastful facade and demonstrates how he compensated with grandiosity of ludicrous proportions. At another time he said, "I do not want to be controlled by a superpower. I myself consider myself to be the most powerful figure in the world and that is why I do not let any superpower control me" (Sunday Times 1978).

He continued to boast of honors he received from countries he claimed to despise, such as Britain's Victoria Cross, the "V.C." of his title. Although he praised Hitler and charged Israel with being the enemy of mankind, he nevertheless was proud of his Israeli connections and displayed the wings of the Israeli airforce on the uniform he wore for his portrait on Ugandan currency.

Although many remarked on Amin's cunning and shrewdness, his intelligence was regarded as limited. Amin himself seemed to sense this. Frustrated by his inability to understand policy discussions with his chief civil servants, he acted without consultation or consideration. "[A]s a military man I know how to act. I am a man of action," he boasted near the beginning of his rule (Melady 1977, p. 167). He confessed to his British former-commanding officer, Ian Grahame, that he could not even follow the English of the British government ministers and journalists, and he asked Grahame to translate for him.

The one-time sergeant was clearly inadequate to the task of nurturing a national economy, of carrying on international relations, and of developing social institutions. One of his ministers reported that Amin could not sit in an office very long and could not concentrate on a single topic for half a morning. The Nigerian journalist Peter Enahero, who spent time in Uganda, observed Amin and interviewed those close to him. He remarked that Amin

> is the kind of man who approaches a thorny problem with an empty mind. It is when he begins to address an audience that solutions suddenly fill his head. Apparently, he then immediately utters these thoughts lest he forget them. And then to prove he does not lack the

> courage of his convictions he orders his ministers to implement "the decisions of my government." [cited in Listowel 1973, pp. 183–184]

Amin always had a tendency to externalize, and with such persons paranoid reactions become a defense against inadequacy. Amin's diplomatic and domestic failures increased the stress upon him, which contributed to his paranoid psychopathology. Criticism could not be tolerated. Failures were the fault of others. Sometimes individuals were blamed for their alleged stupidity or for their individual knavery, but the preferred explanation was conspiracy.

Amin's violence was sweeping, but it focused particularly on intellectuals and the educated elite. He initially courted the intellectual elite, but each intelligent, well-educated, and competent individual was a painful reminder of Amin's own inadequacies. Having left school after the sixth grade, Amin remarked shortly after taking power: "Sometimes people mistake the way I talk for what I am thinking. I never had any formal education—not even a nursery school certificate. But sometimes I know more than Ph.Ds" (cited in Melady 1977, p. 167).

Patrick Marnham, a journalist who spent time in Amin's Uganda, wrote a retrospective of the period six years after the tyrant's fall: "Looking back on the Amin days, it was his fear and hatred of educated people that were both the most characteristic and unpredictable aspects of his tyranny. . . . The better you served him, the more likely you were to attract his resentment" (1985, p. 80). The criticism of Amin's leadership was coming especially from the educated elite. How to eliminate such threats to his self-esteem? Execute the intellectuals. In effect Amin sought to eliminate criticism by literally eliminating the critics who psychologically threatened him.

Narcissistic Insecurity Produces Sycophantic Advisers

Some narcissistic leaders so crave adulation that they surround themselves with individuals who uncritically assure them of the excellence of their plans, protect them from knowledge of public discontent, and so on. These advisors sense their leader's need for uncritical adulation and agreement, and have been sensitized by the abrupt departure of advisors who dared to criticize or who brought unpleasant news. In effect, the self-esteem maintenance function dominates, and the leader surrounds himself with sycophants. A narcissistic leader who has selected his inner circle on this basis may be entirely in touch with psychological reality, as measured by psychological tests, but by dint of surrounding himself with anxious sycophants can be entirely out of touch with political reality. This was the situation with Anwar Sadat. Sadat always had a special sense of his own abilities. In making the overture to Israel, he overrode his advisers' strenuous objections. Rewarded with the Nobel Peace Prize, he became all the more convinced of the preeminence of his own views, further devaluing his advisers. Any advisor who deigned to criticize Sadat was expelled from his position, leading to an increasingly sycophantic leadership circle, who identified external sources of popular discontent, reluctant to suggest that it was Sadat's policies that were producing the unrest.

In the political sphere, because of the leader's control over his environment, he is able to transform his reality and make use of his rage to intimidate subordinates who challenge his narcissistically constructed reality. Thus Hitler, Mussolini, and Stalin used rage to intimidate subordinates.

A particularly telling example is that of Saddam Hussein. In 1982, when the war with Iran he had initiated in 1980 was going badly, Saddam wished to terminate the conflict. But by now Ayatollah Khomeini of Iran was obsessed with Saddam and indicated there would be no peace until Saddam was no longer leader of Iraq. Saddam called a cabinet meeting and described the dilemma, that there would be no peace unless he stepped down. To a man, Saddam's advisers indicated that of course he must stay at Iraq's helm. Saddam then pressed further, asking his advisers for their "frank, candid, and creative suggestions." His Oxford-educated minister of health, Dr. Ibrahim, cleverly suggested that Saddam might consider stepping down temporarily until the goal of peace was achieved, and then resume the presidency. Saddam, as the story goes, gravely thanked him for his candor and had him arrested on the spot. The minister's wife pled with Saddam to return her husband to her, which he did the following day, in a black canvas body bag, cut into pieces. This powerfully concentrated the attention of the remaining ministers, who insisted that Saddam stay in power, which he did, and the war with Iran went on for another bloody eight years. Saddam Hussein's penchant for killing advisors who criticized him led to the construction of a circle of uncritical admirers, who feared for their lives. There is, as Horowitz and Arthur note, no room for independent thinkers in the advisory circle of narcissistic leaders (1988). The group of sycophantic advisors can in effect become a selfobject to the fragile narcissist needing uncritical admiration and agreement.

In contrast to sycophants who tell the leader what they believe he wants to hear, the advisor who performs healthy selfobject functions for his leader both shores up the self-esteem and ensures that the leader is accurately in touch with political reality. Examples of such relationships are Colonel House to Woodrow Wilson, Louis Howe to Franklin Delano Roosevelt, and Theodore Sorenson to John Fitzgerald Kennedy. The foregoing is not meant to imply that Wilson, Roosevelt or Kennedy were full-blown narcissistic characters, but a reading of relevant psychobiographic materials certainly suggests there were significant narcissistic elements in the personalities of each of these leaders. Moreover, the quality of the relationships they had with their close advisors strongly resembles that with "the healthy self-object" as described above.

Belief System and Cognitive Processes

It is hard to identify the narcissistic personality with any consistent beliefs about the world, because his beliefs tend to shift. More than those of any other personality type, narcissistic personality's statements should be viewed as "calculated for effect." *The only central and stable belief of the narcissistic leader is the centrality of the self. What is good for him is good for his country.* The narcissist is capable of changing any position or radically altering previously held benefits if it serves his needs at the moment. Accordingly, placing great weight on the analysis of core determining beliefs from speeches when dealing with a narcissistic personality is apt to lead the unwary political analyst far astray. Words do not convey beliefs for the narcissist. Their only use is instrumental, to gain admiration and support; his rhetoric is calculated to further personal goals. It is not an accurate (conscious or unconscious) depiction of deeply held convictions, for the narcissist does not have deeply held convictions. His beliefs can be discarded fairly easily, and are not strongly associated with particular belief typologies.

In contrast to the compulsive personality, who places high stock on ideas and logical reasoning, and whose decisions are often made in relationship to stable mental schemata or belief systems, for the narcissist, words and ideas are designed to enhance the narcissistic leader's position. Judgments can be changed rapidly and positions reversed without a qualm of conscience in response to changes in the interpersonal environment.

Thus the conscience of the narcissist is dominated by self-interest. Unlike the sociopath, who is without an internal beacon, without an internalized body of scruples and principles, the narcissist does indeed have a conscience but it is a flexible one. Nevertheless, his self-image is of himself as principled and scrupulous, who, if he has reversed himself, did so because of circumstantial changes. Thus he communicates utter sincerity and trustworthiness, so that the unwary may be completely taken in by the trustworthiness of the narcissist who seems to be completely sincere, and indeed, at the moment, he is. The righteous indignation with which he stands in judgment of the moral failure of others often poses a striking contrast to his own self-concerned behavior and seems hypocritical to the outside observer.

By far the most important cognitive heuristic for the narcissistic personality's understanding of the world is by reference to his own personal experiences. Because of the requirement to be seen as all-wise and all-knowing, it is difficult for the narcissist to acknowledge ignorance and seek or accept information or constructive criticism of his ideas. It is difficult for the narcissist to rely on experts, for to do so is to acknowledge someone with superior knowledge. The reluctance to admit ignorance can contribute to flawed information search and problem solving.

Moreover, the centrality of self-interest dominates the search for information. For the narcissistic leader, the problems are not the threats to the country and what can be done to meet these threats, but how he can use this situation to either preserve or enhance his own reputation.

Because the narcissist sees everything as revolving around himself, there is a tendency to equate self-interest with the interests of the nation, a personal corollary of "Engine Charley" Wilson's claim, "What's good for General Motors is good for the nation." This attitude goes beyond naked self-interest, for the narcissistic individual genuinely believes that the national interest and national security are crucially contingent upon his reelection or reappointment. In its extreme form, the narcissistic leader comes to identify himself with his country. Saddam Hussein and his subordinates would regularly proclaim, "Saddam is Iraq and Iraq is Saddam" and for Hussein, the concept of an Iraq without his leadership was inconceivable.

Image of the Adversary

The centrality of the self of the narcissist has interesting implications for his image of the adversary. For one thing, the narcissistic personality has a profound inability to empathize, to understand different points of view, different interests or different perspectives. Perhaps even more importantly, he tends to greatly exaggerate the degree of influence one can have on the internal politics or external actions of other nations. In a negotiation, he may place overly great confidence upon his abilities to influence the other. Moreover, insofar as the narcissist has an exaggerated view of his own abilities and likelihood of success, there is a corresponding tendency to devalue the strength and competence of the adversary.

In a major contribution to political psychology, Volkan (1988) has addressed a human characteristic that is especially pronounced for narcissistic personalities and that has important implications for images of the adversary: *the need to have enemies*. He has observed that externalization of the "bad self" is a normal feature of childhood development. In early and mid-adolescence, targets of externalization can become crystallized; Volkan offers several powerful examples of the crystallization of the enemy during adolescence in situations of ethnic conflict. Volkan has observed the need to deny the sameness of oneself and the enemy and instead to focus on differences—what he calls "the narcissism of minor differences"—in the service of maintaining the psychologically "useful" internal concept of the enemy.

Crisis Decision-Making

These special characteristics of the narcissistic leader's psychology and interpersonal relationships have an important impact upon his leadership behavior and decision-making in general, but particularly in crisis situations. Whether the narcissistic leader is surrounded by sycophants or has selfobject relationships that can assist him in accurately assessing the nature of his adversary, in evaluating the completeness of his plans, and in making mid-course corrections is especially important in crisis situations.

Because of his difficulties in empathizing with others, he will have a difficult time putting himself into the mind of his adversary. Having a tendency to identify himself with the nation, he will have a difficult time in separating national interest from self-interest.

In characterizing practitioners of "hardball politics," Etheredge (1979) describes a variant of the narcissistic personality often encountered in the corridors of power. For these individuals, image and career enhancement are always primary values. Crises do not eclipse this personality tendency; to the contrary, for "hardball politicians" crises are opportunities to seize the moment. It was probably the "hardball" narcissistic personality whom the cynical senior government official had in mind when he described crisis as "an optimal opportunity for a bureaucratic power player to gain senior level visibility and maximize his organizational position." Thus, as he went on to say, the primary interest for such an individual is not the crisis but who goes to the White House for the morning meeting. Since gaining access to power is a primary value for such an individual, knowledge becomes power, a precious commodity to be held tightly and used to one's advantage.

The Optimism of Groupthink

One of the characteristics of "groupthink" identified by Janis (1972) is over-optimism concerning the likelihood of success, and he offers a social-psychological explanation for this over-optimism. Janis sees it as a consequence of unusually high group cohesion, which he treats as a necessary condition for concurrence-seeking to occur as a way of coping with the stress of crisis decision-making. But as we have observed, the narcissist places overly high stock on his own judgments and tends to over-estimate the probability of success for any plans he is formulating. Contributing to this is the sense of omnipotence and invulnerability that leads to a sense that nothing can go wrong with his plans; this in turn leads to the tendency to take risks (Meissner 1979). This narcissistic tendency to over-optimism may well contribute to the overly optimistic group appraisals described by Janis. Moreover, the psychophysiology of stress can lead to an "adrenaline high," which also can lead to over-optimism. The personality and psychophysiologic explanations of over-optimism do not compete with that of Janis. Rather, it is being suggested that the observed over-optimism may be multiply determined. In addition to the social-psychological explanation offered by Janis, it may also be that the psychophysiology of stress and the narcissistic over-evaluation earlier described contribute to this characteristic phenomenon and probably interact. The "adrenaline high" produced by stress may magnify the already present tendency towards optimism in a consensus-seeking group of high-level decision-makers abundantly endowed with narcissistic personality traits.

Malignant Narcissism

In Kernberg's (1975, 1984) view, the development of the pathological grandiose self is associated with primitive and defective superego formation. This combination of extreme grandiosity with a defective superego are core components of a syndrome described by Kernberg (1984), which he considers the most dangerous personality disorder. This syndrome, malignant narcissism, has four core components:

1. Grandiose narcissism with such extreme self-absorption that there is an incapacity to empathize with the pain or suffering of others;
2. A defective superego or conscience;
3. Ego syntonic aggression—the subject's use of aggression in the service of his own needs—is constrained;
4. A paranoid outlook. Highly suspicious and ready for betrayal, the subject views himself as surrounded by enemies (which in truth he often is), but does not comprehend his own role in creating those enemies. He then justifies his aggression in pursuit of his own unbounded needs as required by the enemies without.

A political-psychological analysis (Post 1991a) of Saddam Hussein's personality and political behavior provided phenomenological and longitudinal evidence that Saddam possessed to a significant degree the personality traits characteristic of malignant narcissism. The analysis suggested that it was the political expression of this personality that gave rise to the violence associated with Saddam Hussein's twenty-two years as Iraq's preeminent leader and to his political-military conduct during the Gulf crisis.

Hussein's early life experiences were extremely traumatic. His father died during his mother's pregnancy with Saddam, and an older brother also reportedly died of cancer, during the pregnancy. After a period of depression, his mother in accordance with cultural tradition married her brother-in-law. Saddam's stepfather was both physically and psychologically abusive to the young Saddam, who at age 9 fled to the home of his maternal uncle Khairallah.

In conducting psychobiographic research on political leaders, it is crucial to decipher the personal myth of the narcissist (Lester 1986), the grandiose fantasy that impels action. Saddam's Uncle Khairallah filled his head with dreams of glory, placing him in the tradition of Nebuchadnezzar, who liberated Jerusalem in 597 B.C., and Saladin, who liberated Jerusalem in 1187. He imbued Saddam with the notion that it was his destiny to play a heroic role in Arab history, unifying the Arab nation.

But these dreams of glory were compensating for a wounded self. Saddam climbed a violent path to the leadership of Iraq, ruthlessly eliminating threats to his power, justifying his extremities as "revolutionary pragmatism." This was the same justification he used throughout his career for rapidly changing his course when his decisions were no longer productive.

How was it that the revolutionary pragmatist Saddam Hussein did not reverse his course when confronted with the overwhelming force of the Western alliance? After the invasion, when Saddam Hussein forcefully called attention to the inequity of non-enforcement of United Nations resolutions concerning Palestine, it was not out of a deep concern for the Palestinian people. But they responded by elevating him to heroic status, seeing Saddam as their hope and saviour. Their unanticipated adulation represented the actualization of a long-cherished but frustrated dream, to become the preeminent hero of Arab world, inheriting the leadership mantle of Nasser. Their response engaged Saddam's heroic self, which heretofore had languished in obscurity (Post 1991b). Thus Saddam's personal myth was fulfilled when he was plunged into the spotlight of international prominence and had his self-definition of courageous Arab strongman confirmed by the response of his followers. He was at last where he was supposed to be, on a hero's quest. It was a veritable explosion of narcissistic supplies, and no doubt contributed to over-optimism. At long last Saddam had the recognition that he had long desired, but he never had. At long last he was a powerful world leader. And when the conflict became personalized—George Bush versus Saddam Hussein—this magnified his heroic stature. It also made it impossible for him to back down. Never again would he yield to powerful authority. It would have been an unthinkable capitulation. Moreover, his grandiosity had reached such heights that it was unthinkable that he would not win.

Nicolae Ceausescu of Rumania also demonstrated the characteristics of the malignant narcissist. Like Saddam, he created a cult of personality in his country. For both Saddam and Ceausescu, the architecture of their palaces was a metaphor for their narcissistic psychopathology: each had a grand and opulent palace, under which was a well-fortified bunker with escape routes. Under the grandiose facade of the malignant narcissist is a well-defended siege mentality.

Narcissistic Rage

The grandiose facade of the narcissist rests upon a foundation of insecurity. When a narcissistic wound is suffered, it can promote profound narcissistic rage. Both Kohut (1972) and Kernberg (1975) have addressed the intensity of the rage and the violent actions it can promote. Kohut observes:

> The need for revenge, for righting a wrong, for undoing a hurt by whatever means and a deeply anchored, unrelenting compulsion in the pursuit of all these aims, which gives no rest to those who have suffered a narcissistic injury—these are the characteristic features of narcissistic rage in all its forms and which set it apart from other kinds of aggression. . . . The opponent who is the target of our mature aggressions is experienced as separate from ourselves. . . . The enemy who calls forth the archaic rage of the narcissistically vulnerable,

> however, is seen by him . . . *as a flaw in a narcissistically perceived reality.* [1972, reprinted in Kohut 1978, pp. 637–638]

The target of aggression, the persecutor, is the individual or group that is associated with a flaw in a "narcissistically perceived reality." This is particularly the case when there are significant paranoid features exacerbating the wounded narcissist's tendency to blame others for his disappointment. In the academic world, we are all familiar with the academic denied tenure who becomes obsessed with injustice and the personal pursuit of his persecutors. It is a persistent, smouldering, and all-consuming rage. Kernberg (1975) has emphasized the terror experienced by the individual who has become the target of the wounded narcissist's intense unremitting anger. Because of the "ego-weakening" nature of the archaic defenses of the primitive narcissist, there is apprehension that the rage, which is barely below the surface and barely contained, may at any minute lead to violence.

Kohut cites Captain Ahab in Melville's *Moby Dick* as being in the grip of interminable narcissistic rage, obsessed with the need for vengeance. In the world of politics, the quest for revenge can have major international ramifications and precipitate international crises. One interpretation of Saddam Hussein's invasion of Kuwait is that it was retaliation for the diplomatic "back of the hand" Kuwait dealt to Saddam, refusing even to discuss his grievances over territorial and eoconomic disputes.

The narcissist's rage is a self-righteous rage (Horowitz and Arthur 1988). The narcissist feels entitled, and when that sense of entitlement is disappointed, hurt, rage and retaliation can occur. Underlying the rage is shame and humiliation and a feeling of helplessness to right the perceived wrong. But acting upon the rage converts the sense of helplessness into a sense of mastery. Kohut has suggested that the revenge motive played a crucial role in the destiny of Germany after the humiliating defeat of 1918, leading to the tragic excesses of World War II.

Courage and the Martyr-Hero

In analyzing the role of courage in history, Kohut (early 1970s a) has drawn our attention to the role of the martyr-hero, who at moments of crisis draws strength by establishing a fantasized courage-supporting relationship to an idealized figure. Some, at these crucial moments, will hear the voices of God or see visions in which God appears to them. The narcissistic individual with dreams of glory may feel a profound imbalance when he is unable to meet his heroic destiny. When he does achieve that position, rather than feel anxious, instead he experiences a serenity or calm, for now the destined role of greatness can be played out. Thus, when Winston Churchill achieved the Prime Ministership at a moment of great national turmoil, he felt a great sense of calm descend over him. He was at last where he was destined to be (Kohut early 1970s b).

Narcissism and Charismatic Leader–Follower Relationships[3]

As observed in the discussion of the genesis of narcissism, the two vicissitudes of the "injured self," as described by Kohut (1971), are the "mirror-hungry" personality and the "ideal-hungry" personality. The "mirror hungry" personality requires a continuous stream of admiration to shore up his grandiose self and deny the underlying lack of self-esteem. For such an individual, a career in the political limelight provides a splendid stage. On the surface these individuals convey a sense of certainty and strength. The mask of extreme self-confidence is no mere pose, for so profound is the inner doubt, that a wall of dogmatic certainty is necessary to ward it off.

This strength and certainty are attractive leadership qualities but are particularly attractive to the "ideal-hungry" individual besieged by self-doubt who feels incomplete unless merged with the idealized other. Because these wounded followers seek a God-like leader to

3. This section draws on the author's article "Narcissism and Charismatic Leader-Follower Relationships" (Post 1986a).

follow, these intense attachments may be short lived. For as the leader's human flaws are revealed, idealization may be succeeded by disillusion, and the disappointed followers go on in their never ending quest for a heroic leader. The greater the magnitude of the idealization, the more bitter the disappointment that inevitably follows.

The weak ego boundaries of such individuals lead to a loss of individuality and a merger with the collective as well as with the leader. Thus an expanded "we" substitutes for a limited "I."In becoming such a follower, he is joining other followers and has now acquired an expanded self-concept. His relationship to both the leader and to the other followers is a selfobject relationship. Strozier (1983) has made an important application of Kohut's concept of the "group self" to understanding leader–follower relationships. Abse and Ulman (1977) have usefully elucidated the regression of the followers into a group self, and have depicted the horrifying extremity to which this loss of self-boundaries can lead in their analysis of the group suicide at Jonestown (Ulman and Abse 1983). Observing that narcissistically wounded individuals with a paranoid orientation find the externalizing rhetoric of terrorist groups attractive, Post (1986b) has suggested that a similar group self develops in the closed terrorist group, so that the group ethos becomes dominant. If "they" (the establishment) are responsible for society's (and our own) failures, it becomes not only not immoral to strike out violently against them, but is a moral imperative.

The lock and key fit of "mirror-hungry" leader and "ideal hungry" follower is at the core of charismatic leader–follower relationships. But in times of historical crisis, usually psychologically healthy individuals may temporarily become overwhelmed by external circumstances and will also find the "mirror-hungry" personality's posture of strength and confidence extremely attractive, and will temporarily regress and delegate omnipotence to him. The German people had a selfobject-like transference to the heroic figure of Hitler who, they hoped, would rescue them from their political and economic weakness. But when the moment of historical crisis is past, so too will the neediness of such followers, and they will then cast their charismatic hero in the dustbin of history. The most vivid example of this is the rapidity of the fall from power of Winston Churchill after the conclusion of World War II. His strength of leadership and confidence-inspiring rhetoric, so crucial in time of war, were now no longer necessary.

Volkan (1980) has distinguished between "destructive charismatics," as exemplified by Hitler, and "reparative charismatics," as exemplified by Ataturk, Gandhi, and Martin Luther King. The "destructive-charismatic" splits off the devalued part of himself, projecting it onto an external enemy who is then attacked. This mechanism is reflected in Hitler's scapegoating of the Jewish people, which became institutionalized in the destructive social policy of the Holocaust. In contrast, the "reparative charismatic" heals the psychological splits within himself as he heals the wounds of his nation. He "strengthens his self concept by idealizing his followers, urging them to excel, and seeing them as extensions of himself" (Volkan 1982, p. 345). In both cases, the leader has displaced a private need onto a public object and rationalized it in the public good but with radically different social consequences (Lasswell 1930, p. 76).

Kohut (1976) has distinguished between the charismatic and the messianic personality. The charismatic personality has a fixated grandiose self but has significant elements of conscience. For the messianic personality, the self and the idealized structure are fused and there is no separate superego to constrain behavior. These individuals consider themselves "exceptions," above the law. According to this scheme, "reparative charismatics" would equate to Kohut's charismatic personality, and "destructive charismatics" to Kohut's messianic personality. Both postures are attractive to the wounded individual seeking a source of strength in an omnipotent leader who becomes the admired selfobject, but the messianic personality is particularly dangerous because he is unconstrained by conscience. Should he become the head of a mass movement, so that the messianic self-concept is rewarded, the consequences can be extremely destructive.

The personality constellation of the destructive charismatic or the messianic personality is that of malignant narcissism as described by Kernberg. For the paranoid outlook characteristic of the malignant narcissist justifies the externalization of the aggression, and the absence of conscience permits its expression.

Psychobiographic Analysis of Narcissistic Leaders

In recent years a number of major psychobiographic studies informed by psychoanalytic understandings of the psychogenesis, psychodynamics, and phenomenology of narcissism and self psychology have been published. *The Immortal Ataturk: A Psychobiography* (Volkan and Itzkowitz 1985) is noteworthy for being the first major psychobiographic study to apply understandings of the psychology of narcissism to the study of great men. *Ataturk* literally means Father Turk, and the authors provide a persuasive array of evidence to indicate that Ataturk, who lost his father when he was quite young, sustained within himself an idealized father that was at the heart of his becoming father to his nation. Moreover, the grieving mother who was to cast such a shadow over Ataturk's early years became identified with his grieving nation, so that in healing his nation's wounds Ataturk was healing the split within his own psychic organization. In contrast to the destructive charismatic, as exemplified by Saddam Hussein, Ataturk is an example of the reparative charismatic.

Informed by the self psychology of Heinz Kohut, Zonis (1991) has authored a comprehensive psychobiography of the Shah of Iran that relates his fragile narcissistic grandiosity to the course of his nation's history. Making abundant use of memoirs, Zonis develops a convincing portrayal of the development of the Shah's grandiose narcissism and the manner in which it affected—indeed dominated—his leadership of his embattled nation. The Shah's flying fantasies, first analyzed in an earlier article (Zonis 1985) occupy a particularly powerful place in Zonis' portrayal, which draws on Kohut. Zonis observes that the Shah's capacity to take risks reflected his narcissistic sense of omnipotence and invulnerability, and in the magnitude of the risks he took were the origins of his "majestic fall." Strozier's provocative analysis of Abraham Lincoln's quest for union (1982) and Muslin and Jobe's (1991) psychobiographic study of Lyndon Johnson are also in the Kohutian tradition. What is impressive about these psychobiographic studies as a group is the dimension their authors' psychoanalytic perspective on narcissism and the psychology of the self adds to their portrayals of their subjects.

The Life Cycle of Narcissistic Leaders

The Dream is the driving force of the narcissistic leader. Crystallized during youth or young adulthood, the Dream has its origins during childhood (Post 1984). As Freud noted in "On Narcissism" (1914), parents tend to over-estimate their children, "ascribing to the child all manner of perfections," magnifying their virtues, and ignoring their faults. Reminiscent of Freud's characterization of the parent's view of "His Majesty, the Baby," the mother of Robert J. Hawke, the Labor Prime Minister of Australia, indicated that she looked into the crib and knew that her newborn son would someday be Prime Minister. To be sure, one parental idealization doth not a narcissist make, but such extraordinary over-evaluation, when sustained, may set in motion dreams of glory.

Thus some individuals are raised to be special, to be vehicles of their parents' success. High ambition fused with ability can indeed lead to great achievements, but frustrated dreams of glory in the political arena have been associated with acts of extreme assertion and major changes of political direction.

The gap between the Dream and reality can peak during two of the major transition periods in the life cycle as characterized by Levinson (1978). During the mid-life transition (roughly ages 38 to 43), most individuals go through a period of reevaluation. The end of youth, this transition period is characteristically associated with personal reassessment in both the personal and professional spheres. When an individual measures his life and finds himself wanting, it may impel him to action. Thus the number of divorces and career changes peak at this time. For individuals driven by Dreams of Glory, there is apt to be particular dissatisfaction. There is statistical data suggesting that mid-life psychological dissatisfaction may contribute to the disproportionate number of military coups undertaken by people of this age. When he was 42 years old, Stalin, increasingly anxious to become a leader in his own right, had a major confrontation with his mentor, Lenin (Tucker 1973).

The end of the heroic life can be particularly unsettling for the narcissistic leader. The vicissitudes of old age and illness can impel a leader to exaggerated action to achieve his dream before he dies. In 1973 the Shah of Iran became ill. (The diagnosis of cancer was established by his French physicians in April 1974.) In 1973 the Shah broke with OPEC, quadrupling the price of oil. The sudden infusion of revenues into a society with a poorly established infrastructure led to a revolution, was profoundly destabilizing, and ultimately paved the way for Khomeini's Islamic revolution. In his haste to accomplish his mission for his country, the Shah had superimposed his own personal timetable on that of his nation. Similarly Lifton (1968) has suggested that Mao Zedong's rush to glory in the societally dislocating Cultural Revolution was a response to the approach of his own death. Thus narcissism can impel men to reach for the stars, but when there is a significant gap between the dreams of glory and reality, precipitous actions can occur. The end of life is unthinkable for the consummate narcissist, and the narcissistic leader's reactions to frustrated dreams of glory can produce nightmares for his followers.

Concluding Observations

As the foregoing review indicates, there are many themes relevant to political leaders driven by a quest for power that can be illuminated by psychoanalytic understandings of the psychology of narcissism and of self psychology. Particularly helpful is the insight these understandings provide into the nature of the relationship between the leader and his followers, especially in charismatic leader–follower relationships. Because of the relationship of the narcissistic leader to his advisors, his image of the adversary, and his tendency to over-optimism and risk-taking, his decision-making is subject to distortion, especially in crisis situations. Psychobiographic studies of great men have been illuminated by understandings drawing on this body of knowledge. Because of the prevalence of the Dream throughout their lives, narcissistic leaders seeking glory and omnipotence are especially prone to react to the vicissitudes of the life cycle, and may, at the end of life, confronted with the gap between their dreams and their accomplishments, be moved to actions that history records as tragic.

References

Abse, D. W., and Ulman, R. B. (1977). Charismatic political leadership and collective regression. In *Psychopathology and Political Leadership*, ed. R. S. Robins, pp. 35–52. New Orleans, LA: Tulane University Press.

Akhtar, S. (1989). Narcissistic personality disorder: descriptive features and differential diagnosis. *Psychiatric Clinics of North America* 12:505–529.

Akhtar, S., and Thompson, J. A. (1982). Overview: narcissistic personality disorder. *American Journal of Psychiatry* 139:12–20.

Alford, F. (1988) *Narcissism*. New Haven, CT: Yale University Press.

American Psychiatric Association (1994). *Diagnostic and Statistical Manual of Mental Disorders*, 4th ed. Washington, DC: American Psychiatric Press.

Bacal, H. A., and Newman, K. M. (1990). *Theories of Object Relations: Bridges from Object Relations of Self Psychology*. New York: Columbia University Press.

Bach, S. (1985). *Narcissistic States and the Therapeutic Process*. Northvale, NJ: Jason Aronson.

——— (1990). Narcissism's expression may be mirroring or idealized transference. *Psychiatric Times* 7 (4).

Crayton, J. (1983). Terrorism and self psychology. In *Perspectives on Terror-*

ism, ed. Y. Alexander and D. Freidman. Wilmington, DE: Scholarly Resources.

Etheredge, L. (1979). Hardball politics: a model. *Political Psychology* 1(1):3–26.

Freud, S. (1914). On narcissism: an introduction. *Standard Edition* 14:67–102.

——— (1915–1917). Introductory lectures on psycho-analysis. *Standard Edition* 15–16.

Glassman, M. (1988). Kernberg and Kohut: A test of competing psychoanalytic models of narcissism. *American Journal of Psychoanalysis* 36:597–625.

Greene, M. (1984). The self psychology of Heinz Kohut. *Bulletin of the Menninger Clinic* 48:36–53.

Horowitz, M., and Arthur, R. (1988). Narcissistic rage in leaders: The intersection of individual dynamics and group process. *International Journal of Social Psychiatry* 34:135–141.

Janis, I. L. (1972). *Victims of Groupthink*. Boston: Houghton Mifflin.

Kernberg, O. (1975). *Borderline Conditions and Pathological Narcissism*. New York: Jason Aronson

——— (1976). *Object Relations Theory and Psychoanalysis*. New York: Jason Aronson.

——— (1984). *Serious Personality Disorder*. New Haven, CT: Yale University Press.

——— (1985). *Internal World and External Reality*. New York: Jason Aronson.

Kohut, H. (1971). *The Analysis of the Self*. New York: International Universities Press.

——— (1972). Thoughts on narcissism and narcissistic rage. *Psychoanalytic Study of the Child* 27:360–400. New Haven, CT: Yale University Press.

——— (early 1970s a). On courage. In *Self Psychology and the Humanities*, ed. C. Strozier, pp. 5–50. New York: Norton, 1985.

——— (early 1970s b). On leadership. In *Self Psychology and the Humanities*, ed. C. Strozier, pp. 51–72. New York: Norton, 1985.

——— (1976). Creativeness, charisma, group psychology. In *Freud: The Fusion of Science and Humanism*, ed. J. E. Gedo and G. H. Pollock, pp. 379–425. New York: International Universities Press.

——— (1977). *The Restoration of the Self.* New York: International Universities Press.

——— (1978). *The Search for the Self,* vols. 1 & 2. New York: International Universities Press.

——— (1984). *How Does Analysis Cure?* Chicago: University of Chicago Press.

——— (1985). *Self Psychology and the Humanities,* ed. C. Strozier. New York: Norton.

——— (1991). *The Search for the Self,* vol. 3. New York: International Universities Press.

Lasswell, H. D. (1930). *Psychopathology and Politics.* New York: Free Press.

Lester, E. (1986). Narcissism and the personal myth. *Psychoanalytic Quarterly* 15:453–473.

Levinson, D. (1978). *The Seasons of a Man's Life.* New York: Knopf.

Lifton, R. (1968). *Revolutionary Immortality: Mao Tse-tung and the Cultural Revolution.* New York: Norton.

Listowel, J. (1973). *Amin.* Dublin: Irish University Press.

Marnham, P. (1985). In search of Amin. *Granta* 17:69–82.

Meissner, W. W. (1979). Narcissistic personalities and borderline conditions: a differential diagnosis. In *Annual of Psychoanalysis,* ed. Chicago Institute for Psychoanalysis, 7:161–201. New York: International Universities Press.

Melady, T. P. (1977). *Idi Amin Dada: Hitler in Africa.* Kansas City, MO: Sheed, Andrews, and McMeel.

Muslin, H. L., and Jobe, T. H. (1991). *Lyndon Johnson: The Tragic Self. A Psychohistorical Portrait.* New York: Plenum.

Post, J. (1973). On aging leaders: possible effects of the aging process on the conduct of leadership. *Journal of Geriatric Psychiatry* 6:109–116.

——— (1984). Dreams of glory and the life cycle: Reflections on the life course of narcissistic leaders. *Journal of Political and Military Sociology* 12:49–60.

——— (1986a). Narcissism and the charismatic leader–follower relationship. *Political Psychology* 7:675–787.

——— (1986b). Hostilite, conformite, fraternite: the group dynamics of terrorist behavior. *International Journal of Group Psychotherapy* 36 (2), April.

——— (1991a). Saddam Hussein of Iraq: A political psychology profile. *Political Psychology* 13(2):278–289.

——— (1991b). Saddam Hussein of Iraq: Afterword. *Political Psychology* 13:4.

——— (1993). Current concepts of the narcissistic personality: implications for political psychology. *Political Psychology* 14(1):99–121.

Reid, W., and Wise, M. (1989). *DSM-III-R Training Guide*. New York: Brunner/Mazel.

Strozier, C. B. (1982). *Lincoln's Quest for Union: Public and Private Meanings*. New York: Basic Books.

——— (1983). Fantasy, self psychology and the inner logic of cults. In *The Future of Psychoanalysis*, ed. A. Goldberg, pp. 477–493. New York: International Universities Press.

Sunday Times of London (1978). October 22.

Tartakoff, H. (1966). The normal personality in our culture and the Nobel Prize complex. In *Psychoanalysis: A General Psychology*, ed. R. M. Lowenstein, L. M. Newman, M. Schur, and A. J. Solnit, pp. 222–252. New York: International Universities Press.

Tucker, R. (1973). *Stalin as Revolutionary 1879–1929*. New York: Norton.

Ulman, R., and Abse, D. (1983). The group psychology of mass madness: Jonestown. *Political Psychology* 4:637–661.

Volkan, V. (1976). *Primitive Internalized Object Relations: A Clinical Study of Schizophrenia, Borderline and Narcissistic Patients*. New York: International Universities Press.

——— (1980). Narcissistic personality organization and reparative leadership. *International Journal of Group Psychotherapy* 30:131–152.

——— (1981). Transference and countertransference: an examination of internalized object. In *Object Relations and Self: A Developmental Approach*. New York: International Universities Press.

——— (1982). Narcissistic personality disorder. In *Critical Problems in Psychiatry*, ed. J. O. Cavenor and H. K. Brodie, pp. 332–350. Philadelphia: Lippincott.

——— (1988). *The Need to Have Enemies and Allies*. New York: Jason Aronson.

Volkan, V., and Itzkowitz, N. (1984) *The Immortal Ataturk*. Chicago: University of Chicago Press.

Wolf, E. (1985). The search of confirmation: technical aspects of mirroring. *Psychoanalytic Inquiry* 5:271–282.

Zonis, M. (1985). Fear of flying and phallic narcissism. In *Psychological Approaches to Middle East Studies*. Chicago: University of Chicago Press.

——— (1991). *Majestic Failure: The Fall of the Shah*. Chicago: University of Chicago Press.

7

Omnipotence, or the Delusional Aspect of Ideology, in Relation to Love and Power

Zvi Lothane, M.D.

Editors' Comments

Dr. Lothane, who has written extensively on the Schreber Case, brings to his contribution a knowledge of social theory and philosophy and argues that insufficient attention has been paid to Freud's more sociological essays: "Totem and Taboo," "Psychology and the Analysis of the Ego," "The Future of an Illusion," and "Civilization and Its Discontents." Lothane emphasizes the irrational nature of omnipotence, arguing that love, power, and ideology do not exist in isolation. He states that every communication whether it is verbal or nonverbal is both self- and other-directed, intrapsychic, interpersonal, and transpersonal. He distinguishes between love and libido and argues that Freud paid insufficient attention to power in human relations. Power begins in the family and power is a necessary condition for the preservation of the species. And in the political realm, power and authority define reality as government wields the ultimate power. Any abuse of power, whether it is by a class, a family, or the state, may lead to omnipotence.

Omnipotence in psychoanalytic texts is viewed as descriptive, dynamic, and developmental. Lothane points to the case of "The Rat Man," who succumbed to obsessional belief in his own omnipotence, and he reminds us that Ferenczi very early in the history of psychoanalysis saw omnipotence as a stage in the development of the child. Lothane distinguishes between the power of love and the omnipotence of love and shows how Freud, in the group psychology paper, contrasted social and narcissistic levels of being; he further shows Freud's debt to many of the pioneers in the study of the psychology of crowds, mobs, and masses, including Gustav LeBon.

He studies the Hitler period in Germany and its delusional ideology and demonstrates how injurious are ideologies that from the very beginning bear the stamp of unreason, such as racism, anti-Semitism, and cults and absolute monarchy. He introduces us to a reading of *Mein Kampf* and its irrational ideological roots and shows that Hitler's adherents included not only the masses but even someone as seemingly sophisticated as Carl Jung. Lothane praises the group psychology book, arguing that not since Aristotle has there been such a deep philosophical insight into the human condition and that in every mental act another is invariably involved, thus underlining the power of Freud's sociological writings.

We begin with the connection between omnipotence and the interplay of three social forces: love, power, and ideology. From the outset I emphasize the irrational nature of omnipotence and locate these three forces in social, or interpersonal, relations, because love, power and ideology do not exist in isolation, and because psychoanalysts, due to their traditional preoccupation with the individual, have paid scant attention to Freud's sociological essays. The essays in question are "Totem and Taboo" (1913); "Massen Psychologie und Ich-Analyse" (1921), misleadingly translated by Strachey as "Group Psychology and the Analysis of the Ego," since mobs and masses, very much on the mind of sociologists Le Bon and McDougall, are more than groups; "The Future of an Illusion" (1927); and "Civilization and its Discontents" (1930). Freud is much concerned in these essays with matters of love and omnipotence, much less with issues of power. Ideology became a concern for Freud when he attacked religion as an institution "distorting the picture of the real world in a delusional manner . . . by forcibly fixing [mankind] in a state of psychical infantilism and by drawing them into a mass delusion" (Freud 1930, p. 85).

Due in part to historical causes, interpersonal dynamics have been repressed through the decades both by Freud himself and by psychoanalysts who followed him in favor of intrapsychic dynamics, with the result that preponderantly monadic theories have been applied to the inherently dyadic life of persons in society (Lothane 1984, 1997). Starting with the basic group of two of mother and child, and ending with the twosome formed by analysand and analyst, there is no escaping the fact that every act of thought or communication, whether verbal or nonverbal, is both self-directed and other-directed, both intrapsychic and interpersonal, or *trans*personal, that every action is an *inter*action and a *trans*action. Before Freud turned monadic in his theories, he was himself a dyadic practitioner of the arts of hypnosis and suggestion. At a later phase Freud used the term transference as a synonym for transpersonal influence, such as a patient developing a sense of conviction following the analyst's interpretation. I have chosen to subsume the reciprocal influence and dyadic communication under the rubric of the love relation. This leads to a moral corollary: not just love, but love ruled by ethics (Lothane 1982, 1984, 1986a, 1986b, 1987a, 1987b, 1987c, 1989, 1992, 1994a, 1997). It goes without saying that interpersonal dynamics include both conscious and unconscious processes (Lothane 1994b).

Freud was at first reticent about love, and during the middle phase of his creative years he was mainly interested in libido, for libido as a form of energy seemed to provide a scientific paradigm for psychoanalysis. He was even more silent about power, for like love, power did not fit into any of his theoretical models. Power, not sex, was Freud's last taboo, his denial of the real and causal role of power in human relations, so that in his theories he replaced the lust for power with the power of lust, via those immortal libidinal wishes and aims. Freud identified only two drives: sex and aggression, the latter first called "the death instinct." Had he listened to Adler, he might have also recognized a power instinct or drive, a *Machttrieb*, which may include aggression but is not reducible to it.

That power is a pervasive reality in personal, social, legal, and political relations is self-evident, and Russell (1962) defined it broadly as being able to act in order to achieve an end, to have a sense of mastery in a situation, and, we would add, to have power over oneself and over another. As with love, the question is whether power is used with or without a moral compass, for might turned into right easily leads to the unjust abuse of power: the overpowering of the other by violent brute force.

As love and charity, power begins in the family, where the parents have the physical power to control their children, and where the very notion of authority rests on their ability to command and coerce obedience to their power. Of course, this power is a necessary biological precondition for the preservation of the species. However, parental power is the still-unacknowledged real factor in parent–child relations in the preoedipal and oedipal periods, and especially in adolescence, as are the varieties of its intrapsychic representation. It is that power that makes the child see his parents as not only powerful but omnipotent, and it also creates the images of the good and the bad parent, for that power can be used to heal and to hurt, to protect and to punish. Parental power can be benign and empowering, but it can also be abusive and criminal: parents can overpower their children by enforced deprivation, indoctrination, physical torture and mutilation, and even murder.

In the political realm, power and authority are a most palpable and defining reality. Government in any form means the wielding of power by the rulers over the ruled. Absolutism, or autocracy, the ancient form of government in which power was vested in a monarch, or an oligarchy, could be either enlightened or tyrannical. Its antithesis in ancient Greece and Rome was democracy, a system of government by the people. Different from the ancient model, modern representative democracy was born in England, then spread to the United States and France and the rest of the world. But in spite of this progress, and in spite of the strides made by the sciences in the second half of the nineteenth century, it was in the twentieth century that democracies were swept away by the rising tide of a new form of autocracy, the totalitarian power systems and ideologies in Italy, Spain, Germany, and Japan, culminating in Fascism, Stalinism, and Hitlerism. States have ruled people through their police military power; but, again, it is the totalitarian states of the twentieth century that have created unprecedented forms of mass destruction such as saturation bombing, the Gulag, and the genocide practiced in the concentration camps during the Holocaust.

The defeat of Hitlerism in World War II was followed by the totalitarian aftermath of Soviet domination and ideology during the Cold War. However, after the fall of Russian communism and the emergence of a democratic Russia and a unified Germany, we are now witnessing a new totalitarian threat around the globe in the form of the fundamentalist movements, both secular and religious, bent on the use of violent power.

The abuse of power in the family, a ruling class group or party, or the state, creates the soil for the social and psychological creation of omnipotence, claimed by the mighty on earth and attributed to the Almighty in heaven. In many religions the central attribute of the deity is limitless power, called God's allmight, *Allmacht* in German, and omnipotence in Latin, from *omni* (all and potency, power and might). Mankind can be powerful in many ways, but its power has limits; it is only God who is all-powerful, which brings us into the realm of belief.

Faith moves mountains, we are told; the pen is mightier than the sword: next to the naked power of physical force, there is the power of ideology and belief, the power of persuasion and indoctrination, of commercial and political propaganda, and of image and opinion making, the power of demagogues and messiahs who become the pied pipers of the masses whom they sway, and the media and the meetings through with the masses can be manipulated.

It is also in the family that ideology emerges as the prop of parental power: the various ways in which parents rationalize their power by an appeal to nature-given or God-given authority, sanctified by custom and religion. Such beliefs are based on a complementarity: there is a reciprocal tendency to represent the parents as God-like and God as the heavenly all-loving father. Theists have traditionally believed in God's omnipresence, omnipotence, and omniscience as His unquestionable attributes. Atheists, including nineteenth-century rationalists, of whom Freud was one and Marx another, regarded belief in an omnipotent God as irrational and unscientific, a relic of primitive beliefs of savages and superstitions of priests. They followed in the footsteps of the philosopher Ludwig Feuerbach who attributed religious beliefs to a *projection* of mankind's inherent state of helplessness and dependency onto a nonexistent God imagined as all-powerful.

As expressed by Sartre, mankind's basic project is to be God. But this project to imitate God is acted out in a collusion between the rulers and the ruled to result in mutually shared dreams, or delusions, of omnipotence, contrary to reason and the limitations imposed by reality. The rulers act the part of self-styled gods, and the ruled worship such man-made gods as idols and fetishes in order to partake in the reflected glory of their declared omnipotence; both the ruler and the ruled share a burden of responsibility for this collusion. But there is one social difference: the collusion between the leaders and the led allows the leader what is not allowed to the led. The emperor, the despot, and the Führer have the power to act and speak like gods and are obeyed as gods; ordinary people saying they are god are treated as grandiose madmen and locked up in asylums, even when they are harmless. In turn, when psychiatrists and psychoanalysts are called to explain the behavior of leaders posturing as gods, they are prone to diagnose such leaders as mad, paranoid, or victims of delusions of omnipotence. Do such explanations help us understand or offer a solution to social and political phenomena, such as the rise of Hitler and his ideology or the current menace of fundamentalism?

The Origins of Omnipotence in Psychoanalysis

In many psychoanalytic texts, omnipotence is a descriptive, dynamic, and developmental concept applied in psychoanalysis to persons in health and disease. Descriptively it frequently appears together with such psychiatric labels as grandiosity, megalomania, narcissism, and paranoia. Dynamically it is a mechanism of defense. Developmentally it is assumed to be the most archaic mode of relating to oneself and others. Dialectically, with the widening of the scope of psychoanalytic theories, there has been a trend to apply traditional psychopathological entities to ideas and feelings experienced in the course of ordinary life. Thus paranoia, a severe psychosis, is now every infant's defense at the age of 3 months thanks to Melanie Klein (1932, 1948), while narcissism, highly abnormal until Heinz Kohut (1971, 1977) came along, is now a universal entitlement.

In psychoanalysis, omnipotence is a joint creation of the patient called the Rat Man and Freud (1909). Whenever he raged at his father, the Rat Man would succumb to the obsessional belief in the "omnipotence of [his] wishes [so that] evils would be bound to come upon [his father]" (Freud 1909, p. 226), to a belief in the omnipotence of his "thoughts and feelings, whether good or evil," and to a conviction in the "omnipotence of his love and his hatred" (p. 234). Note the two ways Freud has with omnipotence as a concept: it does not stand by itself, like a thing but is an empty vessel that has to be filled with some content, such as the belief in the omnipotence of thought, or, as here, the omnipotence of love and hatred. Also note that Freud is inclined "to declare that this idea was a delusion" (p. 233), and to explain it as "a relic of the old megalomania of infancy" (p. 234). Freud does not consider the possibility that that attitude of omnipotence could have been a product of a specific interaction between the Rat Man and his parents.

However, such a communicative interaction was taken into account by Ferenczi (1913), Freud's most creative and long-suppressed disciple, in a paper finished before the publication of Freud's "Totem and Taboo" (1913). Starting with the assumption that "this symptom, the feeling of omnipotence," is a throwback to "that stage of child-development characterized . . . by there being as yet no inhibiting, postponing, reflecting thought activity between wishing and acting" (Ferenczi 1913, p. 183), and "not quite satisfied with this explanation of the feeling of omnipotence as an autosymbolic [i.e., a monadic] phenomenon" (p. 184), Ferenczi finds the source of this apparent "delusion" of omnipotence in the mother–child relationship. Originally, omnipotence, as "the feeling that one has all that one wants," is created by life in the womb and "is thus at least no empty delusion" but the basis for subsequent repeated demands for "the return of a state that once existed" (p. 186). The newborn "*longs to regain this situation*" (p. 187, emphasis Ferenczi's), and a good nurse, feeling herself "into the soul of the new-born babe," will minister accordingly to replicate the warmth and comfort of the uterine paradise lost. When such is unavailable, the child will realize it in the form of a wish-fulfilling hallucination, creating within his mind the feeling state of a "magical-hallucinatory omnipotence." The latter then gives rise to "magic signals, at the dictation of which the satisfaction promptly arrives, [such that] the subjective feeling of the child at all this may be compared to that of a real magician [in this] period of omnipotence" (pp. 190–191), the analogy of magic suggested by the assumed equivalence between the psychological makeup of children, savages, and neurotics. While it does no harm to speak in this manner of the magic years of childhood, it should not be forgotten that it is specious to compare the child to a real magician, who was a real social institution in the life of aboriginal tribes.

With the acquisition of symbolic speech the child "thinks himself in the possession of magic thoughts and magic words" (p. 196). It is only with maturation that the "illusion of omnipotence" is replaced with a "sense of reality attain[ing] its zenith in Science," where this illusion "experiences its greatest humiliation" (p. 197). Transposed into the stages of sexual development as delineated by Freud (1905), it can be said that "autoerotism and narcissism are . . . the omnipotence stages of erotism, and since narcissism [i.e., self-love] never comes to an end at all . . . in the matter of love we can retain the illusion of omnipotence throughout life" (pp. 198–199).

Ferenczi, more sensitive to matters of love than any other analyst, would later speak of the *Allmächtigkeit*, or omnipotence, of the parents, and in his posthumous *Clinical Diary* (Ferenczi 1932) would continue his interpersonal line of thought and connect love and omnipotence in ways so different from Freud's:

> Being loved, being the center of the universe is the natural emotional state of the baby, therefore it is not a mania but an actual fact. The first disappointments in love (weaning, regulation of the excretory functions, the first punishments through a harsh tone of voice, threats, even spankings) must have, in every case a traumatic effect . . . [with resulting] psychic paralysis [and] it may be assumed that splitting occurs at this stage. The organism has to adapt itself . . . and lingers for a shorter or longer period in the hallucination: nothing has happened, I am still loved the same as before (hallucinatory omnipotence). All subsequent disappointments, later on in one's love life, may well regress to this wish-fulfillment. [Ferenczi 1932, p. 83]

In "Totem and Taboo," first published as a four-part series in the journal *Imago* under the collective title "On Certain Correspondences in the Mental Life of Savages and Neurotics," Freud (1913) cited Ferenczi and confirmed he had "adopted the term omnipotence of thoughts from a highly intelligent man [living in a world where] only 'neurotic currency' is legal tender . . . [for neurotics] are only affected by what is thought with intensity and pictured with emotion, whereas agreement with external reality is a matter of no importance" (Freud 1913, pp. 84–85). The Rat Man, it is true, feared the power of his thoughts and wishes to destroy his father, feeling correspondingly guilty, and "thus became convinced," Freud said, "of the omnipotence of his love and his hatred. . . . His love—or rather his hatred—was in truth overpowering; it was precisely they that created the obsessional thoughts, of which he could not understand the origin and against which he strove in vain to defend himself" (Freud 1909, p. 234).

But where is the difference between the power of love and the omnipotence of love? Love is powerful, and both lover and beloved will be empowered by it. We fall in love with love, with a person, with ourselves, with ideas, or with power itself, and, as Ferenczi suggested, more narcistically than altruistically. Omnipotence may be said to occur when such love exceeds the bounds of reality, when it is so overpowering or so self-oriented that it become irrational and delusional, thus, a form of madness. But such an assessment of omnipotence, like any other thought or feeling, may be only in the eyes of the beholder, not the upholder of such love: the upholder is convinced he is right, the beholder believes the other is wrong. It then becomes a question of who judges whom, and who has the power to judge whom.

Freud further converted the Rat Man's neurotic currency into inflationary money by applying the dynamics of an individual neurotic man to primitive man in his collective life, first reasoning by analogy and equating *neurotic* and *primitive*, and then extending the analogy to social behavior. This was a momentous transposition: not unlike the primitive man, against whose irrational beliefs Freud was inveighing, Freud himself "transposed the structural conditions of [the individual] mind into the external world" (Freud 1913, p. 91), that is, to life in society, suggesting the following evolutionary sequence:

> At the animistic stage men ascribe omnipotence to *themselves*. At the religious stage they transfer it to the god but do not seriously abandon it themselves, for they reserve the power of influencing the gods in a variety of ways according to their wishes. The scientific view of the universe no longer affords any room for human omnipotence; men have acknowledged their smallness and submitted resignedly to death and other necessities of nature. [Freud 1913, p. 88, Freud emphasis]

But where is the proof that primitive man, like the neurotic, ascribed omnipotence to himself first? Is not rather that such omnipotence, as earlier with the parents, is first attributed by the primitive man to nature itself, and, realizing his powerlessness, he seeks to propitiate nature as god or gods with the magic of incantations, prayers, and offerings? With the advent of the scientific view, intolerant of the prejudices of religion, powerless mankind has nobody left to propitiate except the new gods of the masses: science deified as scientism and the self-styled god-like dictators.

The next step is taken when Freud, like Ferenczi, aligns omnipotence with self-love and the love of others. At this stage, and perhaps without realizing the revolutionary nature of the conjunction, Freud connects the capacity to know reality with the capacity to love and outlines his new ethics of renunciation that would later be embraced by generations of Freudian ego psychologists. Under the influence of the French thinker Comte, Freud universalizes his insight and sees mankind as evolving according to this developmental program:

> If we may regard the existence among primitive races of the omnipotence of thought as evidence in favor of narcissism, we are encouraged to attempt a comparison between the phases in the development of men's view of the universe and the stages of individual libidinal development. The animistic phase would correspond to narcissism both chronologically and in its content; the religious phase would correspond to the stage of object-choice of which the characteristic is the child's attachment to his parents; while the scientific phase would have an exact counterpart in the stage at which an individual has reached maturity, has renounced the pleasure principle, adjusted himself to reality and turned to the external world for the object of his desires. [Freud 1913, p. 90]

But this utopia crumbles under the weight of Freud's inherent skepticism about the powers of the mind to overcome inexorable reality. Freud is driven to the realization that mankind has an Achilles heel: "the primitive belief in omnipotence still survives in men's faith in the power of the human mind, which grapples with the laws of reality" (Freud 1913, p. 88); but Freud also knows that "the human being remains to some extent narcissistic even after he has found external objects for his libido" (1913, p. 89); and, besides, how can the human being give up the pleasure principle? Ineluctably, caught between the pleasure principle and the reality principle, mankind still craves the self-created illusion of omnipotence as a way out. With this we pass to the social uses of omnipotence in the life of groups, nations, and masses.

Love, Power, and Omnipotence: from Individual to Mass Psychosis

Freud's elaborations on individuals in states of love and self-love find their mature expression in his epochal "On Narcissism: An Introduction" (1914), which would become the foundation of his ego psychology and in our days of Kohut's self psychology (Lothane 1987a). In that essay, a continuation of adumbrations in his Schreber analysis (Freud 1911), he delves into megalomania, delusions of grandeur, and paranoid delusions, all viewed as manifestations of narcissism, that is, "grandiose self-love," spanning the spectrum from the normal to the psychotic.

However, in the transition from individuals to groups in his "Group Psychology" a new realization emerges: aware of the "contrast between social and narcissistic" levels of being, Freud now sees that "in the individual mental life someone else is invariably involved, as model, an object, as a helper or an opponent; and so from the very first individual psychology . . . is at the same time social psychology as well" (1921, p. 69). Possibly echoing Nietzsche's saying, the Thou is older than the I, Freud reasons as follows: "the psychology of groups is the oldest human psychology; what we have isolated as individual psychology, by neglecting all traces of the group, has only since come into prominence out of the old group psychology, by a gradual process which may still, perhaps, be described incompletely" (Freud 1921, p. 23).

A crimson thread runs from "Totem and Taboo" (1913) and the

myth of the primal group, or horde, to "Group Psychology" (Freud 1921), in which Freud acknowledges his indebtedness to a number of pioneers in the field of the psychology of crowds, mobs, and masses, among them the French Gabriel Tarde (1890) and Gustave Le Bon (1897), the English Wilfred Trotter (1916) and Harvard's William McDougall (1920). Influenced by the literature on hypnosis and the writings of Tarde, Le Bon (1897) emphasized the unconscious state of fascination, derived from imitation and suggestion, into which a crowd could be hypnotized by a leader like Napoleon. Le Bon was quoted by Freud as follows:

> [F]irst, the individual forming part of a crowd acquires, solely from numerical considerations, a sentiment of invincible power which allows him to yield to instincts, which, had he been alone, he would perforce have kept under restraint . . . a crowd being anonymous [so that] the sentiment of responsibility disappears entirely. The second cause [is] contagion . . . classed among phenomena of a hypnotic order. . . . A third cause is . . . suggestibility. . . . Isolated, a person may be a cultivated individual; in a crowd he is a barbarian—that is a creature acting by instinct. He possesses the spontaneity, the violence, the ferocity, and also the enthusiasm and heroism of primitive beings. [Le Bon 1897, pp. 9–12 quoted in Freud 1921, pp. 74, 77]

Freud adds his own characterizations: "in the group the individual . . . throws off the repressions of his unconscious impulses . . . all that is evil in the human mind, [leading to] a disappearance of conscience. . . . [The group] has a sense of *omnipotence*, the notion of impossibility disappears for the individual in a group" (Freud 1921, pp. 74, 77, emphasis added). But is this the omnipotence of the neonate, or the power intoxication of the crowd in a state of mass hysteria? Freud borrows from McDougall's *Group Mind* the description of mindless mass behavior, an echo of Le Bon:

> [People] become merged in the group and lose the sense of limits of their individuality. The individual loses his power of criticism, [to become] emotional, impulsive, violent, fickle, inconsistent, irresolute

> and extreme in action. . . . [The group is] extremely suggestible, careless in deliberation, hasty in judgment, easily swayed and led, lacking in self-consciousness, devoid of self respect and a sense of responsibility, and apt to be carried away by the consciousness of its own force, so it tends to produce all the manifestations we have learnt to expect of any *irresponsible or absolute power*. Hence its behaviour is like an unruly child or an untutored passionate savage . . . like that of a wild beast rather than like that of human beings. [Freud 1921, p. 85, emphasis added]

Freud also agrees with McDougall that "a group impresses the individual as being of unlimited power . . . and in obedience to the new authority [of the group] he may put his former conscience out of action" (Freud 1921, p. 85). Even though the comparisons to savages and beasts stems from deep prejudices (Le Bon also included women), the obliteration of conscience and responsibility in the group are crucial to the understanding of what Freud, like Kant, called evil, either at the individual or the mass level. Neither Le Bon nor McDougall address the all-important connection of power and love in group dynamics.

Rising to his own challenge to speak of power and love in society, Freud's overarching conception is "the supposition that love relationships (or, to use a more neutral expression, emotional ties) also constitute the essence of the group mind" (Freud 1921, p. 91). Is it more scientific to use neutral expressions, that is, euphemisms, when speaking of love?

The other essential ingredient in the life of the group is work. The popular saying, "a family that prays together stays together," can be used to show that a group that *preys* together stays together; this holds equally well for the primitive hunting horde as well as for its sophisticated modern counterparts: the work place, the corporation, the team. But since, according to Freud (and Plato), "Eros holds everything together in the world" (Freud 1921, p. 92), that cosmogonic Eros is also the source of that force that makes for group cohesion, and it manifests itself as a dual love bond: (a) amongst the members of the group and (b) between the group as a whole and its leader. At this point an additional sublimated, desexualized, ego-psychological emotional tie comes into play: *identification*, "a new perception of a common quality shared with some other person," or persons: "the mutual tie between the members of a group is in the nature of an identification of this kind, based on an important emotional common quality; and . . . this common quality lies in the nature of the tie with the leader" (Freud 1921, p. 108). A good example of a common work and love bond is offered by the army or a church ("a community of believers"), where love gives rise to the same illusion:

> [T]he head—Christ, the Commander-in-Chief—loves all the individuals in the group with an equal love . . . [acting as] a kind of elder brother, [as] their substitute father. . . . [T]he similarity . . . [with] the family is invoked . . . [as well as] the possibility of *a leading idea being substituted for the leader* and upon the relations between the two. [Freud 1921, pp. 94–95, emphasis added]

In this passage we reach the last issue in our analysis of mass mind: ideology. The community of believers, the group that prays together and stays together, is unified by an additional bond: that of commonly shared ideas and ideals. At this stage of delineating his ego-psychological "anatomy" of the person Freud has not yet coined the term *superego*—that is yet to come (Freud 1923)—as his technical term for "conscience, a critical agency within ego, which . . . takes up a critical attitude towards the ego" (Freud 1921, p. 109): here it is called "the 'ego ideal', . . . the moral conscience, . . . the chief influence of repression" (Freud 1921, p. 110).

But since these various parts of the person called ego and superego are only metaphorical parts and truly refer to various functions of the person (Lothane 1987d), I propose to stick to the word *conscience* and to reserve the term ego ideal or ideal ego, Freud's *Ichideal* and *Idealich*, to mean what the words express: the function of choosing and following ideas and ideals embodied in leaders, historical personalities, and ideologies. This will pave the way for combining the forces of love, identification, and ideology into an integrated dynamic whole.

In individual love relations, Freud says,

> everything that the object does and asks for is right and blameless. Conscience has no application to anything that is done for the sake of the object; in the blindness of love remorselessness is carried to the pitch of crime. The whole situation can be summarized in the formula: *The object has been put in the place of the ego ideal.* [Freud 1921, p. 113, emphasis Freud's]

"The object" is Freud's euphemism for person (Lothane 1982, 1987d), and if we restore the superseded term, then the last sentence in the just-quoted passage will read: the (loved) person has been put in the place of the conscience. This applies, of course, not only to lovers, a "group formation with two members," but also to masses in relation to their leaders, where people "*put one and the same object in the place of their ego ideal*" and also "*identif[y] themselves with one another in their ego*" (Freud 1921, p. 116, emphasis Freud's). Keeping the double meaning of ego ideal as conscience and ideology, if we substitute "the leader" for "the object" in the just-quoted definition, we can see that if one replaces one's individual conscience with that of a powerful leader, and accepts his ideals or ideology as one's own, the result is that

> the individual gives up his ego ideal and substitutes for it the group ideal as embodied in the leader. . . . The selection of the leader is very much facilitated by this circumstance . . . the need for a strong chief [who] will often meet him half-way and invest him with a predominance to which he would otherwise perhaps have had no claim. [Freud 1921, p. 127]

In a group of two, shared love and delusional beliefs create a *folie à deux*; in crowds, mobs, and masses we reach the level of mass neurosis (Fenichel 1946, Fromm 1941, Reich 1933, 1942), or mass madness, a *folie à millions*. Faced with a charismatic leader acting on the mass hypnotically and conditions conducive to mass fascination, the mass is only too ready and willing to give up moral conscience and its former ideals and espouse the ideals of the leader, and to act criminally at his behest, as we see repeatedly in the descent to barbarism in peace and war.

The Power of Delusional Ideology: Hitler and the Third Reich

Ideology, the origin, history, and science of ideas, pervades every area of knowledge, be it theoretical or practical, be it in the humanities, the arts, economics, or the sciences. Defined as a *Weltanschauung,* world outlook, or viewpoint, it is a system of ideas and ideals to explain life and to live by—characteristic for an individual, a social class, or a collective, and usually fashioned by adding the suffix *-ism* to some root word—and it plays a role in the life of persons, groups, nations, and governments from democracies to dictatorships. Ideologies often polarize people into adherents and opponents, such as materialism vs. idealism in philosophy, mechanism vs. vitalism in physiology, capitalism and socialism in economics, despotism and democracy in politics. Even when rational in their content and structure, polarized beliefs can lead to rivalry, hatred, persecution, and violent mass wars, as shown in the history of capitalism, socialism, Soviet and Chinese communism, and, last but not least, German National Socialism, or Nazism. How much more injurious are ideologies that from the start bear the stamp of unreason, such as the religious wars over doctrine in the history of the churches; religious persecution of races seen as infidels and heretics, such as anti-Semitism of the churches, a precursor of the secular racial anti-Semitism that followed; and the recurrent mystical secret and esoteric doctrines and cults that have thrived in Europe down the centuries. It is the latter that concern us here, especially in regard to their intoxicating mass appeal and their ability to produce pathological omnipotence. In addition, along with Kant and Freud, I consider that the irrational is not only to be judged by the criterion of truth and common sense, but also by the criterion of ethics (Lothane, in press): the irrational can serve the ends of radical evil and lead to abuses of power and violence, culminating in crimes against humanity.

Absolute monarchies in the nineteenth century were not yet totally despotic, and it is only in our own century, supposedly made safe for democracy under the banner of science, that dictatorships achieved unprecedented control over the bodies and minds of the masses by the use of systematized terror and delusional systems of ideology. This was done in the Soviet Union in persecuting the peasants (kulaks) and other enemy classes, and in the Third Reich in the subjugation of the German people and in the Holocaust of the Jews, the most irrational manifestation of ideology and violence in our time (Johnson 1987). In addition, as Webb (1976) put it, Hitler's Nazi Germany was the place where rejected irrational ideologies and mythologies became the establishment.

In 1933, at the age of 44, the Austrian-born Adolf Hitler seized dictatorial power over the German masses (Hofer 1957, Johnson 1987). After methodically beating the German masses into submission at home (Rauschning 1938), Hitler and his regime went on to arm those same masses for the conquest and subjugation of other nations, in spite of the terms of the Versailles peace treaty, and aided and abetted by the appeasement policies of England, France, and Stalin's Russia. But then something unprecedented took place: a modern totalitarian state, in addition to establishing its economic and political ideology, set up anti-Semitism "as the centre and the end of their programme" (Johnson, p. 472), wrote it into the official state constitution (Huber 1937) and the laws of the land (Hofer 1957), making it into the foundation of both domestic and international politics, and climaxing in the program to exterminate the Jews as a race and a culture. This was not just a matter of Hitler's psychosis or paranoia, of his omnipotence and grandiosity, which are all issues of his individual psychology; nor was it due to the sense of omnipotence he inspired in the masses during the meetings and rallies, with the help of spectacular sound and light effects, or in his own party followers. This vast political program did begin as a romance between the Führer and the nation locked in an ecstatic, orgiastic love embrace, which used all the modern paraphernalia of mass visceral excitement. Huxley (1977) aptly dubbed this phenomenon *herd-poisoning*, "the crowd intoxication that is exploited by the ambitious rabble-rouser for his own political or religious ends. . . . Of course, the greatest virtuoso in the art of exploiting the symptoms of herd poisoning was Adolf Hitler" (p. 125). With Hitler the result was a mass illusion of being loved by the Führer, of forging bonds of comradeship and identification among adherents old and young, and the young abandoning parental values to follow the Führer. No, the "final solution" of the Jewish question was *both* Hitler's personal hatred of the Jews justified by a delusional racial ideology *and* a materialization of that ideology systematically pursued by a state political system (Fest 1973, Heiden 1944). Whether he read Le Bon or McDougall on mass psychology or not, Hitler knew how to move the masses and "the key which opens the door to their hearts." In his *Mein Kampf*, the bible of Nazi political and irrational ideology written in 1924, Hitler proclaimed that

> the psyche of the great masses is not receptive to half-measures or weakness. Like a woman, whose psychic feeling is influenced less by abstract reasoning than by an indefinable, sentimental longing for complementary strength, . . . the masses love the ruler rather than the suppliant, and inwardly they are far more satisfied by a doctrine which tolerates no rival. . . . They neither realize the impudence with which they are spiritually terrorized, nor the outrageous curtailment of their human liberties, for in no way does the *delusion of this doctrine* dawn on them. . . . The importance of physical terror against the individual and the masses also became clear to me. Here, too, we find exact calculation of the psychological effect. *The terror in the workshops, in the factory, in the assembly hall, and on occasion of mass demonstrations will always be accomplished by success as long as it is not met by an equally great force of terror*. [Hitler 1924, p. 56, first emphasis added, last in the original]

Hitler emerges as a master of mass psychology, in ways far beyond the nineteenth-century methods of Le Bon, to wit: first, in the cynical and calculated manipulation of the masses by means of totalitarian tactics of terror and overpowerment, because "only the Jew can praise [present-day democratic parliamentarism,] an institution that is as dirty and false as he is himself. This system is opposed by the true Germanic democracy, the free choice of a *Führer* [leader] with the latter's obligation to take over fully the responsibility for what he does or does not do" (Hitler, p. 116); second, by the psychological bondage to delusional doctrines and by promoting himself as an omnipotent god-like prophet of the millennium: "Man is becoming God—that is the simple fact. Man is God in the making. . . . Those who see in National Socialism nothing more than a political movement know scarcely anything about it. It is more even than a religion; it is the will to create mankind anew" (Hitler, quoted in Berman 1989, p. 253). Like other self-styled gods, Hitler appealed to a recurrent mystical longing of mankind to escape present misery and to achieve salvation and redemption through the establishment of a new race and religion, and a kingdom that would last for a thousand years.

Hitler's anti-Semitic and nationalist Aryan ideology, or his mystical ariosophy (Berman 1989), are fully articulated in his *Mein Kampf*. With the secularization of Western Europe the ancient religious hatred of the Jews was transformed into a new mix of secular religion and pseudo-science that Poliakov (1971) called the Aryan myth. It was a mish-mash of anthropological, mystical, and nationalist myths that had been spreading in a number of European countries since the Enlightenment, enriching the old demonological persecution of the Jews with new conspiracy theories, and it was strengthened by the new middle-class competition in the domains of finance, the sciences, literature, commerce, politics, and the military (e.g., the Dreyfus affair in France).

The irrational ideological roots of Nazism can be traced to a body of popular belief and literature expressing the strivings of the *völkisch* movement, from the German *Volk*, which united the elements of the national, racial, tribal, and folkloric and folksy, and became a defining category of Nazi nationalist occultism and the Nazi constitution (Huber 1937). The distinctive characteristic of the *völkisch* spirit was its preoccupation with race, notably with the doctrine of *ariosophy*, inspired by Blavatsky's theosophy, and so called by its founder, the guru Jörg Lanz von Liebenfels, to mean occult knowledge about Aryans. It also went by such names as armanism, theozoology, and ario-christianity. According to the tenets of ariosophy, touted in Lanz's racist magazine *Ostara*, the blond Aryan hero, the incarnation of God on earth, was threatened by *Tschandala*, the underman, the incarnation of competition and materialism. Another idea promulgated in the *Ostara* was that the original Aryans had copulated with a race of pygmies thereby destroying their racial purity and powers, and the remedies suggested to restore this lost purity were castration and sterilization of the inferior races, as well as slavery, deportation, and forced labor. According to Webb (1974) and Fest (1974), Hitler would have read and absorbed many of the ideas expressed in the *Ostara*, a wellspring of ideology for men who joined both Hitler's *Deutsche Arbeitspartei* (the future Nazi party) and the Munich Beer Hall coup of 1923 (Webb 1974, Berman 1989). Some of the forgotten followers of Lanz and propagators of this mystical *völkisch* occultism, the Aryan myth, and racial anti-Semitism are named in *Mein Kampf*: Dietrich Eckart, Gottfiried Feder, Alfred Rosenberg, Max-Erwin von Scheubner-Richter, Jacob-Wilhelm Hauer, Georg von Schoenerer, and Theodor Fritzsch.

Another major inspiration for Hitler's delusional doctrines was Houston Stewart Chamberlain, the anti-Semitic Englishman who became a German citizen and married the daughter of the equally anti-Semitic composer Richard Wagner. Chamberlain held that "The Jews are neither a race nor a people. . . . They are the unique example of a purely parasitic product of decay" (quoted in the editors' footnote, Hitler 1924, p. 413). Accordingly, Hitler believed and wanted the Germans to believe his doctrine that the Jew

> was never in the possession of a culture of his own, the bases of his spiritual activity have always been furnished by others. . . . Today the Jew is looked upon as 'clever,' yet the most essential presumption for a cultured people is completely lacking, the idealistic disposition. . . . [Their] belonging together is rooted in a very primitive herd instinct . . . [thus they are] counted among the ranks of the *nomads*. . . . The Jews were always a people with definite racial qualities and never a religion, . . . [an excuse] that could divert disagreeable attention from their person. . . . [T]he lie that the Jew is not a race but simply a religion . . . is shown in an incomparable manner in the "Protocols of the Wise Men of Zion." [Hitler, pp. 412–423]

The last mentioned work was a Czarist forgery, a rabid anti-Semitic pamphlet later circulated in Germany by the chief Nazi ideologue, Alfred Rosenberg.

By contrast, according to Hitler, the Aryan was a Prometheus-like "preserver and propagator of the culture" and master of mankind:

> [I]f one were to divide mankind into three groups: culture-founders, culture-bearers, and culture-destroyers, then, as representative of the first kind only the Aryan would come into question. It is from him that the foundation and the walls of all human creations originate. . . . Therefore alone it is not accident that the first cultures originated in those places where the Aryan, by meeting lower peoples, subdued them and made them subject to his will . . . as long as he remained the master. . . . [When] he gave up the purity of his blood . . . he also lost his place in the Paradise which he had created for himself [Hitler, pp. 398–406].

As Chamberlain's disciple, Hitler held that the Jew is a disguised parasite who

> took inside the body of other peoples. . . . [He is] the eternal blood sucker . . . which attaches itself to the body of the unfortunate people . . . the Jewish danger. He poisons the blood of others but he

> guards his own. The Jew does not marry a Christian woman, but always a Christian a Jewess. Yet the bastards take to the Jewish side. Under [his] cloak of social thought, there are hidden some more truly diabolical intentions, . . . the Marxist 'view of life.' The final aims [are] the economic conquest of the world [and] the political subjection of the latter. . . . [and here is another method] For hours the black-haired Jew-boy, diabolic joy in his face, waits in ambush for the unsuspecting girl whom he defiles with his blood and thus robs her from her people. With the aid of all means he tries to ruin the racial foundation of the peoples to be enslaved. . . . [via] the organized mass of Marxism. . . . [T]he blood Jew and the people's tyrant . . . has killed or starved about thirty million people with a truly diabolic ferocity, under inhuman tortures. [Hitler, pp. 425–451]

Hitler's conclusion was that "without the clearest recognition of the race problem and with it, of the Jewish question, there will be no rise of the German nation" (p. 469). It did not matter it was Stalin's regime that starved, tortured, and killed the millions; it is remarkable that Hitler's paranoid vilification of the Jews was a prophetic description of what, a mere fifteen years later, Hitler and his regime would be doing to their own German and other political opponents, to homosexuals, to the feeble-minded and the mentally ill, to the Gypsies, and, above all, to the Jews.

Hitler's ideology found adherents not only in the masses but also in some very high places of learning. An example of the latter was none other than C. G. Jung, who after Hitler's ascent to power extolled the virtues of National Socialism. Although Jung was not anti-Semitic and did not endorse the final solution, in his anti-Judaic and anti-Christian animus (coupled with a pursuit of a heathen Greco-Roman ideal of beauty, power, and freedom from ethical restraint, possibly of Nietzschean inspiration), he nevertheless spoke for many German intellectuals when he said in interview on Radio Berlin on June 26, 1933:

> The self-development of the individual is especially necessary in our time. When the individual is unconscious of himself, the collective

> movement too lacks a clear sense of purpose. . . . As Hitler recently said, the leader must be able to be alone and must have the courage to go his own way. But if he doesn't know himself, how can is he to lead others? That is why the true leader is always one who has the courage to be himself, and can look not only others in the eye but above all himself. . . . Times of mass movement are always times of leadership. Every movement culminates organically in a leader, who embodies the whole meaning and purpose of the popular movement. He is the incarnation of the nation's psyche and its mouthpiece. He is the spearhead of the phalanx of the whole people in motion. The need of the whole always calls forth a leader, regardless of the form a state may take. . . . It is perfectly natural that a leader should stand at the head of an elite, [who] believe by the law of the nature in blood and exclusiveness of the race. [Jung, quoted in Adams and Sherry 1989, p. 366]

If in the next passage, written a year later, we substitute "race" for "unconscious," the similarity between the views of Hitler and Jung is even more striking:

> The Jews have this peculiarity in common with women; being physically weak, they have to aim at the chinks in the armour of their adversary. The Jews themselves are best protected where others are most vulnerable. . . . Because, again, of their civilization, more than twice as ancient as ours . . . they are vastly more conscious than we of human weaknesses, of the shadow side of things . . . [thus able] to put a negative value on [the] unconscious. The 'Aryan' unconscious . . . contains explosive forces and seeds for a future yet to be born. . . . The still youthful Germanic peoples are fully capable of creating new cultural norms. . . . The Jew, who is something of a nomad, has never yet created a cultural norm of his own. . . . The 'Aryan' unconscious has a higher potential than the Jewish; that is both the advantage and disadvantage of youth not weaned from barbarism . . . [which] has been explained as a morass of banal infantilism. . . . This suspicion emanated from Freud. He did not understand the Germanic psyche any more than did his Germanic followers. Has the formidable phenomenon of National Socialism, on

> which the whole world gazes with astonishment, taught them any better? [Jung, quoted in Adams and Sherry 1989, p. 368]

My point is not to so much to damn Jung, for after the war he apologized to Rabbi Leo Baeck for having slipped, but to raise the issue of German responsibility for World War II and the Holocaust. These matters have been most eloquently and ethically discussed by the former President of the German Federal Republic Richard Freiherr von Weizsäcker (1985): "We are all responsible," he declared, "for unspeakable sorrow that occurred in the name of Germany" (p. 86). In a speech commemorating "the dead of the war and the rule of tyranny [but] in particular the six million Jews who were murdered in German concentration camps," he said:

> Most Germans had believed in fighting and suffering for the good of their own country . . . all that was not only vain and senseless, but it served inhuman ends of a criminal leadership [and] a system that despised human values. . . . At the bottom of the tyranny stood Hitler's unfathomable hatred of our fellow men, the Jews. Hitler had never kept it from the public, but rather made the entire nation the tool of this hatred. The very day before his death on 30 April 1945, he concluded his so-called will with the words: 'Above all I place the leaders of the nation and their supporters under the obligation to fulfill scrupulously the laws concerning race, and to resist mercilessly that universal poisoner of all people, international Jewry.' . . . The genocide inflicted on the Jews, however, has no precedent. The execution of the crime lay in the hands of the few. It was shielded from the eyes of the public. Yet every German could witness what Jewish fellow citizens had to suffer, from cold indifference to open hatred. . . . Whoever opened his eyes and ears, whoever wanted to inform himself, could not escape knowing that deportation trains were rolling. The imagination of men is insufficient to encompass the means and the scale of the annihilation. . . . There are many ways of allowing one's conscience to be distracted, of not being responsible, of looking the other way, of remaining silent. . . . Guilt, like innocence, is not collective but individual. Whoever does not wish to remember

> inhumanity, becomes susceptible to the dangers of new infection. [Weizäcker 1985, pp. 44–48]

This constant commemoration continues to be the necessary act of self-healing for the Germans and for the world alike, for it is true of individual and collective trauma as well, that people who do not remember their past are doomed to repeat it.

Concluding Remarks

In his "Group Psychology," the greatest psychological genius since Aristotle recaptured the philosopher's insight into the human condition: that man is a social animal, that "in individual mental life someone else is invariably involved" (Freud 1921, p. 69). This insight tallies with Freud's earlier observation, that "psychical (or psychogenic) symptoms and physical illness are acts detrimental, or at least useless, to the subject's life as a whole" (Freud 1917, p. 358). This is the crucial point: in medicine, symptoms are signs of a physical process; in the social life of individuals, symptoms are acts, and meaningful acts at that. But since all acts are social acts, the difference between any act and an act we call a symptom lies in their social value: thus, acts termed symptomatic are either useless or detrimental to life, and this manner of defining what is useless and what is useful is an ethical judgment.

The foregoing gives us a new approach to Freud's quest for the "sense of symptoms [as] related to the patient's experiences" (Freud 1917, p. 257). Since acts, whether healthy or sick, are by their nature dyadic, they are interpersonal acts, or interactions, and the formulation about the sense of symptoms can now be completed as follows: the meaning of an act is not only related to the individual's experiences but to his interactions: *the meaning of an act is in the interaction*. Hence, *the meaning of an act called a symptom is also in the interaction;* hence, neurosis or psychosis (literally "a state of mind") means neurotic or psychotic *interaction* (Lothane 1997). This should also be valid for the phenomenon in question, omnipotence: it is not only a state of mind, it is a kind of an interaction.

Power, the power to act, was Freud's last taboo, not in his practical life as a citizen, an analyst, or the leader of the analytic movement, but in his theoretical formulations. Since the latter were first developed in the shadow of the monadic or medical model of symptoms, the tendency was to assimilate the power of the act to the power of the wish, especially the erotic wish, to the wish-fulfillment of the night dream or the day dream, that is, fantasy. This led Freud to erotocize politics and to depoliticize eros. This is why only belatedly did Freud realize the importance of power in the life of groups, masses, and the body politic and in the dynamics of groups and their leaders. This is why it is time to combine the dynamics of the power of the wish and the will to power.

We are also faced with the nexus, power of love, love of power. The need to love and to be loved in return is as powerful as the need for food and sex, even though only the last two were classed by Freud as drives, and frustrated love seeks compensation in omnipotent self-love and in acts of aggression, violence, and destruction aimed at individuals and societies. I see lovelessness and the need to find love as the motor of totalitarian, fundamentalist, and extremist movements. Humiliated in World War I the Germans found love in the displays of power and claims of omnipotence offered by Hitler and his party. An important aspect of this self-styled omnipotence was arrogating to himself the power to decide issues of good and evil, of ethics and conscience, thus uniting a compliant nation, except for a small opposition movement, in an escape from free and responsible choice, in obedience to the leader-led dynamics formulated by Freud in his "Group Psychology." Such dynamics pave the way for the coercion of body and mind of the masses, the hallmarks of all expansionist totalitarian systems, whether in Nazi Germany, Communist Russia, or Imperial Japan. Supplied with the right ideology and propaganda against a hated race (in Germany), or a hated class (in Russia), or a hated rival (in Japan), the normal human emotions of love, pity, and sympathy were destroyed in the process of dehumanizing the hated external and internal enemy, and turning it into a scapegoat and a target for the chronic rage that the subjugation of one's own people had caused in the first place.

Irrational aggression against a hated enemy is legitimized by means of an irrational ideology. In addition to biological needs and love needs, people have a metaphysical hunger for ideas and ideals to live by. Irrational ideology, like an obsessional system or a paranoid system, is the dynamism whereby the natural fellow feelings of pity and sympathy are denatured, numbed, or killed so that people can act cruelly and in cold blood toward other human beings who are like themselves, but who have been dehumanized by the ideology and converted into subhuman, despised animals, like vermin or diabolical forms or mere matter, as happened in the religious persecutions of heretics, the Holocaust, the Gulag, the Japanese concentration camps, and the bombings in New York's World Trade Center or in Oklahoma City.

Psychiatry and psychoanalysis have a contribution to make to the understanding of the consequences of love deprivation and the dynamics of violent power. However, states and traits like mania, paranoia, omnipotence, neurosis, and psychosis, elaborated in the realm of individual psychology and useful when dealing with the neurotic conflicts of the person in life and in the psychoanalytic situation, should also be applied to groups and societies. Thus, one should emphasize the difference between harmless paranoid daydreams in an individual like Paul Schreber, seeking to find solace in fantastic ideas, and the paranoia of a group seeking to eliminate another group (Lothane 1996). There are not many totalitarian states left today; however, neo-Nazi type hate ideology is alive and well in the new sociopolitical phenomenon: global fundamentalism and global extremism. The common denominator to these ideological irrational systems is creating a climate of violence and terror. Such an approach is needed, not in order to assign collective guilt, but to realize that a group leader does not operate in a vacuum, that if a Hitler be called grandiose, paranoid, delusional, and omnipotent, then the system that keeps him in power, nay, that requires him to act in such a manner, is no less grandiose, paranoid, or delusional. Similar phenomena were seen in the recent war in Bosnia.

When it comes to ethical issues in society, it behooves us, as citizens and as professionals, to be eternally watchful lest we forget to expose, decry, and oppose any manifestation of irrational ideology, and the hate propaganda and violence promulgated in the name of such an ideology. Not to forget is to remember, as expressed in the Jewish saying quoted by Richard von Weizsäcker:

> The desire to forget prolongs the exile,
> and the secret of Redemption is called memory. [1985, p. 49]

To remember is to understand, to understand is to take a first step toward adopting rational thought and action both on the individual and social levels. Unreason, madness, or psychosis in the individual has been traditionally defined as living by irrational, or delusional, ideas or dogmas, that is, ideas impervious to the criteria of common sense and consensual evidence. Historically, the varieties of delusional ideology are as old as civilization, and organized religions have often been hospitable to delusions, such as the idea that the earth is flat or the dogma that Jews are eternally guilty for the murder of Christ. The progress of the sciences in the last three hundred years has been a necessary antidote to mankind's delusions and superstitions. It was Freud's insight that psychosis is a kind of private religion, and that religion is a communal psychosis. However, winning the war against dogmatic religion did not necessarily save mankind as a whole.

It is shocking to witness the rise of irrational ideologies in the nineteenth and twentieth centuries, in societies driven by science, and therefore, supposedly, by reason and democracy; and this trend is still with us. Historically, Europe saw the birth of new totalitarian states driven by irrational ideologies: fascism (Italy), bolshevism (Soviet Union), and national-socialism, or nazism (Germany). Today totalitarian solutions are still rampant in the Near and the Far East. In all these states the rule of hatred, violence, and terror was and continues to be justified by the irrational-paranoid group ideologies.

Paranoia has traditionally been defined as an individual aberration: feeling persecuted without a cause, within a sane environment. Freud's epochal "Group Psychology" marks a new beginning in two ways: symptoms of disorder are no longer seen as merely monadic events, but as dyadic products of a social interaction; moreover, social action on a mass scale is based on the interaction of leaders and the masses they lead, or by group dynamics. It is no longer the madness of one leader, acting on a passive group, not just individual psychology transposed into a group, but a special group madness that prevails between the leader and the led. While focusing on the historical example of Hitler and the Nazi movement, this dynamics applied equally to Stalin and now to the recent rebirth of totalitarian movements. Thus paranoid can no longer be viewed as an aberration of the individual but needs to be extended to include group, or mass, paranoia, as the special product of group dynamics embracing an irrational, or delusional, ideology, upheld by a group that views another group as an evil persecutor, or enemy.

Today, half a century after the ending of the Second World War, the expected benefits of the lessons of history have not materialized, nor are we even near to realizing the prophet Isaiah's dream of beating swords into ploughshares and not learning war anymore so that nation shall not lift up sword against nation. But we are trying. For the imperative to raise personal, social, and political ethics to the same level of progress as in the sciences is one that will determine the fate of mankind.

References

Adams, M. V., and Sherry, J. (1989). Significant words and events. In *Lingering Shadows: Jungians, Freudians, and Anti-Semitism*, ed. A. Maidenbaum and S. A. Martin. Boston: Shambhala, 1991.

Berman, M. (1989). *Coming to Our Senses: Body and Spirit in the Hidden History of the West*. New York: Bantam.

Fenichel, O. (1946). Elements of a psychoanalytic theory of anti-semitism. In *The Collected Papers of Otto Fenichel*, 2nd series, pp. 335–348. New York: Norton, 1954.

Ferenczi, S. (1913). Stages in the development of the sense of reality. In *Contributions to Psychoanalysis*, ed. S. Ferenczi, trans. E. Jones. Boston: Badger, 1916.

——— (1932). *The Clinical Diary of Sándor Ferenczi*, ed. J. Dupont, trans. M. Balint and N. Zarday. Cambridge, MA: Harvard University Press, 1988.

Fest, J. C. (1973). *Hitler*. New York: Harcourt, Brace, Jovanovich, 1974.

Freud, S. (1905). Three essays on the theory of sexuality. *Standard Edition* 7:125–245.

——— (1909). Notes upon a case of obsessional neurosis. *Standard Edition* 10:153–318.

——— (1911). Psychoanalytic notes on an autobiographical account of a case of paranoia (Dementia Paranoides). *Standard Edition* 12:1–82.

——— (1913). Totem and taboo. *Standard Edition* 13:1–162.

——— (1914). *Standard Edition* 14:67–102.

——— (1917). Introductory lectures on psycho-analysis. *Standard Edition* 16.

——— (1921). Group psychology and the analysis of the ego. *Standard Edition* 18:67–143.

——— (1923). The ego and the id. *Standard Edition* 19:3–66.

——— (1927). The future of an illusion. *Standard Edition* 21:3–56.

——— (1930). Civilization and its discontents. *Standard Edition* 21:59–145.

——— (1932). Why war? *Standard Edition* 22:203–215.

Fromm, E. (1941). *Escape from Freedom*. New York: Farrar and Rinehart.

Heiden, K. (1944). *Der Fuhrer*. Boston: Houghton Mifflin.

Hitler, A. (1924). *Mein Kampf*. New York: Reynal and Hitchcock, 1940.

Hofer, W. (1957). *Der Nationalsozialismus Dokumente 1933–1945*. Frankfurt/M: Fischer.

Huber, E. R. (1937). *Verfassung*. Hamburg: Hanseatische Verlagsanstalt.

Huxley, A. (1977). *Moksha Writings on Psychedelics and Visionary Experiences*, 1931–1963, ed. M. Horowitz and C. Palmer. New York: Stonehill.

Johnson, P. (1987). *A History of the Jews*. New York: Harper.

Klein, M. (1932). *The Psycho-Analysis of Children*. London: Hogarth, 1949.

——— (1948). *Contributions to Psycho-Analysis*. London: Hogarth.

Kohut, H. (1971). *The Analysis of the Self*. New York: International Universities Press.

——— (1977). *The Restoration of the Self*. New York: International Universities Press.

Le Bon, G. (1897). *The Crowd: A Study of the Popular Mind*. London: Unwin.

Lothane, Z. (1982). Dialogues are for dyads. *Issues in Ego Psychology* 5:19–24.

——— (1984). Teaching the psychoanalytic method. In *Clinical Perspectives on the Supervision of Psychoanalysis and Psychotherpy*, ed. L. Caligor, P. M. Bromberg, and J. D. Meltzer, pp. 169–192. New York: Plenum.

——— (1986a). Confrontations: clinical applications. In *Basic Techniques of Psychoanalytic Psychotherapy*, ed. M. P. Nichols and T. J. Paolino, pp. 207–236. New York: Gardner.

——— (1986b). La realltá d'amore, l'amore della realltá. In *Il Foglio e l'Albero*, ed. A Verdiglione. Milano: Spirali/Vel.

——— (1987a). Love, seduction and trauma. *Psychoanalytic Review* 74:83–105.

——— (1987b). The primacy of love: Love ethics versus hermeneutics. *Academy Forum* 31:3–4.

——— (1987c). Love and destructiveness. *Academy Forum* 31:8–9.

——— (1987d). *The self: rhetoric and reality*. Unpublished manuscript.

——— (1989). The nature of love. *Academy Forum* 33:211.

——— (1992). *In Defense of Schreber: Soul Murder and Psychiatry*. Hillsdale, NJ: Analytic Press.

——— (1994a). The revival of ethics. *Academy Forum* 38:4–6.

——— (1994b). The analyzing instrument and reciprocal free association. *Journal of Clinical Psychoanalysis* 3:61–82.

——— (1996). Die Verknupfung von Sohn und Vater Schreber mit Hitler: ein Fall von historischern Rufmord. *Werkblatt* 36(1):108–127.

——— (1997). Freud and the interpersonal. *International Forum of Psychoanalysis*, in press.

——— (In press). Ethics, morals, and psychoanalysis. *Psychoanalytic Review*.

McDougall, W. (1920). *The Group Mind*. Cambridge: Cambridge University Psychological Series.

Poliakov, L. (1971). *The Aryan Myth: A History of Racist and Nationalist Ideas in Europe*. New York: New American Library.

Rauschning, H. (1938). *Die Revolution des Nihilismus*. Zurich/New York: Europa Verlag. Translated as *The Revolution of Nihilism*. New York: Longmans, 1939.

Reich, W. (1933). *The Mass Psychology of Fascism*. New York: Farrar, 1980.

——— (1942). *The Function of the Orgasm*. New York: Orgone Institute Press.

Russell, B. (1962). *Power: A New Social Analysis*. New York: Barnes & Noble.

Tarde, G. (1890). *Le Lois d'Imitation*. Trans. E. C. Parsons from the second French edition (1903) as *The Laws of Imitation*. Gloucester, MA: Peter Smith, 1962.

Trotter, W. (1916). *Instincts of the Herd in Peace and War*. New York: Macmillan, 1919.

Webb, J. (1976). *The Occult Establishment*. La Salle, IL: Open Court.

Weizsäcker, R. (1985). *A Voice from Germany*. New York: Weidenfeld and Nicolson.

Index

About the Editors

Carolyn S. Ellman, Ph.D., is a training and supervising analyst at the New York Freudian Society. A faculty member and supervisor at the Metropolitan Institute, she is also on the faculty of the New York University Postdoctoral Program in Psychoanalysis and Psychotherapy and an adjunct supervisor for the City University Department of Clinical Psychology. Dr. Ellman, a member of the International Psychoanalytical Association, received her Ph.D. in Clinical Psychology from New York University and is certified in psychoanalysis by the New York University Postdoctoral Program. She is in full time private practice in psychoanalysis and psychoanalytic psychotherapy in New York City.

Joseph Reppen, Ph.D., is editor of *Psychoanalytic Books: A Quarterly Journal of Reviews,* President-Elect of Section 1 of the Division of Psychoanalysis (Div. 39) of the American Psychological Association; Vice President and training analyst of the New York Freudian Society: Fellow of IPTAR; and Senior Member of NPAP. A member of the International Psychoanalytical Association and of the International Association for the History of Psychoanalysis, he is editor and co-editor of numerous books including *Beyond Freud: A Study of Modern Psychoanalytic Theorists, Analysts at Work*, and *More Analysts at Work*. Dr Reppen is on the editorial boards of *Psychoanalytic Review* and *Psychoanalytic Psychology.*